Praise for *The North*

'Incorporating sharp questions and big ideas, Ni
culture and literature to offer a fascinating and pr
of the North.'

Madeleine Bunting, a

'Alex Niven's elegant, heartfelt book is the best I have read about the North's subordination by the South in modern England, and about how visionary northern culture of all kinds has defied that imbalance.'

Andy Beckett, author of *When the Lights Went Out: Britain in the Seventies*

'A great book.'

Andy Burnham, Mayor of Greater Manchester

'Alex Niven reveals the north of England in all its variety, potential and vitality. One Nation Under a Groove in book form.'

Lynsey Hanley, author of *Respectable: Crossing the Class Divide*

'A bold, compelling attempt to imagine a new future for England's industrial north by looking at its cultural and progressive past. [...] What Niven gloriously demonstrates is that ... "The ideals of progress must be imagined". A better north is possible and the seeds of its future are in a past of extraordinary achievements, from Redcar to Hollywood.'

John McTernan, *Financial Times*

'*The North Will Rise Again* is thought-provoking, evocative, tenderly appreciative and optimistic.'

Katherine Backler, *The Tablet*

'The history of the North of England is one of astonishing visions, great attempts to realise true progress, and painful deferrals of these dreams, so argues Alex Niven, who constructs this argument incisively, elegantly and movingly in *The North Will Rise Again*. Niven's intervention is a timely one. At a moment where appeals to an insurgent, anti-establishment Northern identity are galvanised by the right and neglected by the left, never before has it been more urgent to revive the modernist, utopian dreams of those who made the region what it is.'

Fergal Kinney, *Tribune*

'[Niven] sees the north as craggy cradle of tradition but also crucible of modernity, from T Dan Smith's doomed architectural dreams of Newcastle as "the Brasilia of the north" to the experimental poetry of the 1960s centred around the Morden Tower poets ... Niven is good on the melancholic, bitter-sweet descant of failure detectable in Victoria Wood, *Phoenix Nights*, Morrissey and others – the sad, plangent bottom note audible beneath the raucous swagger.'

Stuart Maconie, *New Statesman*

'A fascinating, expansive book, which takes in civic architecture, modernist poetry, postmodern art, independent filmmaking, and popular music, from the queer futurism of Frankie Goes to Hollywood to the utopian aspirations of Factory Records.'

James Greig, *Dazed*

'A lively cultural and political history of the lands between the Tweed and the Mersey–Humber line ... Niven skilfully connects Wyndham Lewis's northwards-looking BLAST magazine and the Vorticists' love of concrete and machinery with Yevgeny Zamyatin's inspiration in the "grand mechanised ballet" of Tyneside shipyards, Aldous Huxley's formative visit to the Imperial Chemical Industries's huge plant in Billingham (which "opened the doors of his perception") and on to the influence of industrial Teesside on the aesthetics of Ridley Scott's *Blade Runner*.'

Dan Jackson, *Prospect*

'What makes [Niven] one of the British left's most valuable writers is that he is never embarrassed ... His work is as loud and as achingly sincere as a lay preacher in some rusty methodist chapel. It is motivated by an unfashionable intensity of belief ... By believing once again that the English North is one of the great places on Earth, and taking pride in its achievements and dreaming of new possibilities based upon them, it could be possible to make the first step toward actually accomplishing it.'

Owen Hatherley, *Jacobin*

'A very welcome intervention ... Perhaps the most powerful passages are its most intimate ... Niven has a striking gift for weaving his and his family's personal experiences into a broader project of culture and political critique.'

Luke Cartledge, *Loud and Quiet*

'*The North Will Rise Again* covers, with a huge amount of charm, depth, love and clear-sightedness, the culture of the North of the past few decades: its politics, its position in the UK, and the uneasy relationship the region has between its culture of optimism and hope and the reality that the shiny reformation it reaches for never seems to quite happen.'

Fran Harvey, *NARC*

'A stirring and important book which urges us to rethink how we see the structure of this country and its governance; and even if we are years away from a fairer sharing of England's (and indeed Britain's) resources amongst all its peoples and regions, *The North Will Rise Again* is a reminder that we should never give up hoping for, and fighting for, a more equal world.'

Karen Langley, *Shiny New Books*

'Alex Niven's fascinating new book *The North Will Rise Again* looks at the history of modernism in the north, charting its rise and fall and issuing a call to arms for its return ... It's a lively, opinionated account ... and the author's own life story, recounted here, gives the book a real narrative flow. Highly recommended.'

Robert Meddes, *The Crack*

THE NORTH WILL RISE AGAIN

In Search of the Future in Northern Heartlands

Alex Niven

BLOOMSBURY CONTINUUM
LONDON • OXFORD • NEW YORK • NEW DELHI • SYDNEY

BLOOMSBURY CONTINUUM
Bloomsbury Publishing Plc
50 Bedford Square, London, WC1B 3DP, UK
29 Earlsfort Terrace, Dublin 2, Ireland

BLOOMSBURY, BLOOMSBURY CONTINUUM and the Diana logo are trademarks of
Bloomsbury Publishing Plc

First published in Great Britain 2023

A catalogue record for this book is available from the British Library

Library of Congress Cataloging-in-Publication data has been applied for

ISBN: PB: 978-1-3994-1401-2; eBook: 978-1-4729-9345-8; ePDF: 978-1-4729-9347-2

2 4 6 8 10 9 7 5 3 1

Typeset by Deanta Global Publishing Services, Chennai, India
Printed and bound in Great Britain by CPI Group (UK) Ltd, Croydon CR0 4YY

To find out more about our authors and books visit www.bloomsbury.com and
sign up for our newsletters

For Louise, Ossie, Bobby and the new star

CONTENTS

*We are at last experiencing a new empire, an empire
where the happy South stamps over the cruel, dirty,
toothless face of the northerner. At last Mrs Thatcher is
saying I don't give a fig for what half the population is
saying, because the richer half will keep me in power.
This may be amoral. This may be immoral. But it's
politics and it's pragmatism.*

— Michael Gove, speech at
Cambridge Union, 1987

Never give in, never give in, never, never, never, never.
— David Peace

Richard Carlile, *The Peterloo Massacre* (1819)

It was 15 October 2020, but it might have been any other day over the last 200 years. Against a backdrop of social turmoil, as Covid-19 surged again after a brief pause to wreck countless more lives, Greater Manchester mayor Andy Burnham walked out of the city's Central Library and stood on the edge of St Peter's Square. Dressed casually, rather like a well-preserved member of a Nineties indie band, Burnham gripped tightly onto a couple of typewritten sheets of paper as they quivered in the wind. Then, in a confident, lightly accented voice, he started to deliver a rousing speech to a crowd of local and national journalists.

Almost exactly two centuries earlier, St Peter's Square had been the site of the Peterloo Massacre, when 18 protesters were killed by government soldiers charging into a demonstration calling for reform of Britain's rotten parliamentary system. Now, as anger gathered in the English North about the regional bias of a modern government's lockdown plans, Burnham channelled this radical history as he posed as the champion of a neglected northern heartland. After claiming that Greater Manchester, Liverpool and Lancashire were being set up as 'canaries in the coal mine' for a lockdown strategy which sought to cut government spending, Burnham widened his scope to speak of the past, present and future of the North of England as a whole:

Different rules are always applied to the North of England ...

I think they have been treating the North with contempt ...

The North stands on the brink of being pushed back to where we were in the 1980s, just forgotten and pushed aside. But we won't let that happen ...

People are fed up with being treated in this way. The North is fed up with being pushed around ...

We aren't going to be pushed around any more.

This was, to be sure, slightly hammy stuff. But it was also timely and meaningful. Drawing on a decade's worth of anger at the impact of Austerity on northern communities, as well as much older feelings of resentment and rage, Burnham's speech seemed to confirm some basic truths about northern English existence, which are still – for some reason – often subject to debate.

The first thing Burnham's speech took for granted is that the North is a kind a country of its own within England. Something more than a mere compass point or area, the North he talked about was a definite political realm – a capital-letter affair which demands to be viewed as one of the main fixtures on the map of these islands. In other words, Burnham's North seemed to in some way bear comparison with the neighbouring countries of Britain as a whole: Wales, Scotland, even England itself.

Moreover, and more deeply, the emotional weight of Burnham's words sprang from a basic, time-worn conviction that the English North is severely disadvantaged – in certain clear-cut and statistically provable ways – when compared with the richer, more powerful South. Indeed, he seemed to be suggesting that one of the main reasons the North has such a strong sense of identity is *because* of its difference to the South, *because* of its poor treatment by the political system that has always been based there.

In essence, the story of the North is not very much more complicated than this. And so, with due respect to Andy Burnham's knowing but righteous speech of late 2020, let us lay down a couple of basic assumptions that will underpin everything that follows in this book. First, the North of England is a sort of country unto itself (virtually, if not actually, speaking). And second, the age-old national scandal of the North–South divide definitely exists.

Argue if you like about the details. But both of these points are, I think, fundamentally, undeniably true. It is simply a question of what is to be done about them.

But before we start trying to answer this question – and encounter no end of difficulty in doing so – I should briefly make clear what kind of book this is.

In the pages that follow, we will see various examples of people who have dreamed about what the North of England might look like in a brighter, fairer, more empowered future. More than anything else, as we will see, this is a story about hope rising above despair. Amid the civic crisis and growing inequality that have dominated northern society in my lifetime (and long beforehand), a strong tradition of northern modernism and revivalism has persisted – sometimes staying under the radar, sometimes rising to the surface with explosive but never quite decisive consequences. Driven by a belief that the North somehow holds the key to a freer, more progressive way of organizing and operating the country that has come to be called England, countless artists, writers, musicians, politicians, film-makers and ordinary citizens have used the North as both inspiration and ideal, as they have tried to imagine brave new forms of collective being over the last several decades. Despite recent political setbacks, it is this tradition of passionate northern progressivism – based ultimately on the reasonable, righteous, even inevitable dream of northern renaissance – that I think has something very important to say to us at this chaotic moment in our collective history.

Partly in order to give these sometimes high-flown examples some human grounding – but also because I think that writers should always be truthful and heartfelt about where they have come from – this history of northern revivalism unfolds in the following pages alongside a partial, interwoven memoir of my own northern story over the past few decades. Though I am not the main subject of this book, because it is a study of human emotion arising from attachment to specific places and communities, it seemed important to make clear at certain key moments the links between my own life and the more momentous cultural stories that are the backbone of the chapters that follow.

Aside from anything else, I hope this personal approach will underline that this book is what it could only ever have been – a subjective attempt to sketch the outline of the North's collective character. As will become clear, this is a book that takes a particular line on a particular period in northern history. It is not an attempt to create an exhaustive survey of the varied forms of twenty-first-century northern identity (which isn't to say, of course, that those disparate identities are not important and should not be passionately fought for elsewhere). In a similar vein, neither is this book an attempt to compile a perfectly proportioned encyclopaedia of stories from the various northern sub-regions. As should be fairly obvious from the start, my own understanding of northern history has been most powerfully shaped by my native North-East, which I take to be a kind of quintessence or ultimate example of the

North as a whole far more than another country-within-a-country (though I should also stress that there are plenty of examples in subsequent chapters focusing on the North-West, Yorkshire and the fringe areas of the wider North – this is no narrow essay in Geordie localism). This combination of a core North-East narrative with stories from the wider region will, I hope, back up one of the crucial political arguments in what follows. This is that the North will only ever get to where it needs to be by embracing concrete forms of pan-regional unity, rather than by splitting hairs about minute, mostly rather insignificant differences of opinion, accent and sporting rivalry between its interlocking tribes.

On this last note, before we begin, I should say something brief about the key question of the *where* of the North. For the purposes of this book, I have assumed that the English North begins on the Scottish border and ends somewhere in the northern Midlands. This is broadly in line with the old medieval idea that when you venture into 'England North of the Trent' – that is, past the river which circles the southern tip of the Pennines – you are entering another land entirely to the more settled, more recognizably English parishes of the London-centric South (though we should be mindful here, as always, of the complex example of the deeper South-West, not to mention the many local nuances within London itself). Everywhere from the old county lines of Lancashire and Yorkshire upwards is, I think, pretty unambiguously the North, starting with the classically northern cities of Liverpool, Manchester and Sheffield. But there is also a vaguer borderland slightly below here – including south Cheshire, north Lincolnshire and the land around the Trent-ish cities of Derby, Stoke and Nottingham – which I have often included in my definition of a 'cultural North', even though I know that in many respects they are part of the Midlands (or perhaps even a separate sub-region entirely).

For these and other necessary simplifications – and for the need to leave out so much of the North's myriad history in a normal-sized book like this – I beg the reader's forgiveness. With a bit of luck, the clarity that comes from being selective rather than exhaustive will ultimately seem worthwhile. In other words, I hope it is clear from the start that this is a book in which power and soulfulness are the underlying motives at every moment – and in which details and nuances ultimately come second to the deeper, more valuable goal of beginning to dream a northern rising that will one day succeed.

Part I

DEEP NORTH

The past we inherit, the future we build.
— Various Durham miners' banners

Settlingstones, Northumberland, early 1980s

The Rural Return

On the edge of the seared land of the North Pennines, a single row of houses checks the moorland waste on either side. Sixteen small dwellings form a linear hamlet. Two bedrooms in each, with narrow strips of garden to the front and rear. The north side of the Terrace faces onto bare fields which shoulder a sky that is lead-grey in sympathy with the matter of the earth – a lunar world of rocky grazing land, basalt crags and mounds left by Bronze Age cairns and abandoned mines. If you took a short walk from the houses, following the skyline northwards for a mile over moors scored with burns and sikes, you would soon reach Hadrian's Wall, a neat line ruled across a debatable land which struggles even now to announce its own form. Like the North of England more generally, the story of the Wall goes back centuries and implicates more or less the entire world. Yet it remains a dark tangle of conjecture, half-written history and the endless, overwhelming fissures of the imagination.

This former miners' terrace in the far west of Northumberland – 'Settlingstones' on the maps – was my first home. When I was 18 months old, we moved to a three-bedroom house in Fourstones, the next village along the valley, so I have no memory of living in the Terrace. More to the point, my parents both died when I was 21 (mum, cancer; dad, liver disease), so I cannot now ask them what it was like. But when I was a child we would drive – or rather be driven – to Settlingstones fairly often. My mother would park the car behind the Terrace (nicknamed 'the Knack' by its residents for obscure reasons), then tell my sister and I stories about being snowed in and having to burn Polish coal to stay warm during the long winter nights of the 1984–5 Miners' Strike, a cultural trauma which ravaged the North throughout my first year but mostly didn't touch this hidden corner of its backcountry.

In the Tyne Valley, the mines had nearly all closed in earlier waves of industrial decline. In Fourstones, the colliery was boarded up in 1927. Already ailing by the mid-1920s, the final blow came when 38 men and boys were drowned in its sister pit in Scotswood on the edge of Newcastle. (As the poet Basil Bunting described, with typical modernist frankness, the 'bodies emerged five months later when it was pumped out / and were buried by public subscription'.) The more remote workings at Settlingstones were originally part of a network of lead mines which shaped the life of the North Pennines for hundreds of years. But at some point in the nineteenth century they became the world's main source for witherite, a curious milk-white mineral used in the production of paper, steel and eventually – rather wonderfully – television screens.

After the witherite vein at Settlingstones was abandoned in 1969, the shafts were filled in and landscaped, leaving behind little but the Terrace and a scatter of tumbling red-brick headgear. My childhood best friend, Will Lee, lived in the former mine manager's residence. In the shadow of this strange, belated building, where we would play endless, dreaming games of football in later childhood, an overgrown concrete tennis court, depleted orchard and ruined summer house lingered as gothic reminders of the industrial class which once ruled this part of the Tyne Valley.

For better or worse, no one ever outgrows their origins, least of all northerners. In D. H. Lawrence's 1913 novel *Sons and*

Lovers, an essential text of northern literature, the author gives a semi-fictional account of his childhood in a mining terrace in the Nottinghamshire coalfield, at the other extreme of the Pennines from where I grew up. My mother encouraged me to read Lawrence's great coming-of-age novel when I was a teenager and looking for clues about how to cross over into adulthood. Given the surface resemblance, it wasn't surprising that I would picture the Terrace at Settlingstones as I read Lawrence's portrait of his alter ego Paul Morel – his struggle to escape from his cramped home to become an artist, his smouldering hatred for his miner father, and his Freudian relationship with his mother, Gertrude.

And yet, I was no Paul Morel. For a start, though not free from tragedy, my upbringing was a pretty standard (for the late twentieth century) lower-middle-class one. As a child I felt safe – and mostly happy – because I was supported in various ways by the remains of Welfare State Britain (its historic social equalities, its well-funded hospitals and schools, its securities of employment, housing and benefits, and its atmosphere of artistic freedom and experimentation). This social backdrop, which offered an imperfect but still unequalled model for combating England's ancient class and regional inequalities, combined in my case with the fact that my parents had both passed through the polytechnic education system of the Sixties and Seventies to themselves acquire comfortable (at the time) jobs in state education.

Largely because of these forms of social-democratic privilege, which sheltered me from agonies like the Miners' Strike, I was lucky not to feel the sort of desperation to escape the North and its harsh industrial work culture that, for example, my grandmother had felt in Bolton in the Thirties, and which had earlier inspired novels like *Sons and Lovers* (and countless northern books, films and albums, from *Billy Liar* to *Definitely Maybe*, which followed in its wake). When I did leave the North, as a young adult in the post-Welfare State era, it was as an exile, and after doing so my greatest wish – finally granted – was to return to my homeland to make my life here.

This story of reclamation of the buried good things about modern northern life is central to this book, and it is one of the main reasons why I do not want to lament how dark and depressing the North is (though to be sure, as we will see, there are lots of dismal things about its recent history). Instead, the underlying motive for everything I write here is to show how the North can and should be, and for me always has been, a place of endless subtlety, exceptional generosity, fierce love and utopian possibility.

As I hope I have made clear in starting off this story about the fate of northern hopes and dreams, there is a personal, human factor driving it. Just as I never felt any great desire to leave a North I first knew as a nurturing heartland in the late twentieth century, neither did I take after D. H. Lawrence in wanting to escape from my parents and the grounded childhood they provided for me – starting with the evocative northern beginning of living in Settlingstones in the long winter of 1984. In fact, I loved my mum and dad in a fairly uncomplicated way, and this book is partly a tribute to the various, humane, limitlessly tender North they showed me in my earliest years.

As Albert Camus once wrote, in everything they do writers are engaged in a 'slow trek to rediscover, through the detours of art, those two or three great and simple images in whose presence their heart first opened'. Like so many other people, because of the first and best human landscapes in my memory, my heart will always be of and for the North.

But what does 'the North' even mean at this point of the twenty-first century? And is it really worth fighting for?

One of the starting points for this book is a simple observation that the North of England is changing. Or perhaps it would be better to say that it is *regressing*, and has been for quite a while now. Change, of course, is the one thing that never changes. But I think we can say that the *sort* of change northerners have experienced over the last half-century is of a new and different kind. In fact, it seems clear that the downturn northern citizens have suffered in recent years – an era of deepening civic decay, multiplying foodbanks, failing infrastructure and a more profound crisis of identity – is threatening to undermine the whole essence of what the North has meant to its people, and to the world, throughout its eventful modern history.

Though our subject is the North's more recent development, not its long-term history, we need to begin our inquiry by laying down a brief working definition of northern identity as it has been shaped over time. An obvious starting point here is the idea that if the North has meant anything over the last 200 years, it has meant progress. Because it has tended to look forward to a levelled-up future rather than wanting to remain stuck in an uneven, unequal present, indeed, the North has often resembled a kind of country-within-a-country, as I began this book by saying. In an English nation ruled by an ancient establishment, where the received version of national identity was (and still is) dominated by nostalgia for rural idylls and stately symbols of the past, the rise of the North in the modern period offered a forceful, even violent counter-theory about the sort of country England was – or rather could be.

The crucial development here was of course the technological explosion of the late eighteenth and early nineteenth centuries, which transformed northern society in certain dramatic and long-lasting ways. In recent years, revisionist critics have rightly sought to query the 'heroic' account of the Industrial Revolution, which centres on the biographies of a handful of Great Men and their dazzling inventions. But for all that it was a slower, more complex affair than was once thought – and though it certainly brought plenty of profound moral ambiguities along with it – there is no doubt that the rise of industry in the decades around 1800 was a literally earth-shaking event in northern history. This was, in a sense, the North's creation moment, the point at which the upper half of a provisional country – dimly imagined by the Romans as 'Britannia Inferior', and by late medieval monarchs as the wilderness 'England north of the Trent'– became something more than a backwater defined by its remoteness from civilization. To put it more radically, we might say that after the arrival of the spinning jenny, the steam engine and the steam locomotive sparked the rapid growth of northern towns and cities (and within them, unprecedented new forms of scientific and intellectual discovery), the North of England effectively *became* civilization – or at least, the most vigorous, dynamic existing version of it.

In contrast to much of the South, where the underlying reality of capitalist growth in these years was often obscured by the heavy traditionalism of the political establishment and the overbearing cultural mythology of England's rural southern heartlands, the North was a place where the effects of the Industrial Revolution really were visibly revolutionary. While industrialization in the South outside of London often progressed more gradually, and tended to be focused on marginal parts of its more scattered conurbations, the sudden overhaul of large swathes of the northern landscape – which saw small towns like Leeds and Manchester become sprawling metropolises in a matter of decades – was such a transformative development that it would overwhelmingly define northern culture and society for the next two centuries.

Given this history of sudden, dislocating change, we might in fact say that the English North was one of the original, most complicated and most poignant homes of what we have come to call *modernity*. Much has been written about the rise of this new sensibility (the term is derived from the French *modernité*, and at its simplest means merely the condition of being new and modern) in places like Paris, New York and London at some point in the mid- to late nineteenth century.* But while most commentators have tended to focus on these conspicuous centres of privilege, there is a straightforward case for saying that the industrial heartlands of northern England – in particular, the large conurbations surrounding Manchester, Leeds, Liverpool, Newcastle and Sheffield, but also smaller cities and towns such as Middlesbrough, Bolton, Sunderland, Bradford, Halifax, Darlington, Preston, Barrow and Hull, and not forgetting rural-industrial village-scapes like much of County Durham, Derbyshire, Staffordshire and Nottinghamshire – were the real historic capitals of modernity.

Cotton weaving mill, Bolton, early-twentieth century

*For a typical example, see the title and content of the geographer David Harvey's fine 2003 book *Paris, Capital of Modernity*.

Certainly, in the context of England itself, it is the North which has so often embodied a sort of rebel commitment to modernism and progressive change, against a contrasting backdrop of deeply ingrained traditionalism in the English system as a whole. As with all attempts to define large-scale collective identities, we have to be careful here to avoid sweeping, binary notions of the divide between North and South (which is, it should go without saying, complicated by a thousand nuances, exceptions-to-the-rule and local variations). Even so, there is surely something to be said for a comparison between the North's fundamental civic bias towards modernity at certain crucial moments, and the more entrenched, Home Counties-centric stereotypes of Englishness which continue, even now, to play a starring role in British politics, from the House of Windsor and the House of Lords to the tweedy, Middle England mannerisms of politicians like Boris Johnson and Nigel Farage.

Partly because it has never been very well treated by the political system which supports such conservative clichés, the North of England has historically tended to privilege radically different forms of cultural being (though again, we should stress that there are plenty of northern conservative exceptions to the rule, as anyone who has ever been to Harrogate or Knutsford knows all too well). As we will see, from its history as the birthplace of the steam train, the light bulb, hydroelectric power and modern computing, to its shaping influence on twentieth-century sci-fi novels and films, the *idea of the future* has tended to be at the forefront of northern culture, in a way that simply hasn't been the case – at least not so openly nor to the same extent – in England's cultural mainstream. As large numbers of people who have navigated the North–South divide can attest, this contrast between a mostly stable, tradition-loving English centre and a mostly restless, unfulfilled periphery in search of future empowerment is one of the major cultural facts of life in the British Isles.

In any case, it is one of the central themes of this book. As we will see, the North of England is defined by many things, from the landscape of the Pennines and the ruins of heavy industry, to a maddening mass psychology which alternates fitfully between overconfident brashness one minute and terminally low self-esteem the next – often within the space of a single line of poetry, passage of prose or fragment of political rhetoric. But at the most basic level, I think we can say that the North is a country apart from England because it is a place where a mostly forlorn desire for things that might be, rather than things that have been, is a sort of unshakable collective inheritance.

So much for the long view. What about the present tense? Rather tragically, in spite of its high-speed modern history, there is a sense in which the North has lately given up the ghost when it comes to envisioning a future above and beyond English tradition. In fact, as we will see, even before recent disasters, the North has often embodied instincts of self-destruction and self-loathing alongside its basic vernacular commitment to modernization. Over the last few decades, aided by an overarching English system which has never had very much time for northern interests (let alone protests), it is this negative tendency that has started to gain the upper hand in northern society.

The historical backdrop to these years – broadly speaking, the post-Second World War era – is fairly well known. Throughout the later twentieth century the process of 'deindustrialization', which saw almost all of the North's identity-shaping manufacturing industries decline and then finally vanish, gradually withdrew the material foundations on which the North's progressive culture had arisen in the first place. Meanwhile, successive Labour and Conservative governments routinely failed to find any long-term replacements for the vanished industries of the past – often putting little effort into

11

the task, and mostly remaining fairly relaxed about the drastic deepening of regional inequality which occurred as a result.* Bearing in mind this recent narrative – which has only got worse since climactic confrontations like the 1984–5 Miners' Strike – we might say that the English North has, for some years now, been the graveyard of modernity.

The ongoing nightmare of the North's prolonged civic death was brought powerfully home to me when I returned to the North-East in 2015, after a decade or so of living down South following my childhood and adolescence in Northumberland. After studying and working for several years in a series of mainly very wealthy southern cities (none of which, of course, was without its own inequalities), it was a profound shock to move back to the North-East in the mid-2010s, at the end of a period during which the Austerity policies of an especially South-East-centric Westminster government had devastated much of the North's communal infrastructure. As I settled back into the North-East in the second half of the 2010s, it soon became

---

*I take it is a given that the North–South divide exists, irrespective of stock – and often rather irrelevant – quibbles that severe poverty exists in the South too (which is, of course, absolutely true). Partly as a result – and also because of this book's mainly literary-cultural focus – I don't think it would be profitable here to reel off the many statistics that prove this to be the case. Those who remain sceptical about the irrefutable scientific basis of the North's disempowerment would do well to explore the findings in multiple recent reports by the think tanks IPPR North and the Centre for Cities, and the broader structural summary in an excellent recent study: Tom Hazeldine's *The Northern Question: A History of a Divided Country* (2020). On a parallel track, those in search of a more exploratory portrait of modern northern identity (and its problematic aspects) will likely find much of interest in Anita Sethi's lyrical travelogue *I Belong Here: A Journey along the Backbone of Britain* (2021).

12

painfully clear that my home region had relapsed in visible ways since I had last lived there in the millennium years – a time when it had seemed to be, at least superficially, recovering from the effects of deindustrialization.

To be sure, there were lots of good, even great things about being back up North. The move happened because I somehow managed to get a university lecturing job, which offered a form of professional stability that was once commonplace, but that is now increasingly a privilege for members of my generation (especially those, like myself, who had been stupid enough to think that a career in the arts would be viable in twenty-first century Britain). In another stroke of luck, my partner Louise was able to get a job working remotely as a medical writer. Now that we were both gainfully employed, and able to move up North together, we could start to think about having a family – another growingly rare privilege for millennials like us (as it turned out, our first son Oswald, named after the Northumbrian saint, was born about a year after we got to Newcastle). We could also find time to explore the more luminous side of the modern North-East: the enduring friendliness of its people, the freeing mix of urban and rural spaces in the land around Newcastle, the peerless Metro train system, spectacular architecture and, perhaps most wonderful of all – on blue-skied weekends and holidays – the well-kept post-industrial secret of its many vast and gorgeous sandy beaches. For the most part, we felt lucky and grateful to have exchanged the rat-race of 2010s London for an airier, less frantic, more nurturing way of life.

But while the basics of our life were mostly sound thanks to certain forms of privilege (and frankly sheer luck), there was quite a lot that was disturbing, even nightmarish around the edges. As we made our way through our new surroundings in urban Newcastle, we encountered large numbers of homeless people, where previously – I could clearly recall from my younger years – there had been none. Savage council cuts had left much of the city centre looking badly unloved and untended, as weeds sprouted out of the cornicing of elegant neo-classical buildings on the main shopping thoroughfares. If we wandered to the end of our street in Fenham, we would be confronted by the harrowing sight of the West End Foodbank – the largest of its kind in the country, and scene of one of the most traumatic scenes in Ken Loach's 2016 film *I, Daniel Blake*, a howl of protest against the deadly impact of Austerity on places like the North-East. Venturing into the wider Tyneside conurbation, and into former industrial areas like County Durham and south-east Northumberland, we would see settlements almost wholly without amenities and full of boarded-up shops and closed-down pubs. The local BBC radio station continually ran features about the snowballing legal-high epidemic and the soaring child poverty rate (a chilling 48 per cent in central Newcastle), jarringly interspersed with the usual commentary about the canny North-East people and the rare beauty of the local landscape. After seeing how much money was continuing to pour into London's commercial districts throughout this whole period, arriving in a region that seemed to have been mostly cut loose from the staggering wealth of the world's fifth-largest economy was disorienting and upsetting in the extreme.

But I don't think I fully grasped how much the North had changed (or rather regressed) in the early twenty-first century until the very last weeks of the 2010s. Partly because of the experience of living through the Thatcher, Major, Blair, Brown and Cameron years, when Britain became a harsher, less equal place (especially for northerners, public sector workers and people born after circa 1980), and also because of growing anger at the devastating impact of Austerity on British communities, by the late 2010s I had become a fairly committed political radical. In making this ideological leap of faith, I had been influenced by a left-wing family background, a fair bit of wide reading and discussions throughout my twenties with people in various walks of contemporary politics. But for the most part, my growing political engagement in these years was a simple response to the social hardship I saw around me. This was combined with a rational, even moderate belief that some sort of alternative to a society of funding cuts, proliferating foodbanks, student debt, exploitative landlords and declining living standards was surely not so hard to imagine in an economy as wealthy as Britain's.

Like many millennials, it seemed to me that, for all its flaws, the Jeremy Corbyn-led Labour Party of 2015–19 offered at least a fighting chance of achieving this rather humble goal. And so, with this assumption in mind, I became a card-carrying Labour member just prior to moving up North in 2015. In between heavy work and childcare duties, I managed to do a little campaigning for Labour in the 2017 general election, when the party somehow managed to force a hung parliament, which hamstrung the Tory prime minister Theresa May for the next couple of years, effectively ending the most wantonly cruel phase of Austerity. Then, when yet another general election was announced towards the end of 2019, I threw myself much more wholeheartedly into Labour's campaign in the North-East. In a timely coincidence which spoke of the ongoing decline of the public sector in modern Britain, university lecturers were striking over pay and working conditions in the last weeks of 2019. Temporarily unemployed by this walkout in the days before the election on 12 December, I was able to spend a solid fortnight canvassing, leafleting and trying to get the vote out for Labour, both in my own constituency, Newcastle Central, and in various marginal (or so we thought) seats throughout the wider North-East.

The author canvassing in the Bishop Auckland constituency,
December 2019

The final result of the election announced on the evening of
the 12th – a clear and devastating defeat for Labour – marked
the end of a profoundly depressing few days for me and for
my fellow Labour canvassers. Every one of the supposedly
marginal seats we visited fell heavily to the Conservatives, some
for the first time in their history. Meanwhile, the wider picture
suggested that the prospect of a government committed to major
reform of British society had been ruled out for the next several
years at least. Having already lost most of its former heartlands
in Scotland, and now much of the so-called Red Wall of once
safe seats in the North and Midlands, it was clear that Labour

16

would struggle in future to win a majority without a momentous reversal of electoral geography and allegiances (or, equally likely, a return to the managerial, cautiously inactive centrism of the Blair years, which had helped to get the party into its mess in the North in the first place).

But there were other, more historic, more place-specific sides to the narrative of the 2019 general election besides the downfall of the national Labour Party. Away from the nuances of the result and its political aftermath, the election seemed to underline just how dramatically the social landscape of the twenty-first-century North had changed (or rather regressed) during the course of my lifetime. In analysing events likes this, it is important to remember what conservative journalists embarking on 'northern safari' excursions in the wake of Brexit have tended to forget: that ad hoc interviews on pavement and doorstep can never take the place of rigorous sociological research. Nevertheless, our canvassing odyssey of December 2019 was at the very least a stark and visceral lived experience of a series of diverse northern parishes. During the course of the campaign, in damp, gloomy December weather, we traipsed for days across the council estates, suburban backstreets, shopping districts, former mining villages, Edwardian terraces and unregenerated small towns of Tyneside, County Durham and Teesside. Though this was a brief, subjective endeavour, I think it would be fair to say that, combined with our knowledge of the North-East as long-term residents, we got a pretty clear insight into the collective mood in the region on the eve of a new decade.

There were some brighter moments in the campaign, mainly in urban Newcastle, where twenty-something football fans talked of Corbyn as a hero, and where, during one leafleting session outside a mosque in Fenham, we were told that we were wasting our time, as 'everyone here votes Labour'. But as time went on, it was increasingly hard to ignore the deepening sense

17

that something terrible and profound had happened to many of the former Labour heartlands in the North-East. In myriad doorstep conversations, we heard plenty of regurgitated tabloid slurs, of course, about Corbyn being an IRA sympathizer (sometimes just 'a terrorist') or thinly veiled racist attacks on Labour's 'disgusting' and 'stupid' shadow home secretary, Diane Abbott. Just as often, there were more reasonable digs at Labour's confused, confusing stance on Brexit, which, at the behest of party centrists like Keir Starmer, had led to a clause in the manifesto promising a second referendum with the option to remain in the European Union. Whatever the rights and wrongs of Brexit (I had been a cautious Remain voter in 2016 myself), the second referendum idea quite rightly struck many voters in these Leave-supporting areas as an insult to their democratic prerogative, and fed into a wider sense – especially acute since the Blair years – that Labour had become a party controlled by an aloof, London-based elite.

But while Brexit, Corbyn and the legacy of the Blair years clearly played a part in the hostility many voters seemed to feel towards Labour in the 2019 campaign, it was also clear that something more was going on here than could be explained by recent party-political shenanigans. In fact, the experience of campaigning in 2019 seemed to underline that these former industrial areas had declined, and perhaps finally crossed over into another realm, for much deeper, longer-term reasons than had anything to do with either Labour or the insurgent (but hardly popularly adored) Conservatives, who many people seemed to be voting for out of a mixture of morbid curiosity and vague fondness for the clownish media persona of Boris Johnson.

The main, slightly melancholy thing I realized while campaigning for Labour in 2019 was that much of the North-East – like much of the rest of the North – had in a sense finally returned both to nature and to the past after two centuries of being dominated by industrial technology and various forms of belief in the future. While this process – I suppose we could call it deindustrialization in the fullest sense of the term – had been ongoing for perhaps a hundred years, it was clear that by this point of the twenty-first century it was definitely, absolutely, irreversibly complete. Now that the cultural residue as well as the actual workplaces of industrial community in places like rural County Durham had disappeared for ever, we were now looking into the void on the other side and seeing nothing but a sort of untended social wasteland.

Viewed in the most extreme terms, this regional regression represents nothing less than a total transformation of the northern landscape on a par with the radical overhaul which gave rise to the Industrial Revolution in the first place. This is not, we should be clear, a green activist's dream come true. If England north of the Trent has become a kind of wilderness once again, it is not because of any large-scale 'rewilding' process, of the kind that an increasing number of ecologists are recommending as a way of reintroducing biodiversity to the countryside. Such projects are indeed beginning to make their mark on the contemporary North, notably through proposals for a new 'Northern Forest' stretching from Liverpool to Hull, and plans to reintroduce apex predators (such as lynxes) to places like Kielder Forest in Northumberland. These sorts of schemes belong to a very different, potentially progressive northern narrative (indeed, despite some contentious aspects, just possibly they will allow the North to offer the world a kind of historic recompense for all those years when it was the global centre of the environmentally disastrous coal industry).

No, rather than offering optimistic signs of an innovative green future, the 2019 general election seemed to underline that the North had retreated from progress and development in a more banal, more pitiful sense. The whole thing struck me as

19

the ultimate outcome of the ruins I had grown up surrounded by in Settlingstones and Fourstones in the late twentieth century, while speaking of something much more final and far-reaching. Knocking on door after door in the countryside around Darlington and Bishop Auckland, where dynamic collieries had once dominated the landscape, and where the world's first modern railway line was built in the 1820s – but where there were now very few amenities, let alone large-scale workplaces – it was hard to avoid the conclusion that this part of the world had left behind the vital, technologically advanced phase of its history once and for all. To put it bluntly, after many years of being an energetic landscape of progressive politics, new machines and futuristic innovation – and then, for a long time, a transitional site of deindustrialization – at some point the countryside in this part of the North had been reduced to just that: countryside.

There are, of course, plenty of good and indeed great things about rural life in England, as elsewhere in the world, and it would be a huge oversimplification to view rural areas as mere underdeveloped poorer relatives to their urban counterparts. Nonetheless, it does seem that the specific aspects of rural life which have become prevalent in recent years in places such as County Durham (and the same might be said of countless areas throughout the new England north of the Trent) tend to speak of a lack of development – and indeed basic civic care – rather than any more idealistic return to rural community. For the most part, the disappearance of heavy industry in much of the North has given way to nothing very much at all – or rather, to a scattered, sequestered, extra-infrastructural way of life, which has seen the North revert to being a kind of postmodern, twenty-first-century version of the social and political no-man's-land it was prior to the rise of industry in the long nineteenth century.

While the culture of the mines, factories and foundries of the North is now definitely gone for ever, there has also been a profound long-term failure, for more than half a century, to replace them with any really viable alternative, forcing many of its former industrial areas to retreat into a state of intermittent organic decay. The effect of this process of deliberate socio-economic abandonment has been bad enough in the North's many large and proud cities, where, with a couple of exceptions, an atmosphere of civic downslide and disillusionment still reigns in the wake of the Austerity of the 2010s. But though once electric northern cities like Newcastle are, as I discovered on returning to the North-East in the mid-2010s, still searching for a future on the other side of the Industrial Revolution, at least, as we will see, these inner-urban areas have benefited from various attempts at revival and regeneration since the Sixties. In stark contrast, outside of the major urban centres, much of the rest of the North is a place of crumbling amenities and non-existent economic growth, where railway lines don't dare to reach, and where the only residents able to secure a decent quality of life are the privately wealthy (and, more ambiguously, the much larger demographic of solvent but hardly affluent pensioners, who have benefited from decades of sympathetic government policy). Meanwhile, young people escape as soon as they can, in ever increasing numbers, leaving behind even less favourable conditions for a revival of innovation and collective purpose.

Though the North is still a distinct region which retains the potential to offer an alternative to the traditionalism of mainstream English culture – and indeed, with six out of eight of the country's so-called Core Cities, it is still, even now, the apex of urban England – we have to face the fact that at this point of the twenty-first century many northern areas are simply vastly less wealthy versions of the southern pastoral heartlands of Middle England. In the gap where industrial

21

community and infrastructure once were, something like the classic Middle England worldview built on individualism and selfishness has rushed in, to be joined by a newly virulent strain of northern bitterness at being so flagrantly marginalized for so many years by the Westminster system. Whereas in the past the latter emotion might have given rise to more coherent forms of radical rebelliousness, now, in the ageing, weary communities of the twenty-first-century North, a lethal combination of petit-bourgeois narrow-mindedness and genuine 'left-behind' grievance simmers under the surface. These impulses might come to the fore at intervals in the form of spasms of indignation like Brexit – or indeed the 2019 general election, which was, in much of the North, a vote to maintain the integrity of the 2016 referendum, mixed with widespread fogeyish dislike of Corbyn, long-brewing hatred of local Blairite Labour councils and a more indefinite, misguided belief that Tory promises to 'level up' the country might actually amount to something.

But underneath these superficial narratives, we have to accept a simple underlying truth about the sort of place the North of England is as we approach the middle decades of the twenty-first century. If it was once something like the global-historical capital of modernity, the North is now – like much of the rest of England – a place that is trading on dimly remembered past glories, and seemingly unable to reinvent itself in a changing, increasingly ominous contemporary world. Of course, there are isolated pockets of optimism, and recent examples of northerners doing extraordinary things – from tech start-ups in Leeds and social housing initiatives in Salford to renegade artists in Gateshead and experiments in community wealth-building in Preston. Probably, there always will be. But for the most part, most of the time, I have to say that I'm not so sure how many of us in the bewildered, still marginalized, post-everything North have a really clear sense of what progress looks like any more.

***

What, then, is to be done about all this? Is it possible that the North might rouse itself from socio-economic slumber, and find a way forward which builds a new, more energetic, more youthful society on top of a landscape that is still – after all these years – full of boarded-up towns, ruined mills and abandoned mines?

It should go without saying that I don't personally have any simple answers to these questions, or any kind of miraculous, magic-bullet remedy for northern problems. Nonetheless, when it comes to the contemporary North, I think there is some urgency in the need to respond as boldly and radically as possible to some primal existential sighs which demand an urgent response at this moment of crisis and confusion: namely, *Where do we come from? What are we? Where are we going?*

My basic approach to these questions in writing this book has been that in order to get to the future, you have to venture a little way back into the past. From this point on, following on from the preamble laid down in this introductory chapter, we will explore the various ways in which the North has tried but failed to rise over the last few decades, by examining a series of cultural and political stories from the last half-century or so (with glances at related episodes from my own life).

In organizing these examples to serve a coherent narrative, I hope it is clear that my goal is to endorse the cultural livelihood of the North, broadly defined. Certainly, I hope I have managed to avoid the sort of bigoted parochial boasting which James Joyce satirizes in his great novel *Ulysses* in the figure of the nationalist 'Citizen' character (a modern version of Homer's Cyclops – who makes all manner of exaggerated claims for the supremacy of native Irish culture, and who is therefore unable to appreciate that good things might sometimes happen elsewhere). In exploring a series of sometimes only provisionally 'northern' case studies, I am aware that I am casting a net into the ocean of collective identity, and hoping that something solid and valuable might be dragged to the surface. I am absolutely not mounting any kind of essentialist or nativist argument which suggests that northerners are an exclusive tribe destined for the Promised Land. Rather, the writing in this book is guided by a fundamental belief that the two most important things in life are loving yourself and loving your neighbour (which means fellow human beings all over the world just as much as those in neighbouring parts of the British Isles). It's just that, as will become clear in subsequent chapters, I think that people in the North of England should probably learn to love themselves a bit better – or at least in more nuanced and confident ways – and then try to work out how to make a concrete political reality of such deepened forms of collective self-worth.

As well as making clear that this is not a study in myopic 'northern nationalism', I should stress that this is very much a book of two halves – or rather, three thirds – which moves gradually from the ghostlier demarcations of cultural history to the more tangible debates of the political present. In the remainder of this first section, we will mainly examine the North's deeply embedded modernist culture, which underwent a spectacular revival in the post-war years (ironically, just as deindustrialization was starting to peak). Then, in the second section, we will look at the pivotal moment of the Long Eighties, a moment of defeat for the North's modernizing ambitions – though one which also saw a final flourishing for various progressive, countercultural schemes. Finally, before an Epilogue which speculates more broadly on the North's collective fate, a third section focuses mainly on the present tense of northern politics, considering the current state of regionalist debates and the various twenty-first-century attempts at regeneration and regional devolution which have led us to the derisory moment of 'levelling up'. (Readers in search of material focusing on the contemporary State of the Region, and the current prospects for northern renewal, might therefore like to skip the first two sections and head straight for the more urgent political discussions which begin with Chapter 8 – perhaps especially those in Chapter 10.)

As well as providing some sense of who we are and where we came from, the hope is that maybe, at the end of this inquiry into the recent dream-life of northern faith and failure, we will get a very initial imaginative sense of where we are going, and of how northerners might start to think about escaping from the endless loop of decline – followed by botched recovery – which has dominated their history for 50 years and more.

But first of all, before we get anywhere close to this endpoint, I should probably paint a slightly more detailed picture of the specific places and people which made me care so much about the North in the first place.

In order to do this, we will have to head briefly backwards and inwards once again.

Newcastle Civic Centre, 1969 - a proto-parliament in all but name

Walking on the Moon

In the basic version of my story, I grew up in the North because my dad got a lecturing job at Newcastle Polytechnic in 1977, a few years before I was born. My parents were both children of working-class migrants from textile towns on the margins of Britain and Ireland (Derry, Dundee and Bolton). These clever, dislocated men and women, my grandparents, had washed up in London during and after the Second World War, for all the usual romantic and economic reasons. After this migration to the centre, their only children, my parents, grew up mainly in certain rather anonymous suburbs of the capital in the steadily improving post-war years. But soon enough both families would drift back to the fringes of the islands. After meeting in the hippy vortex of student East London in the very early Seventies, my parents bumped into each other again at a party later that decade. They then began a long-distance relationship, which led eventually to my mother joining my dad in a rented Tyneside flat in Newcastle – as far as I know, within a couple of years of him getting the job at what was then known locally as the Poly.

Not long after moving in together, my parents were driving back to the North-East one day after visiting dad's grandparents in Cleveleys in Lancashire. When they reached Haltwhistle on the A69, they decided to take a meandering detour through Hadrian's Wall country. Somehow, randomly, they ended up at Settlingstones. This was why, a short while later, despite my dad's reluctance to leave urban Newcastle, they moved into one of the 16 terraced houses on the edge of the leaden fields of the Pennines.

After embedding themselves in rural Northumberland, my parents would pass through a surreal, very northern sliding door as they drove daily between their moorland home in Settlingstones and their workplaces in urban Tyneside. My mother got a job as a teacher at Westgate Hill Primary School in the Arthur's Hill area of Newcastle, on the north side of the old road which follows Hadrian's Wall westwards out of the city. Here, 80 per cent of the children were of Pakistani and Bangladeshi heritage – highly unusual in the North-East, where the population was nearly all white from the end of the Roman Empire to the first years of the twenty-first century. At Westgate Hill, mum got to know one of the parents, the owner of perhaps the only South Asian food outlet in Newcastle at this point: Brighton Oriental Food Stores, on Brighton Grove in Arthur's Hill. In later years, this friendship would be the cause of regular, mind-altering family shopping trips to this numinous corner of Tyneside, where hippy communes and vegan cafés were mingled with sari shops, Balti houses and Hindu temples.

Meanwhile, dad's workplace, the Poly, was also seemingly the polar opposite of isolated, outmoded Settlingstones. At the same time, on a more essential level, these two locations shared a sort of stark, obdurate grandeur which placed them broadly in the same northern ambience.

Newcastle Polytechnic would turn into the more traditional-sounding Northumbria University after British higher education was given a major overhaul in 1992. But back in the Seventies it was a shiny new institution housed in a compound of hard-edged modernist buildings on the edge of Newcastle city centre. Arguably the most successful of the Polytechnics to emerge from the 'white heat' education reforms of the Harold Wilson years, Newcastle Poly was, in design and outlook, a kind of urban spaceship. It had been built on the scorched earth left behind when several redbrick Victorian terraces were demolished by the gleefully modernizing city planners of the post-war years. In fact, the Poly was the only really lasting outcome of plans for a 'Central Education Precinct' – a sort of HQ for the North-East intelligentsia – championed in the Fifties and Sixties by the controversial council leader T. Dan Smith, a man who famously dreamed of transforming Newcastle into a gleaming city-state to rival ultramodern locales like Milan, Manhattan and Brasilia. We will explore the backdrop to this enterprise in a short while; but I should make clear from the start that my personal stake in the schemes and dreams of Smith (one of the heroes or anti-heroes of this book) goes back a long way – all the way to the beginning of my life, in fact, if not a little earlier.

Contrary to lazy clichés about northern backwater towns and their 'concrete monstrosities', late twentieth-century Newcastle was an incredibly exciting, visually dramatic place to be – in large part because of the energetic building projects of the Sixties and Seventies. The surroundings of Newcastle Polytechnic were a perfect example. Because neither of my parents is still alive, I can't recover and relate to you much about their first encounters with the North-East in that transitional time, the late Seventies and early Eighties (though I do have some paper heirlooms, like a flyer for a 'Psychology and Science Fiction' conference my dad organized in Newcastle in 1979, along with a polite handwritten note from the author J. G. Ballard regretting that he couldn't deliver the keynote address). But some of my most evocative childhood memories, which now form the bedrock of my subconscious, are of the blasted, lunar landscape of the Poly and its imposing surroundings in the late Eighties and early Nineties, when I first began to gain a glimmer of civic awareness.

I can clearly recall being driven into Newcastle at weekends from our home in the Tyne Valley and being totally awestruck and overwhelmed by the council headquarters, Newcastle Civic Centre, a sublime modernist structure built around a Pharaonic tower of milk-white stone. Designed on a Scandinavian model, and opened by King Olav V of Norway in 1968, this building resembled a prospective regional or national parliament far more than a mere provincial town hall, as though it were pointing away from tired old England and towards a brave new constitutional future.

After parking opposite the Poly in the Civic Centre car park, or else a short distance away beside the futuristic charity office MEA House, we would make our way through the eastern swathe of the city centre, climbing over concrete walkways, down spiral stairwells and past radiant entrance halls of new underground Metro stations, before coming to the gilded Georgian heart of town. Often we would end up at Eldon Square, a plate-glass shopping mall built at the height of the T. Dan Smith era. In keeping with the astral ambitions of the post-war years, a bizarre suspended café resembling a flying saucer loomed strikingly here in the central courtyard.

Moving through this cityscape always felt like a spacewalk on a shifting terrain of glass and concrete, like we were wandering over a wild and thrilling man-made moon.

But there were deeper reasons than childish amazement why Tyneside circa 1989 made me and many others feel so cosmically transported. In fact, along with the other great northern cities – especially Manchester – Newcastle and its surrounding areas had played a central, even dominant role in shaping the futurist dreams of the twentieth century. The fact that original moonwalker Neil Armstrong (whose surname has echoed through Tyneside since the building projects of the Victorian inventor William Armstrong) was descended from a family from the sparse 'debatable land' between northern England and southern Scotland is of merely poetic relevance to this narrative.* Far more important, if we are searching for the remains of northern futures, is the fact that a large number of the modernist and science-fiction narratives of the last century were directly inspired by northern English backdrops.

Whatever the nuances of industrialization (and later deindustrialization), there is no doubt that the *idea* of an alternative England – one in which machines rather than symbols of tradition defined cultural life – was the starting point for the futurist aesthetic in the British Isles. Right from the start, modernism in England was driven by this pro-industrial, very often pro-northern impulse. Beginning in the 1910s, a series of major literary endeavours would look determinedly northward to try to imagine what England might be like once it was freed from the mind-forged manacles of its ancient traditions.

The first of these experiments was perhaps the most intellectually provocative. In 1914, as he translated Italian futurism into English with the first issue of his *BLAST* magazine and its 'Vorticist' rallying cry, the modernist artist–writer Wyndham Lewis was at pains to emphasize that Britain's industrial landscape would offer a much-needed escape from

---

*In the same vein, it is surely not completely irrelevant to note that another northern celebrity, the Wallsend-born popstar Sting, would channel the vaulting energy of his shipyard birthplace in Tyneside to top the British charts in 1979 with a song about taking giant steps while walking on the moon.

the 'bourgeois Victorian vistas' of the nineteenth century. In place of the 'wild nature cranks' and 'raptures and roses' of Victorian art, Lewis celebrated an England he reimagined as an 'industrial island machine'. With bracing iconoclasm, the manifestos in *BLAST* offered a vision of a future that might emerge from the 'scooped out basins', 'insect dredgers', 'heavy chaos of wharves', 'steep walls of factories' and 'lighthouses blazing through the frosty starlight' of Britain's modern urban panorama. *BLAST* asserted that the modern world had 'reared up steel trees where the green ones were lacking', and 'found wider intricacies than those of Nature'.

Like many of the modernist outbursts of the 1910s, *BLAST* and Vorticism were based in London, where the vast majority of the island's museums, publishing houses and media outlets were – and still are – located. Yet there was no doubt that, in common with much English modernist art, Lewis's project was driven by a fierce desire to move British culture away from the hidebound institutions of its geographical centre. For Lewis, this decrepit establishment mainstream was embodied in both the aristocratic fantasies of the Victorian era and the tamer version of modernist innovation typified by the upper-middle-class aesthetes of the Bloomsbury Group (Clive and Vanessa Bell, Virginia Woolf, Duncan Grant, Lytton Strachey), whom Lewis hated with a very personal passion. In opposition to such tendencies, *BLAST* advised its readers to 'ONCE MORE WEAR THE ERMINE OF THE NORTH', stating yet more boldly: 'We assert that the art for these climates … must be a northern flower.' In saying such things, Lewis was gesturing at a more general northern *European* sensibility, to stand in counterpoint to the 'southern' (i.e. Mediterranean) aesthetic of the Italian futurism he was plagiarizing. Yet there was no doubt that the radical northward reorientation Lewis desired also applied to England itself.

Newcastle.   Edward Wadsworth.

Edward Wadsworth's 'Newcastle' woodcut from *BLAST* (1914)

Amid all the abstract sloganeering – which also, to be sure, found time to praise the more dynamic side of post-Victorian London – this foundational British modernist text was clearly yearning for an upending of Britain's power structures that would have to involve some sort of raising up of 'the North', variously defined. In *BLAST*, evocatively, the London-centric bias of England or Britain was inverted, so that the island became a 'pyramidal workshop' with 'its apex in Shetland, discharging itself on the sea'. Notably, the magazine's first illustration – a woodcut by the West Yorkshire artist Edward Wadsworth – was a powerful depiction of the Newcastle Quayside, its bridges, docks and dredgers caught in a livid monochrome stasis. Newcastle native Frederick Etchells also contributed several, equally assertive Vorticist sketches to the issue. Meanwhile, a majority of the ports the magazine singled out for special praise (Newcastle, Hull, Liverpool, Glasgow, London and Bristol) were in Britain's upper reaches. If *BLAST* was the first really vigorous announcement of modernism in the British Isles, it said much about the nation's deeper cultural geography that the new style was christened by way of an attempt to put the island's northern enclaves on a par with – and perhaps above – imperious London.

If the futurist strand of high modernism had strong northern roots, the same might be said for some of the most influential texts in European sci-fi, though here it was the dystopian side of the industrial North – now beginning its slow, century-long downslide – that would be pushed to the fore. Shortly after Lewis's *BLAST* was published, a Russian naval engineer called Yevgeny Zamyatin was sent to Newcastle to supervise manufacture of polar icebreaker ships in the Swan Hunter and Armstrong Whitworth docks of Wallsend and Walker. During his 18-month spell in the North-East, Zamyatin would find time to visit local landmarks such as Hadrian's Wall, assist with design of the ships that would later achieve Soviet glory under the monikers *Krassin* and *Lenin*, and write a satirical novella about English bourgeois life (*The Islanders*) based on his experiences of living in suburban Jesmond.

More importantly, while he was in Newcastle, Zamyatin would also store up material for later use in the seminal sci-fi text for which he is best known. Written in 1920–21, and often viewed as a veiled critique of the new Soviet Union by a disillusioned

Bolshevik, Zamyatin's *We* was also an attempt to render the capitalist, industrial landscape of 1910s Newcastle in allegorical prose. Zamyatin's descriptions of a global landscape dominated by a despotic 'One State' are in fact far more redolent of the modernist critiques of British Imperialism found in Wyndham Lewis's *BLAST* than they are of much later texts like George Orwell's *1984* (published in 1949), which fairly blatantly borrowed from the template of *We* as it sought to attack the nightmare of mid-twentieth-century totalitarianism.

As in *BLAST*, which celebrates the *surfaces* of industrial capitalism while attacking its central political institutions (partly because Victorian English culture had done precisely the opposite), *We* manages to derive great excitement and energy from its descriptions of a machine-dominated dystopia. Witness the following description of the building of the great 'Integral' spaceship in the novel's first pages, which seems to derive fairly directly from Zamyatin's encounters with the docks of Wallsend and Walker:

> For instance, this morning I was at the hangar, where the Integral is being built, and suddenly: I noticed the machines. Eyes shut, oblivious, the spheres of the regulators were spinning; the cranks were twinkling, dipping to the right and to the left; the shoulders of the balance wheel were rocking proudly, and the cutting head of the perforating machine curtsied, keeping time with some inaudible music. Instantly I saw the greater beauty of this grand mechanised ballet, suffused with nimble pale-blue sunbeams.

Reading such passages, and taking into account the rigid work environments, mathematical theorems and perfunctory daily routines we find in *We*, the technologically primitive landscape of Bolshevik Russia in the very early 1920s does not in fact seem like a very plausible inspiration for Zamyatin's alternative fictional universe, which laid down the basic blueprint for the grand tradition of dystopian sci-fi in the twentieth century. Instead, it seems fairly clear (especially when comparing them with similar descriptions in *We*'s Newcastle-based companion text *The Islanders*) that Zamyatin was basing such visions of a 'grand mechanised ballet' on his first-hand experiences of the alien, automated sublime of urban northern England in the last really confident days of its industrial heyday.

After texts like *BLAST* and *We* had helped to establish the modernist and sci-fi strands of twentieth-century art, the North continued to be a dominant influence in inter- and post-war culture, especially for those seeking to imagine a future beyond the traditionalism of the English cultural mainstream.

One of the first attempts to create an English version of Zamyatin's seminal dystopian novel (though with a much more overtly consumer–capitalist emphasis), Aldous Huxley's *Brave New World* was directly inspired by its author's visit in the late 1920s to the recently built Imperial Chemical Industries (ICI) factory in Billingham, County Durham. On encountering this sprawling industrial complex, which Huxley rhapsodized as a 'triumphant embodiment' of the principles of planning as well as an 'ordered universe [...] in the midst of the larger world of planless incoherence', the imaginative world of *Brave New World* suddenly fell into place, after a long period during which Huxley had tried but failed to sketch out a H. G. Wells-style dystopia (almost certainly also with Zamyatin's *We* acting as a major influence). In tribute to the role played by industrial Teesside in offering up a contemporary model for his great novel, Huxley duly named his paternalistic World Controller character 'Mustafa Mond', after ICI's chairman Sir Alfred Mond.

In Huxley's case, as in Zamyatin's, the modern North seems to have provided inspiration for sci-fi fantasy because it appeared to him to be something like another planet. The alien landscape of Billingham clearly liberated Huxley's creativity in some profound way (a little like mescaline would do in the Fifties); encountering it allowed him to step outside and above the traditional Englishness of his background in one of the elite families of the London intellectual establishment. (Like Wyndham Lewis, Huxley was deeply scornful of the Bloomsbury Group, whose mild-mannered version of modernism he had witnessed at close quarters in the 1910s.) In this sense, the alternative, ultramodern version of England that Huxley found in Billingham played a crucial part in opening the doors of his perception, allowing him to become one of the most prophetic novelists of the twentieth century.

As the century wore on, and as the spread of democracy (especially post-war social democracy) allowed for greater social mobility in Britain, seminal modernist and sci-fi narratives produced by people who had actually grown up within earshot of the industrial North began to appear. In the next chapter we will see how a particular strand of post-war modernist art coincided with the rise of civic regionalism in the Sixties and Seventies, to offer powerful suggestions about how the North might rouse itself from its post-industrial torpor. Alongside this more affirmative tradition, there were also some darkly visionary northern elaborations of the dystopian model laid down by Zamyatin and Huxley, all of which reflected and helped to shape the distinctive cultural atmosphere of Cold War Britain in some essential way.

Published in 1962, as Britain teetered on the brink of a transformative white-heat modernity, Anthony Burgess's *A Clockwork Orange* condensed an array of disparate influences in a caustic sci-fi novella which argued for the importance of theological free will in an increasingly scientific, rationalist epoch. Enormously influential on the counterculture of the Seventies and Eighties (especially in the wake of Stanley Kubrick's brutal 1971 film adaptation), *A Clockwork Orange* was also very much the product of Burgess's chaotic upbringing in interwar south Manchester.

As lyrically described in the first volume of Burgess's autobiography, *Little Wilson and Big God*, this was an environment in which Manchester's amorphous sprawl of brick terraces, factories and textile mills was beginning to buckle under the weight of the first really severe onslaught of deindustrialization. These surroundings were a key formative influence for Burgess. Passed between a series of surrogate parents after his mother died in the influenza epidemic of 1918, he grew up in a place where economic conditions meant that 'ragged boys in gangs' would pounce on grammar school boys like him, and where a new, consumeristic world of cinema matinées, phonograph records and jazz dances was asserting itself with a kind of abrupt violence. This shifting, ominous cityscape would later reappear in his imaginative life, to spectacular effect, in the nightmarish urban reverie that was *A Clockwork Orange*.

By the early Eighties, modernism was largely on the retreat in England, as throughout the world as a whole. But there would be one last flourish for sci-fi futurism in these years, as US president Ronald Reagan talked of a 'Star Wars' nuclear warfare programme, and as the counterculture enabled by the Welfare State enjoyed a late moment of avant-garde audacity. It was in this context that the director Ridley Scott, who had grown up in Stockton in County Durham, and whose family had helped to establish most of the state-of-the-art cinemas in interwar Newcastle, would launch *Blade Runner* into the world. Released in 1982, as the final, most aggressive phase of northern deindustrialization was kicking into gear, this visionary film was something like the swansong of a particular tradition in twentieth-century art – of using an industrial northern backdrop as both creative inspiration and a means of hallucinating an evocative impending future.

Though it would later become an archetype of northern backwater decline (in the context of early 2020s debates about so-called Red Wall and 'left-behind' areas), it was in Hartlepool on the County Durham coast that Scott would pick-up the inspiration – and the professional training – for *Blade Runner*'s spectral premonition of the year 2019. An early beneficiary of the British state education system of the post-war years, Scott studied at West Hartlepool College of Art between 1954 and 1958, an experience he would later describe as a 'revelation', because of its 'weirdly dressed students' and 'passionate teachers'. In this nurturing creative environment, and later as he enrolled at the Royal College of Art in London, Scott would absorb certain key high modernist influences while giving them a distinctively northern twist. His first film, *Boy and Bicycle* (made in 1962), featured stream-of-consciousness voiceovers indebted to James Joyce's *Ulysses*, underlain with footage of his brother Tony cycling over a landscape of cooling towers and blast furnaces in West Hartlepool and Seaton Carew, on the north-east edge of industrial Teesside.

There is little doubt that such vistas would remain lodged in Scott's mind, so that when he later came to create the cosmic chiaroscuro of twenty-first-century Los Angeles which supplies the backdrop to *Blade Runner*, he would ensure that it looked a lot like the brooding panorama he had once seen at the mouth of the River Tees. In this weirdly generative space, which had also given Aldous Huxley the imaginative jolt to create *Brave New World*, Scott would be one of the last in a long line of twentieth-century writers and artists to uncover a sublime other England – one rooted in the urban North rather than the rural Home Counties, and which looked forwards to a technological future, not backwards to a rustic past. As Scott commented in a 2007 interview:

> There's a walk from Redcar into Hartlepool ... I'd cross a
> bridge at night, and walk above the steel works. So that's

probably where the opening of *Blade Runner* comes from. It always seemed to be rather gloomy and raining, and I'd just think 'God, this is beautiful.' You can find beauty in everything. And so I think I found the beauty in that darkness.

Redcar Steelworks, Teesside

An awful lot of claims have been made over the years about Englishness and English tradition. But what is often neglected or ignored completely in these discussions is the rather obvious fact that northern English identity is, most of the time, a completely independent country of the mind. As the above examples have begun to show, one of the ways in which the North is distinct from the rest of the country is that its mainstream cultural tradition since the Industrial Revolution has been, broadly speaking, one of modernism and futurism. To an appreciably greater extent than in the heartlands of England's cultural Establishment, where conservative and pastoral clichés are, on the whole, far more dominant, in the North technological idealism and futurist imaginings are, as it were, simply a part of the soil.

If this seems like a sweeping statement – and of course it is to an extent, though not, I think, unforgivably so – then let me offer some more fragments from my own biography to flesh out this notion of a futurist cultural *terroir* for the North.

When my parents were expecting me, and shuffling daily for work between far-flung Settlingstones and cosmopolitan Newcastle, they compiled a 'birth tape' to play to their future child *in utero*. According to family friends, in the months after I was born, one of the songs on the tape would be played over and over to usher me into a kind of infant nirvana. Apparently, in these infant weeks my parents would often place me in a baby-harness suspended from one of the beams on our living room ceiling. They would then turn on the hi-fi system, and cue up the shimmering electro soundscape of 'Relax' by Frankie Goes to Hollywood. It's probably safe to say that I was ignorant at this point of the queer subtext to this glorious piece of music, the artwork for which had stirred up huge controversy in late 1983, with its pornographic innuendos and frank references to gay culture. On the other hand, it would seem that I was fully on board with the more instinctive side of 'Relax'. As Holly Johnson's searing Scouse voice intoned a barely coded lyric about delaying sexual climax, so the story goes, I would bounce maniacally up and down on the baby-harness, keeping loose time to the heartbeat of a tune which – in its dark, mechanized splendour – perfectly captured the ominous, martial mood of the early Eighties.

Aside from being an unwitting early experience of the camp sublime – and though I obviously didn't know it at the time – this was my first real encounter with twentieth-century popular futurism. And in fact, we do not have to dig very deeply before we discover that, beneath its radio-friendly surface, 'Relax' was a repository for layer upon layer of modernist subtlety.

'Relax' was in fact the greatest and most successful single released by the provocative indie record label ZTT, a collaboration between producer Trevor Horn, businesswoman Jill Sinclair and music journalist Paul Morley. While Sinclair helped to ensure that records like 'Relax' and its follow-up, 'Two Tribes', sold many millions of copies (both were among the top-selling singles of the decade), her two northern sidekicks would both have a distinctly avant-garde influence on ZTT's creative identity. One of the new breed of superstar producers who came to dominate the digital age, Horn was brought up in post-war County Durham, in a place called Neville's Cross on the edge of Durham City. Relocating to London in the early Seventies, he forged a career as a jobbing session musician, songwriter and producer. After steadily building his music industry profile, he formed the Buggles with keyboardist Geoff Downes in 1978. The band's signature tune, 'Video Killed the Radio Star' (inspired in equal parts by a J. G. Ballard short story and the German electronic band Kraftwerk), was originally a UK number 1 hit in late 1979. But it would help to usher in the new era of global mass media when it was picked to be the first song played on MTV in August 1981. (Rather fittingly, its iconic video was a montage of consumer imagery and glam sci-fi design, which opened with a shot of a luminous artificial moon mirrored in shimmering water.) After a short spell in the prog-rock band Yes in the early Eighties, Horn became the in-house producer at ZTT when it was founded in 1983. Here he was responsible for innovating a dazzling approach to music production, which became hugely influential in shaping the cut-glass electro house-style of Eighties pop.

The deeper intellectual basis of ZTT, meanwhile, was laid down by Morley. After growing up in Stockport in Greater Manchester – not far, incidentally, from the childhood home of sci-fi novelist Christopher Priest – Morley moved to London at the tail-end of the Seventies. On arriving in the capital, he quickly became the precocious star journalist at the *New Musical Express*, just as punk and its aftershocks were forcing the music industry to turn to face an ambiguous postmodern future. Morley started out as a music writer by covering the Manchester post-punk scene of the late Seventies – especially Joy Division, a stark, anti-art rock band, whose sound was sculpted into visionary post-industrial contours by the producer Martin Hannett and distributed by the neo-modernist Manchester indie label Factory Records (the narrative of which is explored in more detail later on). The subversive business model Factory innovated – which combined an avant-garde pop aesthetic with situationist gestures like giving the company cat a serial number – would supply Morley with many of the key influences for his own label, ZTT, when it was founded in 1983.

Cover art for Marinetti's *Zang Tumb Tumb* (1914)

But Morley was also interested in venturing further back than recent northern cultural history as he co-ordinated a 'strategic assault on pop', which triumphed spectacularly with release of the chart-topping 'Relax' in 1983. ZTT was in fact an abbreviation of 'ZANG TUMB TUUM' (or ZANG TUMB TUMB), the title of a famous 'sound poem' written between 1912 and 1914 by Italian poet F. T. Marinetti, founder of the futurist movement. Marinetti's *Zang Tumb Tuum* – with its declaration that there was 'No poetry before us / with our wireless imagination / and words in freedom', and its uncompromising attempt to capture echoes of the violence of the First World War in onomatopoeic verse – was an ideal mascot for a record label that was also attempting to embrace the modern world in all its high-octane intensity. If Ridley Scott's *Blade Runner*, released in 1982, lay at the end of a long tradition in twentieth-century art of using northern heavy industry as creative inspiration for sci-fi reveries, there was deep resonance in the fact that Morley's ZTT project of 1983 was also founded (as Wyndham Lewis's *BLAST* had been 70 years earlier) on an attempt to translate Italian futurism into the context of the industrial or post-industrial city – to demand, as it were, that the art for these climates must be a northern flower.

In one sense, of course, it's a simple accident of fate that the first work of art I ever loved was a high-energy futurist sound poem sculpted by a visionary electro producer from the outskirts of Durham City, sung by an S&M-clad eccentric from Liverpool and packaged for commercial release by a situationist music journalist from Stockport. I don't know what else was on my birth tape, but I suspect that not all of it was quite as cool – and as fitting to this book's narrative – as 'Relax'. (Billy Joel's 'Uptown Girl', for example, would have been much less apt, though I credit my parents with better taste than to have forced that musical calamity on even an unborn baby.) But in another, more

44

important sense, the fact that 'Relax' was my first encounter with the mechanized human world is no coincidence. In another sense, that is to say, these things matter and are meaningful.

I was born into a society where, for various concrete reasons, people were able to create complex works of mass art, based on the belief that there was a viable – if not necessarily always utopian – future on the other side of Britain's so-called twentieth-century decline. As we have seen, and as we will see again in the next chapter, this socially licensed belief in the future was especially prominent in the North of England, where for several decades modernist and sci-fi dreaming became a kind of regional vernacular style – even, we might say, a folk culture.

Throughout the twentieth century, and especially in its later decades, the North was undergoing a painful kind of counter-revolution, whereby the modest forms of power and prestige it had acquired in the Industrial Revolution were being comprehensively dismantled, along with the material basis of industry itself. However, for all that the later twentieth century was a time of rapid industrial decline and social implosion for the North, there is a strange, paradoxical sense in which the structures of social democracy seemed to offer a basis for the region to recover and revive itself after the wrecking ball of deindustrialization. Certainly, for all their dystopian digressions, the cultural artefacts of the Welfare State era were far more confident in gesturing at a future tense for the North than those produced after say 1984 – the year I was born (along with many other 'millennials'), the year the Miners' Strike began, and the year in which Ridley Scott decided to follow-up the futurist *Götterdämmerung* of *Blade Runner* with a big-budget TV commercial (titled simply *1984*) in honour of the launch of the first Apple Macintosh computer. Depending on your perspective, this was either the beginning or the end of something or other – a brave new world perhaps, or maybe just Orwell's dystopia made flesh.

45

As we have seen in this chapter, the basic atmosphere of modernism which persisted in northern areas up to the Eighties was partly the result of a more general tradition in national and European culture, which saw some form of potential or at least possibility lurking in the remains and ruins of industry – even when the surrounding landscape was in other respects rather bleak. Out of this popular futurist tradition emerged many of the key works of science fiction of the middle decades of the twentieth century – up to and including the daringly progressive musical products of record labels like Factory and ZTT. In the next chapter we will zoom in to look at the more grounded side of northern modernity – by exploring the ways in which the late modernist art, architecture and poetry of the post-war years intersected with concrete campaigns for regional and civic empowerment in the North.

But let us return, finally, if you will forgive the egotism, to one of the primal scenes of my earliest years. This is, I hope, no mere self-indulgence. The landscape and environment I was born into profoundly influenced the definition of northern modernity I am trying to elaborate here. And anyway, I do not think that my own story is all that atypical of many people's better experiences of life in northern England in the years either side of the Miners' Strike.

Of all the photographs my parents left behind of their time in Settlingstones in the early Eighties, the one I like best is of a geometric pod greenhouse, pictured against a backdrop of bare moorland stretching up to and beyond the ruins of Hadrian's Wall. Piecing together what I remember my parents telling me when I was a kid, and what family friends have said in the years since they died, it would seem that this dome of plate-glass triangles – a popular futurist object if ever there was one – was a sort of sanctuary my dad would retreat to of an evening in the years before I was born. Here he would open a can of beer, check on the marijuana plants he was illicitly growing, start listening to German space-rock through his first-generation Walkman headphones (Tangerine Dream, Neu!, Amon Düül II), then sit back on a deckchair and watch the constellations of the northern sky as he read sci-fi novels by the likes of Ursula K. Le Guin, Samuel Delany and Christopher Priest.

Dad's greenhouse, Settlingstones, early 1980s

When I think of him in this setting – and of the levelled-up, future-facing society that had allowed it to come into being – I find it hard to accept that it is mere nostalgia which makes me see the residue of a very real utopia in this strange enclave in space and time. In fact, even allowing for the distorting pain of loss, I often think that human history reached one its rare pinnacles in certain buried places like this subtle civic moonscape of the twentieth-century North.

Newcastle Central Station, circa 1900

The Future We Build

The world dominated by its phantasmagorias – this, to
make use of Baudelaire's term, is 'modernity'.
    – Walter Benjamin, *The Arcades Project*

On 22 May 1965, the American Beat poet Allen Ginsberg got off a train at Newcastle Central Station and stepped into the morning light. He did so feeling energized by one of the most dramatic northern vistas imaginable. A few seconds earlier, after a three-hour journey from London (where he had just met the Liverpudlian Beatles for the first time), Ginsberg's train had glided over one of the soaring kinetic bridges spanning the River Tyne, rounding the last curve of track into a vast station concourse sheltered by a rippling canopy of glass, iron and wood.

The Sixties were a decade of decline for the British railway system – a time of line closures and upheaval of the landscape to allow for the rise of the motor car. But in spite or perhaps because of this fact, Ginsberg was surprised and elated to enter Newcastle through the portal of its mouldy, soot-blackened but still astonishingly elegant and modern-looking Victorian station (a memorial of sorts to the site where George and Robert Stephenson had designed *Rocket*, the world's first widely usable steam locomotive, in 1829).

After disembarking from his train, Ginsberg wandered to the station toilet, where he was 'greeted by the most furious display of Gnostic [i.e. mystical] graffiti in the gentleman's room walls that [he] had ever seen on the planet'. Feeling 'like a bearded emissary from another hemisphere', he was then ushered through the centre of Newcastle by a 19-year-old local poet called Tom Pickard.

Working alongside his partner Connie, Pickard had recently hired a room in Newcastle's old medieval walls from the city council. Here, this enterprising couple set about organizing a series of freewheeling poetry readings, which invigorated the youth culture of the post-war North-East. Morden Tower, as it was known, soon became a sort of countercultural mecca – a place where veteran modernist writers such as Stevie Smith, Hugh MacDiarmid and Herbert Read rubbed shoulders with younger radicals from all over the world. Among the angel-headed hipsters who visited the Tower in the heady early days of its new incarnation were the novelist Alexander Trocchi, the musician Bryan Ferry, the artist Richard Hamilton and the poets Robert Creeley and Lawrence Ferlinghetti – all of whom, in some way, shared its intrinsic values of spontaneity, experimentation and vigorous social engagement.

Perhaps most remarkable of all, the Morden Tower scene also enabled a long overdue breakthrough for the local modernist poet Basil Bunting. A one-time member of the interwar circle of T. S. Eliot, Ezra Pound and William Carlos Williams, Bunting had for several decades failed to find a home in England's staid literary culture for his densely carved experiments in poetic form. But after being rediscovered at the age of 64 by Connie and Tom, and welcomed into the youthful setting of Morden Tower, Bunting was inspired to write his masterpiece – the 1966 long poem *Briggflatts* – an extraordinary affirmation of northern identity, and one of the major modernist poems of the twentieth century.

Lawrence Ferlinghetti reading at Morden Tower, 1965
(Basil Bunting is on the far-right, wearing glasses)

Alongside Bunting, and coming from a very different place in every sense, Ginsberg was the perhaps the most celebrated contemporary poet yet to agree to give a reading at Morden Tower. He was also, more crucially, one of the first people to note the vital connection between the literary happenings taking place in the Tower and the deeper modernist heritage of the North of England. Drawing a line between what he had seen of Newcastle city centre (especially its evocative railway station) and the 'celestially decorous' scene he witnessed when he gave his poetry reading at Morden Tower later that evening, Ginsberg said that he

> realized for certain that the bardic rituals of Morden Tower were not merely the propriety of youthful cognoscenti continuing traditions of old, but that the magic enacted in the Tower articulated the unconscious of the entire city slumbering in the mechanic illusions of the century.

As this slightly rambling beatnik tribute suggests, Ginsberg felt powerfully that in coming to Newcastle he had arrived at a place where post-industrial decline was being offset by more modern, more vital forms of art and activity.

Ginsberg's notion of a modernizing tradition salvaged from the ruins of industry strikes at the heart of the whole narrative of northern revivalism explored in this book. So let us look a little more closely at how it came about. We saw in the last chapter how modernism and futurism became embedded in the twentieth-century North to become a kind of regional house style – and how the northern landscape was itself the inspiration for a series of visionary dreams about the future of humanity. But in many of these cases the future tended to function as an abstract idea rather than a more concrete reality.

Sci-fi dreaming is all very well. But what about actual, everyday manifestations of progressive culture and society in the late twentieth-century North? And what does examining such examples teach us about the longer-term prospects for renewing a national culture in which the North is often marginalized – a culture in which northern areas are, if you like, continually prevented from rising above their station?

If there is one really essential message underlying the postwar examples explored in this section, it is something like this: at certain crucial moments in these years, a mood of modernist revival managed to win out against a more deep-seated feeling that deindustrialization marked the beginning of the end for northern society. To be sure, the North's industrial culture had been in slow decline since the high-water mark of the Edwardian era – and it would continue to deteriorate, much more drastically, in the Thatcherite Eighties. Nonetheless, beginning in the Sixties, as the British economy recovered from wartime and underwent a many-sided cultural boom, there was a dramatic upsurge of creative activity throughout northern cities, which both continued and overhauled the region's deeper traditions of modernist innovation.

The dominant cultural mode of the post-war years has sometimes been described as 'popular modernism', a moment when the radical avant-garde experiments of the early twentieth century – especially those in literature, architecture, film, visual art and music – crossed over into ordinary walks of everyday life. According to this theory, while the modernist activity of earlier decades had been a mostly leftfield, marginal affair, in the Fifties and Sixties the modernist sensibility became a basic template for mass culture of all kinds, from furniture and fashion to the newly electrified pop music which changed the whole fabric of contemporary life. This trend was visible right across social-democratic Britain (and of course, with different accents, in other parts of the world). But in the English North it was perhaps more than usually prominent, partly because modernizing renovations of Britain's centralized system will probably always involve some form of unchaining and upraising of its so-called provincial cities.

As we delve deeper into the post-war history of one of these northern regional outposts (Newcastle), to try to work out why grassroots happenings like Allen Ginsberg's 1965 reading

THE NORTH WILL RISE AGAIN

at Morden Tower came about, it makes sense, for the sake of historical understanding, to look at this narrative from both cultural and political angles. On the cultural side, to begin with, two individuals in particular exemplify the strident forms of popular modernism that began to take root in cities like Newcastle in the Fifties and Sixties.

The first of these figures, the poet Basil Bunting, is a good example of the essential relationship between the new modernizing instinct and dreams of regional empowerment in these years. Prior to his belated breakthrough in the Sixties, Bunting had faced many years of hostile reception from London publishers and literary tastemakers – largely, it would seem, because of the singular mix of modernism and northern-ness to be found in his poetry. Born and brought up in Newcastle in the first years of the century, Bunting subsequently integrated with the lively London and Paris modernist scenes of the post-First World War period. As a close friend of Ezra Pound – and an acquaintance of Pound's modernist ally T. S. Eliot – he might have been expected to have found an easy reception in the publishing culture of the Thirties. But Eliot (by this point deep into his self-described 'Anglican-royalist-classicist' phase) would not publish Bunting at the main British poetry publisher Faber & Faber, apparently because his writing was too radical in the style of Pound. Meanwhile, the leading British poet of the Thirties, W. H. Auden, rather snootily rebuffed Bunting's attempts to strike up a literary friendship in the first years of the decade. Unable to break into the elite English literary scene, Bunting stopped writing completely after publishing a handful of well-regarded but little-read poems in the early Thirties. Over the next three decades, a series of itinerant jobs in sailing, journalism and the RAF would take up much of his time, at the expense of any original creative work.

In fact, Bunting would most probably have died in obscurity if he hadn't been suddenly transported into the Sixties and their counterculture by the Pickards and their friends at Morden Tower in the spring of 1964, after Tom Pickard took the train to visit him in his home in Wylam – incidentally, the birthplace of George Stephenson – following a random tip-off from a mutual American contact. Perhaps the gratitude Bunting felt for this remarkable turnaround is one of the reasons why he would embrace an often exaggerated version of 'Northumbrian' identity after his belated breakthrough in the Sixties. After being coaxed back into creativity by a youthful northern community, Bunting became one of the key figures in the development of regional-separatist ideas in the late twentieth-century North. With excessive northern chauvinism, Bunting liked to claim that 'Southrons' would 'maul the music' of his signature work *Briggflatts*, by mispronouncing its melodious northern refrains. Perhaps encouraged by the example of his friend and drinking partner, the Scottish nationalist poet Hugh MacDiarmid, Bunting offered reduced reading fees to 'Northumbrian' event organizers (rather eccentrically defined as people living north of the Humber and Ribble rivers), advocated devolution of the English regions along the lines of the Anglo-Saxon kingdoms (Northumbria, Wessex, Mercia, East Anglia, Sussex, Essex, Kent) and was fond of citing a series of historic northern rebellions – especially the pro-Catholic 'Rising of the North' against Elizabeth I in 1569 – as he made the case for Northumbrian separatism. Bunting liked to joke that he wanted to set up passport control checkpoints at the Humber. But in reality he believed in a form of federalism which would see England divided up into federal units in the manner of, say, Germany or Switzerland – very much like those which are increasingly being talked about in the 2020s.

55

However, while Bunting ventured back into the history of regional inequality in arguing for the northern cause, his poetic style looked determinedly to the future. Against the received version of modern English literature, which is mostly based on lingering pastoral and nostalgic clichés, Bunting's poetry offered a glimpse of a different kind of English identity – one that was, in essence, derived from the iconoclastic traditions of his northern homeland. After many decades spent on the margins, following his discovery by the youthful counterculture of the mid-Sixties, Bunting was finally able to put into practice a bold, sharp-cut modernist aesthetic with the aid of the supportive live environment of the Morden Tower. Here, rather miraculously, ordinary Newcastle citizens seemed to show natural sympathy for a brand of modernist poetry which looked and sounded as though it had emerged directly from the soil of a still uncharted northern landscape. As Tom Pickard would later put it, the Morden Tower scene was 'cross-discipline and cross-class too ... it was an adoring, attentive audience. They had no literary ambitions, so Basil had to make it work for them, and he did.'

Bunting's example, then, underlined ways in which northern regionalist ideals could be combined with a modernizing aesthetic which thrived at far remove from the traditions of the English centre. But more fundamentally, his literary project was also a simple attempt to render homage to a region that tended to be ignored, patronized or stereotyped by the central institutions of English cultural life.

A love letter to the Rawthey Valley, an archetypal Pennines landscape where Westmorland and the Yorkshire Dales overlap, *Briggflatts* celebrates the distinctive ambience of the wider 'Northumbrian' countryside. It is full of the sounds of machinery thudding over crushed grit, the music of farm animals, the melody of flowing streams and the lively cadences of northern speech, which are a continual rebuke to clichés of English reticence:

Gentle generous voices weave
over bare night
words to confirm and delight
till bird dawn.

This extraordinary poem is far from a straight romantic idealization of the North: as a faithful-ish 'autobiography' of its author, it also expresses a good deal of the self-loathing Bunting felt as an outsider from the institutions of the English centre. (As well as being repeatedly rejected by the London publishing industry, as a Quaker of sorts Bunting had suffered a brutal few months in Wormwood Scrubs in 1918–19 for conscientious objection to the First World War.) One especially vivid passage in *Briggflatts* is based on Bunting's experience of 1920s London. A 'sick, self-maimed, self-hating' protagonist tells of the feelings of alienation and inadequacy felt by so many young northern exiles in the capital, both then and now:

Poet appointed dare not decline
to walk among the bogus, nothing to authenticate
the mission imposed, despised
by toadies, confidence men, kept boys,
shopped and jailed, cleaned out by whores,
touching acquaintance for food and tobacco.

But on the whole, the northern tale of the tribe that is *Briggflatts* is remarkable for what it affirms rather than for what it laments. Named after one of the sacred foundational sites of Quakerism – a tiny hamlet in the Pennines where Quaker divine George Fox delivered a momentous open-air sermon to rural labourers in 1652 – *Briggflatts* is a radical spatial reimagining of English literature, which pushes a distinctive northern nonconformist sensibility to the front and centre. Rather predictably, it has been somewhat forgotten and marginalized over the years, largely at the expense of less threatening, more genteel poets like John Betjeman, Ted Hughes and Philip Larkin. But when taken together with the vibrant anti-institutional culture of the Morden Tower which spurred its existence, Bunting's *Briggflatts* remains a lasting testament to the potential for an assertive regional province of the mind to arise in England's northern half.

After Bunting discovered the Morden Tower scene in the mid-Sixties, his poetry was published (for the first time in many years) in two successive books designed by the pop artist Richard Hamilton. The first of these, 1965's *King Ida's Watch Chain*, combined a prankish title which nodded at the ancestor of the Northumbrian kings with experimental packaging and contributions from northern, Scottish and American modernist writers. The pamphlet's content was mostly literature of a rather serious kind. But Hamilton's 'passion for designing things ran away with him', as Bunting put it, to produce an artefact that was decentred, playful and egalitarian, very much in the spirit of the pop *annus mirabilis* that was 1965. Each contribution to *King Ida's Watch Chain* was printed on a separate piece of paper, and slotted into a mysterious, minimalist envelope featuring Hamilton's Jesmond address and the simple description 'Printed Matter'. With typical grouchiness, Bunting claimed that the 'idea was that all the bits and pieces should be one size, so that they could be filed by anyone who thought fit and used for arsewipes by the rest'.

Whatever its intended function, *King Ida's Watch Chain* was among other things the summit and summary of an extraordinary decade of activity in the North-East for Hamilton. He had grown up in London and studied at the Slade School of Fine Art. But in 1953 his career took a fateful detour when he accepted a lecturing job at Newcastle University (at this point still officially called King's College, a part of nearby Durham University). In making the journey northwards from the capital – where he had recently integrated with the seminal Independent Group of neo-modernist artists and writers – Hamilton was venturing to a regional art school where staid naturalism was still the dominant house style, and where the students followed a traditional curriculum based on life-drawing and study of perspective. But this would all change, with explosive consequences, when Victor Pasmore became Master of Painting at the university about a year after Hamilton had relocated to Newcastle. A very different figure from Hamilton, Pasmore had started off as a member of the stylistically conservative Euston Road School in the interwar years. But after an abrupt change of direction in the later Forties, he quickly built up a reputation as a radical innovator of continental-style abstraction – a master of large, often monochromatic canvases in which strange, UFO-like shapes were arranged in dynamic tension.

After Pasmore arrived in Newcastle in 1954, he collaborated with Hamilton in developing a groundbreaking foundation course inspired by the blend of applied and fine arts pioneered at the Bauhaus – the German art school which had been at the centre of European modernism in the Twenties and Thirties. The 'Basic Course' developed by Hamilton and Pasmore, which became the standard model for British art degrees from this point on, was largely the

59

result of a commitment to the *Gesamtkunstwerk* (the total, multimedia work of art), which Hamilton and Pasmore shared, despite their differences in artistic style and temperament. For Pasmore, the interest in combining fine art with more engaged, multimedia forms of artistic activity would result in a series of major architectural and public art commissions throughout the North-East from the Fifties to the Seventies. (He designed abstract murals for Newcastle Civic Centre, for example, and built a large, other-worldly sculpture for Peterlee New Town in County Durham, which he named the Apollo Pavilion in honour of the spacecraft involved in the first moon landings.) Hamilton, meanwhile, took a more youthful, irreverent approach. In his view, blurring the boundaries between disparate art forms was a way of innovating a new, provocative aesthetic, which reacted against the high seriousness of both English tradition and continental high modernism by embracing twentieth-century life in all its tacky, technicolour glory.

In a crucial development, as he searched for an authentic artistic style for the post-war years, Hamilton set a trend for his Basic Course students by immersing himself in the American-led pop culture of the day. Influenced by discussions with fellow Independent Group members, such as the Scottish artist Eduardo Paolozzi (a visiting tutor at Newcastle in 1965), during return trips to London in the early Fifties, Hamilton had become fascinated by the American consumerist iconography that was beginning to infiltrate British life, as the austerity and gloom of the immediate post-war years gave way to a more liberated cultural atmosphere. Just as Bunting provided a living link between the literary modernism of the early twentieth century and the younger, freer literary scene of post-war Newcastle, so Hamilton and his Independent Group colleagues would combine respect for the fundamentals of earlier avant-garde movements like futurism, surrealism and Dada, with an openness to pop-cultural references (science fiction and Western films, advertising, comic books, pop music, fashion magazines and so on).

In practice, this meant a continual reshaping of modernist models with the aid of contemporary influences, as Fifties and Sixties Newcastle played host to Hamilton's development of a sophisticated version of what would come to be called pop art. On the one hand, Hamilton would coax his students into relocating the *Merz Barn* sculpture frieze (by the legendary German modernist Kurt Schwitters) from the Lake District to Newcastle University's Hatton Gallery in 1965 – and, in the same period, he would embark on a daring reconstruction of Marcel Duchamp's multi-dimensional art work *The Bride Stripped Bare by Her Bachelors, Even* in his Newcastle studio. At the same time, the desire to give modernism a radically democratic update for the Space Age led Hamilton to encourage his students to derive inspiration from the fairground kitsch of the Hoppings (a yearly funfair on Newcastle's Town Moor) and lunchtime dances at the Majestic Ballroom, where office workers danced to rock 'n' roll and pop records by Elvis Presley, Chubby Checker and The Shirelles, before going back to their humdrum desk jobs. Hamilton himself was always impeccably dressed in the latest Levi jeans and cowboy shirts bought from influential Newcastle menswear boutique Marcus Price on Percy Street; and, slightly later on, as the Sixties began to pick up pace, he would become a regular attendee at the Club A-Go-Go nightclub, a few doors down from Marcus Price. Here, a house-style based on the importation of American rhythm and blues provided a nurturing home for local band The Animals (who began life with a residency at the club). A natural predisposition to this strand of mass culture had, some years earlier, lurked behind Hamilton's famous summary of pop art, as communicated in a 1957 letter to fellow Independent Group members Alison and Peter Smithson: in Hamilton's definition, 'Pop art is Popular (designed for a mass audience), Transient (short term solution), Expendable (easily forgotten), Low cost, Mass produced, Young (aimed at youth), Witty, Sexy, Gimmicky, Glamorous, Big Business.'

As we will see, there was a problematic side to this enthusiastic celebration of consumer capitalism, which in certain key ways pre-empted and prepared the way for the postmodern turn of the Eighties and Nineties. But with hindsight, the actual material products of Hamilton's Newcastle phase now strike us as unmistakably modernist artefacts: more futuristic than the present-tense ephemera of Andy Warhol and Roy Lichtenstein, and with an eye on *tomorrow* as the ultimate goal of all this elaborate attention to the minutiae of the Nuclear Age. Certainly, when we now look at archive images of the *Man, Machine and Motion* exhibition which Hamilton assembled at the Hatton Gallery in 1955 – the pinnacle of his early career and a Big Bang moment for British pop art – we are reminded of modernist precursors (futurism, the Bauhaus, Kurt Schwitters, Marcel Duchamp) far more than of the leading lights of American pop, still less the jaunty postmodernism of the decades to come. In part, this is because Hamilton's work for the Hatton exhibition was above all a celebration of *technology*. In thirty modular frames made of black steel, Hamilton arranged monochromatic installations on four themes: 'Aquatic', 'Terrestrial', 'Aerial' and 'Interplanetary'. Photos of deep-sea divers, early motor-car races and aeroplane fuselages were juxtaposed with antique drawings of fantastical flying

62

machines and up-to-date images of rockets and astronauts. The underlying narrative of this overtly sci-fi presentation was, in Hamilton's words, the 'mechanical conquest of time and distance [by way of] structures that man has created to broaden his ability to travel and to explore regions of Nature that were previously denied to him'.

Even setting aside the internationalist ethos of *Man, Machine and Motion*, it is important to remember that it was a product of London just as much as Newcastle. Or perhaps, more accurately, given that Hamilton was commuting between his northern day job and weekend meetings with the Independent Group in the capital throughout this whole period, we should place it in a tradition of post-war inter-city travel, which saw increasingly fertile creative networks

Victor Pasmore's Apollo Pavillion, Peterlee, County Durham

develop all across Britain (despite the rapid decline of its railway system from the mid-Sixties on). Nonetheless, while Hamilton was certainly no cheerleader for regionalism, it is also clear that *Man, Machine and Motion* – and indeed Hamilton's output throughout the whole period from 1953 to 1966 – was in certain key respects the natural outgrowth of a specifically northern urban environment. The material basis of Hamilton's development of a neo-futurist, technology-oriented version of pop art was, as we have seen, partly the result of his engagement with the specific pop culture of post-war Newcastle – its fairground rides, mod boutiques and rock 'n' roll ballrooms, not to mention the state-funded Newcastle University photography and print departments which Hamilton relied on when preparing exhibitions like *Man, Machine and Motion*. (The university's historic expertise in marine technology, reflecting Tyneside's nautical heritage, was especially useful in providing archival material for the panel displays.)

But there was also a deeper sense in which Hamilton's pop modernism captured the northern spirit of place. Hamilton's work in Newcastle throughout the Fifties and Sixties would seize on the city's collapsing industrial identity to revive its underlying sense of forward momentum – just as Basil Bunting's readings in the Morden Tower bypassed the reactionary culture of English literature to achieve a kind of unlikely, long-delayed grassroots breakthrough for intricate modernist poetry. Quite aside from its origins in a newly empowered regional art school, an exhibition like *Man, Machine and Motion*, with its imagery derived from the history of industrial technology, was clearly in one sense an organic product of the North-East – a place where the modern steam locomotive was created, the steam turbine was invented and electric lighting was patented. *Man, Machine and Motion* was a work-in-the-round which revived modernism's celebration of the machine and its ability to liberate human beings, even in a rapidly deindustrializing, post-atomic world, where such technological optimism was starting to seem slightly questionable. In this sense, and in keeping with both its roots in a Bauhaus-influenced tradition of socially engaged design and the populist backdrop of the post-war years, *Man, Machine and Motion* was a work which took inspiration from its immediate surroundings as it sought to lay down a path to tomorrow.

In remembering the dynamic cultural era which produced *Briggflatts* and *Man, Machine and Motion*, we might think finally of the powerful symbolism of Richard Hamilton passing through Newcastle Central Station before starting his teaching week at the university, and of Allen Ginsberg's similar arrival at the birthplace of *Rocket* on his way to meet Basil Bunting and Tom Pickard in May 1965. If art and atmosphere are at all intertwined, it seems highly likely that both of these figures would have been profoundly affected by this echoing vault of the century's 'mechanic' illusions – and also, maybe, more deeply moved by its howling, haunting potential for renewal.

As the examples of both Richard Hamilton and Morden Tower show, the modernist revival of the North in the post-war years was all about *surroundings*. Neither *Briggflatts* nor *Man, Machine and Motion* was very different, in its fundamentals, from the major works of early twentieth-century modernism. But as we have seen, it was the manner in which these works and their creators engaged with the North's grassroots – in particular, the new, exuberant culture of the post-war young – which made all the difference.

In fact, the new emphasis on social engagement combined with affirmations of northern place was being more widely sponsored by the political culture of the post-war North. In Newcastle, much of this civic backdrop was shaped by the leading local politician of the era, T. Dan Smith, whose story is perhaps the saddest and pithiest in the whole narrative of northern revivalism since the Second World War.

A direct heir to the North's industrial culture (and its unhappy fate), Smith was born in the Tyneside shipbuilding hub of Wallsend in 1915, shortly before Yevgeny Zamyatin began working in the docks there. His parents were working-class radicals and autodidacts: his father a communist coalminer fond of quoting Plato and Marx to his son, his mother (also a communist) a cleaner who worked double shifts to keep the family solvent. With this blend of hardship and literacy as his bedrock, the adult Smith integrated with radical leftist circles after working as a painter and decorator at the tail end of the Depression. Then, in the later Forties, he wandered into the mainstream, defecting to the Labour Party to become a driving force in Newcastle's post-war council. By 1960 he had become its charismatic leader – variously dubbed 'Mr Newcastle', the 'Mouth of the Tyne' and the 'Voice of the North'.

In the wider context of social-democratic Britain, forces were aligning to empower figures like Smith. The progressive mood of the time encouraged a multitude of ambitious proposals for overhauling Britain's antiquated, London-centric political scaffolding. These movements would culminate in the (mostly unimplemented) Redcliffe-Maud Report of 1966–9, which called for a two-tier system of government based on devolution of power to eight regional 'provinces'. Smith was eventually one of the architects of Redcliffe-Maud. But even prior to its publication, he benefited from – and helped to intensify – a climate of regional boosterism enabled by the hefty government spending increases of the Keynesian post-war years. As the buoyant Sixties dawned, Smith embarked on a serious of ambitious building projects, which made the most of this political zeitgeist. At the start of his tenure as council leader, he made sure that Newcastle was the first city in the country to have its own planning department – a shot in the arm for regional autonomy. From this point on, his administration was responsible for one of the most imaginative modernizations of any British city since the Industrial Revolution.

At the heart of Smith's programme was a fierce determination to rid Newcastle of its slums – the row upon row of crowded terraces which curved down to the polluted River Tyne in areas like Byker, Elswick and Scotswood. He spearheaded council projects which demolished these unpopular buildings and replaced them with modern public housing, most of which is still standing over half a century later. Smith also ordered the construction of a motorway system to alleviate the city's traffic congestion problems (at the time, the main shopping thoroughfare formed part of the busy road between London and Edinburgh). The murky, coal-blackened Tyne was cleaned and purified with the aid of new sewage pipelines, and plans were eventually laid for the creation of a European-style metro train network. (At the time of writing, the eventual product of this scheme, the Tyne and Wear Metro, is still the only full-blown rapid-transit system in England outside London.) On top of such achievements, Smith's council was partly or wholly responsible for developing Newcastle Airport, the shopping centre Eldon Square, the Civic Centre, Newcastle

Polytechnic, the independence of Newcastle University from Durham, the Northern Stage theatre, the arts organization Northern Arts, the City Library, the preservation of the medieval town walls and the expansion of Tyne Tees Television – basically, the vast majority of the city's modern infrastructure, even to this day.

Smith's vision of a regional metropolis was inspired by the cities of the Renaissance and the ancient world, as well as more contemporary models like Manhattan and the post-war modernist showpiece Brasilia. He was driven by a rare sense of metaphysical urgency, which could be breathtaking in its determination to turn his home city into a modernist capital. Indeed, at times Smith seems to have envisaged Newcastle to be something like a culmination of Western civilization as a whole. A passage from his 1970 autobiography shows this idealistic instinct in full flight:

Why do you like water or mountains? ... Think about it, talk about it. Why is it that when buildings are put on the landscape they appear to offend[?] Yet cows don't, sheep don't, dogs don't, trees don't, and flowers don't, no matter what their colours or what their shapes, whether it's calm, whether the wind's blowing, whether the trees are blowing about, whether it's autumn, spring, summer or winter; Nature has a way of integrating its own objects into the landscape. Can we do this consciously as human beings? Of course we can. We can give just as much attention to a street lamp, or a litter bin, or a bus station, or a bus shelter, or a house, or the colour of a house, or the colour of a brick ... These details are essentially in the mind of the artist and this is why I need to try to direct the discussion towards the creation of a city in the image of Athens and Florence and Rome.

This was, apparently, the sort of thing Smith would say while chairing council planning meetings. Truly, this was urbanism as a fine art.

But tragically, there was also a dark side to Smith and to his planned northern renaissance. In the first years of the Sixties – the time of Richard Hamilton's pop experiments and Basil Bunting's improbable modernist rebirth – Smith's overhaul of Newcastle received broad support, both in the North and further afield. He was named *Architects' Journal* Man of the Year in 1960, and at the same time enjoyed considerable popularity on his home turf, in spite of occasional grumbles about his glam lifestyle as signalled by dapper suits and a Jaguar with the personalized number plate 'DAN 68'. The general consensus in Newcastle was that many of the city's more eccentric Victorian buildings – from the slum terraces of Scotswood to the gawky, unloved old Town Hall – were simply not fit for purpose. As a result, Smith-aided replacements like the ultramodern social housing high-rises of Elswick and the no-expenses-spared local government complex of the Civic Centre were mostly seen as positive, even lavish developments. (Notably, the de luxe Civic Centre was designed by city architect George Kenyon, who had earlier worked on the construction of the Empire State Building in New York.) They seemed to suggest that the region was recovering and thriving again after the interwar nadir of the Depression – the first really major cataclysm in the century-long tragedy of northern deindustrialization.

However, Smith's reputation started to collapse fairly rapidly after his Sixties zenith. In part, this was due to changing attitudes in the later twentieth century to civic modernism and its social-democratic underpinning, such that many of Smith's building projects came to be seen as 'concrete

T. Dan Smith (left) in front of a social housing development in Newcastle, early 1960s

monstrosities' created by a technocratic elite with scant regard for Newcastle's traditional urban fabric. It is true that in some cases the replacements for demolished nineteenth-century buildings were not much of an improvement (such as the rather dully designed Eldon Square shopping centre – its awe-inspiring flying-saucer café aside – which replaced one half of a pleasant if unremarkable Georgian piazza). But for the most part, such criticisms of Smith and his modernizing dreams for Newcastle were and are unfair. Most of the buildings demolished to make way for social housing and infrastructure projects like the Central Motorway were over-elaborate, awkward and, crucially, under-used products of the later nineteenth century (whereas Smith's administration ensured that more valuable early Victorian set-pieces like Grey Street were preserved).

But the main cause of Smith's ultimate downfall was a more human failing. The received narrative, enthusiastically promoted in national newspaper accounts from the Seventies on, is that Smith was a crooked, Chicago-style city boss, whose personal flaws embodied the sinister totalitarian impulses of post-war planning – and by extension, perhaps, left-leaning regionalism in general. In this reading, Smith's public disgrace after he was imprisoned on corruption charges in 1974 was the Profumo Affair of the Seventies – and he eventually brought Newcastle and the wider social-democratic experiment down with him, just as John Profumo's misdeeds had fatally wounded Harold Macmillan's Tories ten years earlier.

The fact of Smith's six-year prison sentence in the mid-Seventies is inescapable, though the actual charge brought against him (gifting the contract for a £1,000 model of Peterlee New Town to corrupt property developer John Poulson) has been disputed. Smith's biographer Chris Foote Wood (the brother of seminal northern comedian Victoria Wood) argues that he pleaded guilty to the charge because he 'was told by his legal team that if he didn't plead guilty, the powers-that-be would come back again and again until they got a conviction'. Going by the available evidence, and at the distance of several decades, it seems probable that Smith was guilty of at least some of the corruption charges levelled against him. More recent cases of prominent politicians consorting with the likes of Vladimir Putin, Donald Trump and the Saudi government help to put Smith's relatively minor misdemeanours in perspective. But arguing that he was not quite as bad as the racketeer democrats of the twenty-first century is not much of a defence, still less an excuse.

Ultimately, there is little doubt that Smith's fall from grace was at least partly deserved. This is not to say, however, that we should let his personal flaws obscure the memory of his ambitious plan for a bold, energetic, far-reaching revival of a slumbering northern town. Indeed, as we try to work out how to build new renaissance cities on either side of the modern Pennines, we must try to learn from Smith's successes, as well as his failures.

As the story of T. Dan Smith underlines, the modernist revival which peaked in Sixties Newcastle was a relatively fleeting one. The mid-Sixties were a remarkable high-water mark for the city's cultural scene: from the foundation of Morden Tower as a poetry venue in 1964 and the publication of *Briggflatts* in 1966 to Richard Hamilton's renovations of Duchamp's *Bride* and Schwitters's *Merz Barn* throughout 1965–6, to the completion of the T. Dan-powered Civic Centre in 1967, there is no doubt that this was an interlude of rare optimism and renewal for this long marginalized corner of the North of England.

But for all the durable achievements of this period – many of which, like the Civic Centre and Morden Tower, are still just about standing – there is a sense in which the assertion (or re-assertion) of the modernizing impulse in places like Sixties Newcastle was built on shifting sands. By the mid-Seventies, Smith was in jail, Hamilton had long since left Newcastle and Bunting was a depressed OAP writing very little new poetry. While the cultural and building projects of the Fifties and Sixties had done a decent job of checking the march of post-industrial decline – ongoing since the early decades of the century – the rocketing unemployment figures and recurrent economic crises of the Seventies were a sign that it would take far more than a handful of art works and even a concerted campaign for modernist housing to revive the North in more permanent ways.

In fact, as we will see, instead of a lasting reversal of regional inequality, the post-war northern revival epitomized by the case study of Sixties Newcastle was merely the prelude to the wholesale dismantling of northern society in the Eighties and Nineties. In the broad historic view, this was a classic northern case of taking one step forward before several light years back.

The deserted Grove Rake Mine, North Pennines
(territorial cousin of the American West)

England's Unconscious

How, after all that modernist dreaming, did the North continue to slide downwards after the bold egalitarian strides of the post-war years? As we will see in the next section, the reactionary movements of the later twentieth century were partly to blame. At the same time, it is important to stress that the North's problems are much older and more deep-seated than the rightward turn in British politics over the last few decades, which sought to eradicate northern communal structures, from the grassroots of the Labour Party to the civic initiatives of people like T. Dan Smith. In fact, if we are trying to work out how to achieve a truly lasting regional levelling, we need to realize that the North's modernizing culture has been fighting a mostly losing battle against England's unequal power structures for centuries rather than just decades. Another detour back – or rather forwards – into my own story will, I hope, help to give this harsh underlying reality some fuller human context.

In the first decade of the twenty-first century I helped to start an idealistic, future-facing pop band called Everything Everything. Like all meaningful adventures, and unlike the many hundreds of pop bands driven by artifice and opportunism, this project was the outgrowth of deep roots in place and time. For the most part – and certainly the better part – these roots were both northern and modernist, in the sense that I have been using those terms up to now. The immediate northern context for the formation of the band (Manchester) will come to light in more detail in a later chapter. But its basic outline was first sketched in a very different part of the North, a place that in its strange marginality contains certain buried clues about what has happened to the northern idea of the future over the last century – and where it is now heading as we burrow deeper into the twenty-first.

Three of the four founding members of Everything Everything (myself included) first got to know each other at Queen Elizabeth High School, a large comprehensive in Hexham in the west of Northumberland. To the untrained eye, Hexham is a sleepy district capital – an ancient market town and pushing-off point for excursions to Hadrian's Wall and the Northumberland National Park. But here, as elsewhere in the rural North, the tourist-board clichés are complicated if not wholly undermined by the presence of a neighbouring backcountry that is desolate, neurotic and wild, in both scenic and psychological ways. This still mostly undefined rural space is quite literally England's Deep North, and it played a crucial role in shaping the project that would later become Everything Everything.

On the surface, the origins of the band were ordinary enough. Myself and the other founding members would tend to meet on schooldays in respectable, well-connected Hexham (after Manchester's Liverpool Road, Hexham's railway station is the oldest in continuous use in the world). Here, at QEHS, we benefited from a liberal, arts-oriented education, which embodied most of what was good about the British comprehensive system, in the last days before Ofsted, academies and league tables obliterated its finely developed extracurricular culture. During breaktimes and music lessons, we would make the most of this state-sponsored laxity by embarking on endless psychedelic jam sessions at the back of the flaking Victorian 'hydro' hotel which formed the top half of our school grounds.

In spite of such shabbiness, there was an atmosphere of cosmopolitan worldliness about the school as a whole. Many of the teachers commuted from urban Newcastle, and the outgoing headmaster was Patrick Eavis (brother of Glastonbury Festival founder Michael), a lovely man who would usher pupils through crowded corridors while instructing them to 'keep to the left, as in life'. Eavis's successor as head was married to the drama teacher, a one-time partner of Mark Knopfler from Dire Straits; together with the populist head of music, Len Young, this hippyish school executive would organize large yearly youth theatre events featuring hundreds of cast members, elaborately crafted stage sets and high-octane musical provision, which offered band members like us a way of integrating our grungy eccentricity with the norms of the mainstream school community. For all its bitter and often violent internal class divides, I will always be grateful for the nurturing culture of our comprehensive school, which made the most of the now lost educational freedoms of social-democratic Britain, and which empowered us to think we were at the centre of a world of creative possibility. More than anything else, it was this environment which literally brought Everything Everything together, and which gave us the confidence and the leeway to be as weird and as wayward as we liked.

But while Hexham and its school provided the future members of the band with a testing ground for ideas, we would find deeper inspiration in a more impenetrable northern locale. Outside of the school day, the band's eventual lead singer Jonathan and I spent most of our time in our family homes, both of which were in more remote villages on the edge of the vacant moorlands of the North Pennines and the National Park. This gave rise to a kind of doubleness in our lives, which embodied the deeper tension between primitive marginality and advanced creativity which has defined northern culture since at least as far back as the eighth-century Lindisfarne Gospels.

The author (left) playing guitar in Everything
Everything, 2008

There is no doubt that both our friendship and the project which became Everything Everything arose from the specific combination of loneliness and intense dreaming Jonathan and I felt while growing up in the isolated countryside of this peculiar hinterland. To begin to understand its atmosphere, you could do a lot worse than think of the famous setting of Emily Brontë's *Wuthering Heights*. Underlying Brontë's unsurpassed Pennines novel is a profound truth about existence in the rural English North: it suggests that while the expansive moors offer a mirage of emotional liberation, the more dominant reality in this part of the country is the cloistered space of the domestic home (and indeed this is precisely *because* the ocean-like moorlands surround and isolate dwellings which can, therefore, resemble desert islands). In *Wuthering Heights*, this theme takes shape in the form of the brooding gothic farmhouse at the centre of the

78

novel, a place where all the unbridled urges of the unconscious are permanently, nakedly on show.

One of the main things Jonathan and I had in common was that we both experienced a sort of pared-down, millennial version of Brontë's northern rural domestic prison. Our mothers were both primary school teachers (and in fact, after my mother died, Jonathan's mother would replace her as headteacher of a small village school on the other side of the Tyne Valley). Meanwhile, our dads were both somewhat eccentric, mentally unstable scientists, both of whom, I think, felt in some sense stranded in the inland desert of west Northumberland after their professional lives faltered. This family subplot meant that we both grew up in the thick of claustrophobic, emotionally volatile home lives – hardly helped by our socially barren surroundings.

I don't know whether this is a northern or a national or even a global phenomenon, but it always strikes me as absurd to the point of hilarity when people – often city-dwellers indulging in *Escape to the Country* reveries – talk about the 'greater sense of community' in the countryside. No doubt communities and community feeling exist to a degree in rural settlements everywhere. But I have to say that in the part of the Tyne Valley where I grew up there was very little of it – and certainly much less than I have found as an adult living in a series of disparate but usually very friendly urban neighbourhoods. Perhaps the ancient, dispersed settlement patterns of upland areas in the north and west of England are ultimately to blame. (There are very few village greens, for example, in west Northumberland, where the villages tend to have a scattered layout and few communal spaces.) Or maybe it has more to do with the anti-social trajectory of modern life. Contemporary existence almost everywhere now tends to centre on a kind of domestic fortress; but while urban areas have many more civic amenities to tempt people to venture outside, in the countryside homes are increasingly inhabited by people who commute to nearby towns and retreat into their TV and laptop hideaways at evenings and weekends, leaving little room for anything resembling the older structures of rural community. As home-working professionals flock to the countryside in the wake of Covid-19, the situation seems likely to get worse to the point of social crisis. And so, as in so many other walks of contemporary life, it seems clear that only cities can save us.

Whatever the causes, the reality of living on the western edge of Northumberland was – and probably still is – remarkably lonely, often boring and psychologically enervating for anyone wanting to engage with the basic infrastructures of human civic life. Faced with this unforgiving backdrop, and the fraught family life which follows from being cut off from amenities and social outlets for much of the year, Jonathan and I developed separate but parallel coping strategies. We both sought solace in art, music and writing – as contained in a private technology of books, CDs, musical equipment and, eventually, the internet. And we both ultimately evolved separate but parallel canons of belief in the supreme value of futurist innovation. Though neither of us was much aware of it at the time, this was perhaps the truest possible expression of our surroundings in the Deep North – England's remote, rarely heeded unconscious.

―――――

Moving westward from Newcastle and the relatively sedate landscape of the eastern Tyne Valley, you feel a creeping wildness with every mile. This is, as the tourist brochures are keen to point out, England's last wilderness. For once, they are not exaggerating. Out of all the sparsely populated upland areas of northern England, the North Pennines and their environs (which reach up to the Scottish border in the extended form of the Cheviot Hills and the Northumberland National Park) are surely the most extreme in atmosphere – in part because they are so seldom visited, especially when compared to holiday-home theme parks like the Lake District and the Yorkshire Dales.

Over the years, a long line of artists and writers have been both traumatized and inspired by encounters with this part of the country. The poet W. H. Auden was one. Writing at the height of the Second World War, while in exile in the United States, Auden wrote about the North Pennines in his poem 'New Year Letter':

Those limestone moors that stretch from BROUGH
To HEXHAM and the ROMAN WALL,
There is my symbol of us all.

As we can see from this fragment, this overlooked backcountry was a precious, even sacred space in Auden's private mythology. But even for him it was not always such a cosy one. For Auden, and for many others, the North Pennines have often acted as a kind of brutal polar opposite to that other great inspiring space of the English literary imaginary – the tamer, wealthier pastoral landscape which lies somewhere on the far side of the Home Counties, perhaps specifically within a 50-mile radius of Oxford (a major source of inspiration for a long line of canonical authors, from Shakespeare to J. R. R. Tolkien). While the nearby Lake District was long ago assimilated into the mainstream of English culture (partly because the London and Home Counties rich bought up much of the housing stock there), the North Pennines have remained a refuge for those writers and artists in search of a shadowy *terra incognita* which seems somehow to exist beyond England itself.

In another version of Auden's 'New Year Letter', we can see this idea at work as he offers a more ominous portrait of the abandoned mining country around Rookhope on the

Durham–Northumberland border, where he spent several childhood holidays:

> In ROOKHOPE I was first aware
> Of Self and Not-Self, Death and Dread:
> There I dropped pebbles, listened, heard
> The reservoir of darkness stirred.

A strange episode from Auden's teenage years lies behind this passage. While wandering on nearby Bolt's Law at the age of 15, Auden apparently had an epiphany after dropping a handful of pebbles down a disused shaft of the Sikehead lead mine (then, as now, a cluster of ruined workings grouped around a lone brick chimney in the nowhere land around Rookhope). As the stones hit the bottom, Auden felt a profound terror. Realizing the deep oblivion at the heart of this landscape, he underwent 'the seminal moment of his life as a civilised human being and as an artist', as one critic later put it. For Auden, the memory of encountering a place utterly devoid of people and littered with the ruins of an extinct technology seems to have acted as a kind of provoking, productive fear in the years to come. Auden himself described his epiphany as a discovery of *Urmutterfurcht* ('fear of the original mother'), a compulsion which, he claimed, 'drives / Us into ... / The far interior of our fate / To civilise and create'. There is perhaps some cod-psychology – and some very dodgy gender politics – behind this description of a suffocating, womb-like space. But the more general portrayal of this post-industrial wilderness as a foreboding interior is a suggestive one, which certainly had a powerful impact on Auden himself. Whatever dark mystery he felt or heard in the Sikehead mine, it apparently spurred him on to write poetry for the remaining several decades of his life.

Auden was not alone in coming to this view of the North Pennines and its 'reservoir of darkness'. Indeed, you do not have to be hell-bent on searching for occult weirdness to get a sense of the savage sublime which dominates this locale and cultural responses to it. As we will see in Chapter 6, another, very different poet, Barry MacSweeney, chose the land around Allenheads as the setting of his radiant verse tragedy *Pearl*, a 1995 poem sequence which narrates the visceral struggle of a mute, illiterate young girl to make her voice heard against the backdrop of a 'white water upland empire' where nothing and nobody is listening. Similarly (and again we will return to this narrative later on), MacSweeney's fellow Newcastle poet Tom Pickard also found creative impetus in this alternately hellish and holy terrain, when he sought refuge in the wind-raked land around Cross Fell during a period of break-up and breakdown in the early twenty-first century.

John Martin's *The Destruction of Pompeii and Herculaneum* (1822)

But there are yet more definitive examples from cultural history which help to describe the Deep North's distinctive *genius loci.* Venturing further back than the poetry of the last hundred years, there is the extraordinary case of the painter John Martin, who grew up in Haydon Bridge, some 7 miles west of Hexham. Martin's apocalyptic paintings based on biblical and classical episodes – notably *Belshazzar's Feast* (1820) and *The Destruction of Sodom and Gomorrah* (1852) – are sometimes associated with the industrial landscape of urban Newcastle, where Martin underwent professional training in his teenage years. But the hallucinatory juxtapositions we see in Martin's canvases, which combine vast, unpeopled mountain scenes with demonic tricks of the light, underground caverns and furnace-like recesses, are probably best seen as an exaggerated depiction of Martin's actual native environment – the paleo-industrial countryside of the South Tyne Valley at the turn of the nineteenth century. More to the point, Martin's paintings certainly give expression to the febrile, fiercely autonomous worldview that is more than usually common among the Deep North's inhabitants.

I can't speak for everyone from this part of the world, but for me, being a teenager in west Northumberland often felt like being trapped inside a John Martin painting. This was partly due to fairly typical adolescent mental-health wrangles and family psychodramas. But it also had quite a lot to do with the gothic-industrial panorama of the landscape itself. Largely because of its history of depopulation and deindustrialization, which has given rise to a haunting sense of bareness and void, the greater North Pennines can often seem like a nightmarish place – perhaps especially to its scattered, hedged-in citizens. Up here in the unconscious of the island, the disembowelled remains of the ambitions and failures of technological progress are everywhere to be seen. Deserted mine shafts and smelting chimneys appear suddenly in landscapes mercilessly cleared of trees to make way for grouse killing fields. Ornate electric powerhouses lurk at the back of Victorian mansions hidden on the edge of villages now deprived of their occupational heart. Old wagonways which once carried the world's first train carts trail away and vanish in blood-red moors.

At its most basic level, Everything Everything took root as an inchoate idea in this ultra-specific setting, as Jonathan and I were brought together by our shared experience of a depleted northern wilderness where the future often feels like it has been derailed. The nuances of our friendship – which tended to alternate between magic empathy and sullen incomprehension – supplied the personal backdrop to the development of the band. But there was also a geographical influence at work here. In a fairly obvious, if sometimes unwitting sense Everything Everything was our attempt to follow on from – and perhaps resurrect – the tradition of northern modernism I have described in previous chapters. (The seed of the idea for the expansive band name, for example, came from Paul Morley's 2004 book *Words and Music*, which I read one summer while working in a car-panel warehouse on the site of the old colliery in Fourstones, and which argued that the rise of the internet suggested infinite new possibilities for musical novelty and experimentation.) But perhaps we should have known, from looking at the technological ruins surrounding us in our corner of the North, that this enterprise would be far from straightforward in practice.

Jonathan and I first met in 1993, when our small village schools came together for a residential week in Ford Castle in the far north of Northumberland. But it wasn't until we arrived at QEHS in 1997, when we were 13, that we became close friends. As already mentioned, we both lived in outlying villages of the western Tyne Valley – an area slightly but definitely beyond the more urbane commuter strip which stretches from the Newcastle suburbs to Hexham, the district capital. My village, Fourstones, lay some 5 miles to the west of Hexham. Meanwhile, Jonathan was stranded even further out. The garden in his home – in an ambivalent village called Gilsland, some two hours by public transport from urban Newcastle – was in fact so far into the debatable land of the Deep North that it literally traversed the Northumberland–Cumbria border, and therefore also the ambiguous boundary line between North-East and North-West.*

Both Fourstones and Gilsland had been radically detached from the modern world and its networks when the Beeching cuts decimated the British railway system in the late Sixties, around about the same time as the last mines in the area – such as Settlingstones – were finally abandoned. In common with many train routes in the North (especially those in the North-East, where the invention of *Rocket* had turbo-charged the growth of global rail transport), the Tyne Valley railway line arrived very early on the scene. Indeed, it slightly pre-dated even the heady Victorian era, having been constructed in the last days of William IV's reign. A train service started running to Gilsland in the summer of 1836, with Fourstones following a few months later in January 1837. Rather astonishingly – and yet utterly in keeping with a quintessential northern habit of taking sudden, dramatic leaps forward (and back) – this meant that these formerly remote borderland settlements contained two of the first passenger railway stations in human history. However, an equally drastic reversal would occur just over a century later. In the mid-Sixties, two infamous government reports were written and published by the engineer Richard Beeching (ironically, just as urban Newcastle was caught up in the modernist convulsion of Basil Bunting, Richard Hamilton and T. Dan Smith). The

---

*Though not directly relevant to our narrative, the fact that recent historians have surmised that Gilsland may have been the childhood home of St Patrick adds a further layer to its recherché spirit of place.

so-called 'Beeching Reports' argued that 'lightly used' train stations were a pointless waste of public finances. As a result of these recommendations, the Fourstones and Gilsland termini were closed, seemingly forever.

By the time our families came to live in the two villages in the early Eighties, the railway stations had been out of use for over a decade, more than doubling the time it took to get to Newcastle (and therefore the wider world) by public transport. Middle-class families had long since colonized the old station outbuildings, incorporating waiting rooms and ticket offices into oddly structured, warren-like but fairly respectable family homes, which passengers on shabby, underfunded trains tended to ignore as they swung past on journeys between Carlisle and Newcastle.

Though it had often been idyllic in childhood, with its poor transport links, small population and almost total lack of amenities (aside from a small shop and a largely redundant pub, rather forlornly called the Railway Inn), Fourstones was a pretty gloomy place to be an adolescent. But Gilsland was on a whole other level. As well as the foundation text of northern isolationism that is *Wuthering Heights*, there are other, more recent cultural examples that will help to provide some context for this singular place. *The League of Gentlemen*, an exquisite BBC sitcom of 1999–2002, created a permanent memorial to such outposts in the form of its central fictional location, the surreal Pennine backwater of 'Royston Vasey'. However, it must be said that the show's creators (Steve Pemberton, Reece Shearsmith and Mark Gatiss) all grew up in relatively well-populated areas of Lancashire, Yorkshire and County Durham. Judging by the comparatively tame portrait of remote northern existence to be found in *The League of Gentlemen*, I strongly suspect that none of these men has ever set foot in Gilsland.

Throughout my teenage years, visiting Jonathan in his cluttered Victorian terraced house at the centre of this strange village was an often terrifying experience. Afterwards, I would usually take a day or two to recover my mental composure, trying desperately to banish the terror of social desolation I had felt in Gilsland by watching multiple DVDs of *Friends* and dreaming of living in a major city. Much of the feeling of mental disturbance centred on Jonathan's house itself – part of another slightly incongruous terrace in the middle of nowhere, which had been built in the late nineteenth century when the railway station briefly connected the village to the North's expanding trade and tourist networks. After the long journey by bus or car through Hadrian's Wall country, you would tend to arrive at Jonathan's house feeling slightly carsick. Then, venturing inside, you would be confronted by a startling spectacle – shelf upon shelf stacked with dead rodents contorted in formaldehyde-filled jars, animal skulls of various kinds, and other taxidermic oddities. To be clear, I am not making this up, or exaggerating for poetic effect. The animal remains had been collected by Jonathan's dad, apparently in the service of amateur science, but probably in reality to stave off the boredom of living in such an obscure outpost of human civilization.

After we started to experiment tentatively with recreational substances when we were about 15 – exactly the age, coincidently, at which W. H. Auden first discovered the 'reservoir of darkness' beneath the North Pennines – excursions to Gilsland became quite literally psychedelic and often profoundly disquieting. In Jonathan's garden there were hives of barely domesticated bees, discarded kitchen units and a satellite dish which testified to his dad's membership of the research organization SETI (the Search for Extraterrestrial Intelligence). Even without any chemical aid, this backdrop would come to life, in my mind at least, as a waking nightmare of northern badland *grotesquerie*. This was certainly the extreme edge of something – sanity perhaps – and for better or worse it helped to define the shape and the limits of the people we were growing to be.

Unsurprisingly, given the focus of our ambitions, it was music that was best able to help us understand our surroundings. In the thick of the still postmodern millennium years, we were eclectic connoisseurs of a wide variety of musical styles, from drum 'n' bass to the futuristic Y2K pop of Destiny's Child and TLC (another eventual motivation for the all-embracing band name). But there were some more local musical artefacts which had a profound influence on how we made sense of our place in the world. For me, *Storm in Heaven* – a 1993 album by the Wigan band Verve – was one. When I started listening to it, aged 15, the geological psychedelia of tracks like 'Star Sail' and 'Beautiful Mind' would unlock my unconscious, bringing to mind second-hand memories of my first home in Settlingstones – and beyond that the landscape around Hadrian's Wall, which stretches past Gilsland and down into the Pennine hills which give the North its shared scenic heritage. If any piece of music *sounds* like a John Martin painting, it is this remarkable, undervalued album.

Further afield, our group of friends heard other, more distant sonic echoes of the way the Deep North made us feel deep down. As well as selected works by weird avatars of the British periphery (Mogwai, the Beta Band, Super Furry Animals, the KLF, Aphex Twin), we found a special object of worship in the form of *The Sophtware Slump* by the Californian band Grandaddy. This singular 2001 album offered a lyric portrait of a western American wilderness full of broken household appliances, obsolete robots and visionary crystal lakes glimpsed amid plantations of trees and rubble-strewn hillsides – all of which was instantly recognizable to us. Allowing for a few minor differences, it might have been written about the countryside around Fourstones and Gilsland.*

A final musical example will, I hope, get to the source of this occluded northern outback, which had such a profound impact on us as we tried desperately to find a way to get to the future in an era terminally obsessed with the past. It is important to emphasize, when all is said and done, that the eerie, discomfiting atmosphere to be found on the Northumberland–Cumbria border arises not from any arcane mysticism, but from certain enduring socio-historical conditions, most of which go even further back than the notable recent example of civic decline that is deindustrialization. Specifically, the Deep North's distinctive atmosphere is the result of two fundamental factors: first, a lack of people; and second, a surplus of ruins.

The truth of this formula would be brought vividly to life on visits to see Jonathan in Gilsland, where its proofs were quite literally all around us. At a certain point in the day, for chemical–recreational reasons, we would tend to wander to the back of the village in search of a place beyond parental eyes and ears. In a short while, after passing under the railway bridge which leads out of Gilsland's historic disused station, we would arrive at the maze-like remnant of the Poltross Burn Milecastle – a well-preserved former stronghold on Hadrian's Wall, the high ramparts of which offered perfect cover for smoking illicit substances.

---

*Like much of the wider North Pennines hinterland – which underwent its lead-mining heyday at roughly the same time as the California Gold Rush, and which spawned many of the so-called Scots–Irish immigrants who would go on to profoundly shape the culture of the US frontier – this is the only part of England to come close to resembling the landscape and mentality of the American West.

While we were ensconced in the Milecastle on these teenage pit-stops, I always for some reason used to think of the Smiths song 'Still Ill', from the 1984 album *Hatful of Hollow* (a discount CD of which I had bought on a trip to the Gateshead MetroCentre just prior to my first encounter with Gilsland). Like many of Morrissey's early lyrics, which are heavily indebted to kitchen-sink writers like Shelagh Delaney and Victoria Wood, 'Still Ill' emerges from an archetypally northern landscape. This is an imaginative space where everything good seems to have happened in the past, and where all that remains is a fierce, probably doomed yearning to upend an English system that is continually trying to suppress the northern locales that once drove its historic rise to power. All of these feelings are condensed in the song's keening refrain about kissing under an iron bridge and nothing being like it was in the old days. This lyric in particular would often come to my mind unbidden as we ambled, slightly stoned, around Gilsland's ancient ruins on the edge of England's unconscious.

As a teenager, I couldn't quite put a name to the powerful mixture of melancholy, belatedness and fear of decay that would surge inside of me on such occasions. But I'm now sure that on moments like this I was looking right into the heart of the English North at its furthest, deepest extremity.

There is one last cultural narrative which must be mentioned in any discussion of Gilsland and the Deep North. This brief, haunting biography has a special kind of relevance at this point in our story, as we try finally to decipher the legacy of the modernist dreams of the twentieth century – and work out why they have so often seemed to melt without trace into the northern landscape.

In the mid-Seventies, for reasons that remain slightly obscure, the pioneering electronic composer Delia Derbyshire relocated from London to live in a small house on the edge of Gilsland. For much of the previous decade Derbyshire had been at the heart of the Sixties metropolis. Working from her base at the BBC Radiophonic Workshop in Maida Vale, she was responsible for a seminal series of recordings which far surpassed even the most innovative and freakish products of the Sixties pop scene, in both their experimental daring and their ambitious harnessing of new technological forms.

Drawing on elaborate tape effects and the new paraphernalia of synthesizers and sequencers, and working with a series of brilliant collaborators, Derbyshire created a body of work that is now rightly regarded as one of the foundation stones of modern electronic music – a key influence on everything from post-Eighties techno to the more experimental wing of contemporary classical music. Perhaps the most famous of Derbyshire's works is the theme tune to the BBC TV series *Doctor Who*. Though it was originally written by the Australian composer Ron Grainer, Derbyshire's ingenious arrangement transformed a relatively straightforward melody into a cavernous electronic masterpiece, which became a fitting anthem for the Space Age and its sci-fi subculture after it was first funnelled into British homes in November 1963. For some early twenty-first-century commentators, works like Derbyshire's *Doctor Who* theme – and the output of the BBC Radiophonic Workshop more generally – represent the pinnacle of post-war popular modernism, by which the experimental practices of the modernist avant-garde were distributed to mass audiences through publicly funded institutions like the BBC.

No one knows quite why Derbyshire moved to Gilsland after she left the Radiophonic Workshop in 1973. Perhaps, as the daughter of working-class Catholic parents from Preston in Lancashire, she felt a kind of deep spiritual affinity with the North-West, which just about includes Gilsland in the broadest definition. Or maybe, more likely, she simply wanted to get as far away from London as possible, and found an ideal bolthole in this far-flung settlement on the edge of everything.

Delia Derbyshire in the BBC Radiophonic Workshop, 1960s

What is certain is that Derbyshire was deeply unhappy for much of her time in the Deep North. Her marriage to a local labourer, David Hunter, was a spectacular failure, and her already chronic alcoholism – which would eventually cause her death in 2001 – accelerated dramatically, perhaps exacerbated by the demoralizing mood of isolation and marginalization that can hold sway in this part of the country. Eventually, in 1978, she returned to London, before moving back to her native Midlands in 1980 to look after her elderly mother. Though recent critics have tried to shed some light on what happened after this final migration, the last two decades of her life were chaotic, mostly unproductive and largely obscure.

But despite the fact that it seemed to mark the beginning of the end for her creative career, there was one major source of solace for Derbyshire during her Gilsland phase. After moving northwards, she worked for the most part as a radio operator for labourers installing local gas mains. But away from this mundane day job – which must have been a big culture shock after the Radiophonic Workshop – she also spent large portions of her time volunteering at a curious building in the tiny hamlet of Banks, a couple of miles west of Gilsland on the line of Hadrian's Wall.

This was the LYC Museum and Art Gallery, brainchild of the visionary Taiwanese artist Li Yuan-chia. Li had come to the Deep North in the late Sixties to stay with a local friend, Nick Sawyer, eventually buying a tumbledown old farmhouse in Banks from the post-impressionist painter Winifred Nicholson. In this unlikely sanctuary, Li engineered extraordinary multimedia exhibits incorporating painting, sculpture, video, crafts and poetry. As well as providing a home for Li's own spectacularly varied artistic output, the museum hosted exhibitions of work by major artists, displayed archaeological fragments from nearby Roman sites, organized community projects for children and local artists and ran an in-house publishing press. By the time it closed in the early

Eighties, the LYC had made a profound impression on the arts culture of the North – despite the fact that Li himself was financially ruined (and physically depleted) after a long struggle to evict a 'lodger' who moved into the Banks farmhouse and took advantage of Li's weak grasp of English property law.

Although there is scant documentation of Derbyshire's engagement with the LYC during her time in Gilsland, she was certainly involved in curating exhibitions there – and her future partner Clive Blackburn would later recall that she loved the Museum and mixing with its visiting artists and sculptors. On one level, this seems like a fairly random piece of luck – a fortunate development in an otherwise bleak period for Derbyshire, during which time she saw her artistic potential, and her mental health, begin to fall by the wayside. But in another sense I think that Derbyshire's exile in Gilsland, and her discovery of the remarkable LYC, says something important and deep-reaching about the nature of this part of the North, which is really just an exaggerated, more extreme archetype of the region as a whole.

As we have seen time and again in this book up to now, and as we will continue to see in more complicated ways in future chapters, one of the things which defines the history of the North is that it has often seemed to exist above and outside the mainstream of English culture. Combined with the legacy of a now mostly ruined industrial infrastructure, this means that the North has frequently provided the conditions necessary for the creation of a series of ghostly, never-realized alternative futures – creative dreams which have often stood in stark opposition to the nostalgic, unambitious images of Englishness typically found in the poetry, art and writing of the English establishment, whose natural habitat is institutional London and the Home Counties (which is not to say, of course, that other, more aberrant and interesting forms of art and experimentation are not to be found in the South-East outside of its dominant power structures).

Given all this, the combination of dazzling innovation and tragic marginalization we find in the narrative of Delia Derbyshire and her encounter with the LYC Museum and Gallery seems fitting, even fated. It would appear that the progressive sensibility Derbyshire and Li shared led them both to a place which seemed to offer them the freedom to experiment and the space to create vigorous modern art works resembling the pioneering technological inventions of the North's industrial past. At the same time, in spite of the fact that they were able to derive brief inspiration from the environment of the Deep North, like many of the creative figures in this book they could not escape the surrounding reality that northern society was dying, if not totally dead, in the late twentieth century. As such, the most they could do was offer glimpses of how the North's modernizing traditions might be rediscovered, even though their life and work was shot through with the sadness that comes from awareness of a region that has been deliberately abandoned over the course of many decades, if not centuries.

While we can be excited and inspired by looking back at these historical examples, we also have to acknowledge that the culture of late twentieth-century Britain, with its dreams of a future salvaged from the ruins of deindustrialization, is now gone for ever. One of Li Yuan-chia's simplest, most enigmatic poems acts as a kind of oblique epitaph to the whole panoply of Sixties and Seventies art, music and writing, and its ultimately failed attempt to open the door to radical northern reform and revival:

a point
is a beginning

of everything,
as well as
an end
of everything.

In the wake of the end of everything that was late twentieth-century culture, we will have to look beyond vanished modernist schemes as we try to work out how the North might somehow find its way to a new beginning.

Part II

LAND OF THE GOAFS

goaf, *n.*
Originally English regional (northern). Coal Mining.
An empty space from which coal has been extracted in a longwall mine,
sometimes filled with waste material.
— Oxford English Dictionary

MetroCentre, Gateshead, 1987

County Durham to Eldorado

*Mr. Parker has chosen a subject comprehensive of every grace and
variety, and has levied a pleasing tax upon a whole galaxy of
female beauty and masculine character. The effect is bewildering
and overpowering, reminding us of the magnificent but incongruous
assemblages of an opium dream.*
— Description of Henry Perlee Parker's
'Fancy Dress Ball in the Mansion House',
Newcastle Journal, 29 September 1832

Near the start of a film released in 1988, Melanie Griffith
emerges from a jewellery shop and wanders through the
white-walled arcade of a sun-drenched shopping mall. In keeping
with the signature look of the High Eighties, she is wearing a
grey suit jacket with shoulder pads, high-waisted trousers and
wide-frame sunglasses. Her red hair is worn in a neatly styled
mullet. After walking past a Yamaha piano trilling out classic
jazz, she strides coolly into another shop nearby, where she
tries on a red dress, twirls in front of a mirror, then pays at the
counter with a showily flashed credit card. The scene then cuts
to a shot of Griffith's character gliding through artificial palm
fronds, as she descends an escalator with a cargo of shopping
slung over her shoulders. At the bottom of the staircase, she
collides head-on with a sexy young man – Brylcreemed hair,
Walkman headphones, Levi jeans, black leather jacket. After

collapsing in a mildly erotic tangle on the floor, and before going their separate ways, they smile awkwardly at each other in a way that suggests they are destined to meet again in the film, probably sooner rather than later.

Perhaps surprisingly, this is not a description of a scene from the era-defining film *Working Girl*, which featured a similarly attired Melanie Griffith in its lead role, and which was also released – to much fanfare and commercial success – in 1988. In fact, this dreamlike, Lynchian summary of Eighties consumerism was one of the opening sequences in a relatively little-known British film called *Stormy Monday*. The scene's location was a gargantuan shopping mall called the MetroCentre, which had appeared a few months before filming in an unlikely setting – the swampy terrain of an industrial wasteland (formerly part of the northern border of County Durham) in Gateshead on the banks of the River Tyne.

Both film and location said much about their historical moment. Directed by Tyneside native Mike Figgis (who would later create the nihilistic Hollywood masterpiece *Leaving Las Vegas*), *Stormy Monday* brought together an improbable cast – Griffith, Sean Bean, Tommy Lee Jones, Sting – to offer a *noir*-ish portrait of the late Eighties North-East. A jazz soundtrack composed by Figgis himself made this haunting, understated film all the more strange and enigmatic. But even more intriguing than *Stormy Monday*'s atmospheric backdrop was the social symbolism of its central narrative, which hinges on a portrait of a northern city (Newcastle) approaching the end of the twentieth century.

After his breathless meet-cute with Griffith in the MetroCentre, Sean Bean's character tumbles quickly into a Chicagoan demi-monde of gangsters and crooked city bosses. In some ways, this is a straightforward (if exaggerated) depiction of Newcastle's frequently corrupt post-war culture. But it is also a more abstract riff on the idea that American-led capitalism was increasingly eating British cities alive as the Eighties progressed. If you want to know how the civic dreams of the Sixties and Seventies had degraded by this point of the Thatcher years – and where places like Newcastle seemed to be heading on the eve of a new *fin de siècle* of rampant globalization – *Stormy Monday* wouldn't be a bad place to start.

The portrayal of the urban North as a site of American-style mob corruption had also been at the heart of the 1971 film *Get Carter*, starring Michael Caine, another gangster-*noir* set in Newcastle (and reputedly a source of inspiration for Figgis's film). But in *Stormy Monday* this subtext is literally in the foreground of almost every shot. The main narrative takes place during 'America Week', apparently an attempt by the local authorities to attract US investment for redevelopment of the region. This results in an undulating backdrop of Uncle Sam paraphernalia: red-white-and-blue balloons, Fourth of July rosettes and – at one bizarre moment – a corporate junket in which a New Orleans jazz band careens towards Newcastle's Quayside area (a scene which resonates with the fact that, in the real-life Eighties, a new government quango called the Tyne and Wear Development Corporation had recently embarked on a swanky regeneration of this former industrial hub).

As well as nodding to the Thatcherite schemes of the late Eighties, the elaborate civic reception which takes place at the climax of *Stormy Monday* (ostensibly in honour of a shady tycoon character played by Tommy Lee Jones) is a sort of warped parody of Jimmy Carter's celebrated tour of the North-East in May 1977. At the height of this visit, the 39th President of the United States stood in front of Newcastle Civic Centre and greeted a rapturous crowd with the trademark local phrase: 'howay the lads'. Despite everything, T. Dan Smith's Sixties dream of turning Newcastle into a northern city-state with global influence echoed throughout the Seventies and Eighties, albeit in sometimes surreal ways.

But let us look a little closer at *Stormy Monday*'s sun-drenched shopping mall in the middle of Gateshead's post-industrial desert – and at the circumstances which brought it into being.

Most people who grew up in the late twentieth-century North, like people almost everywhere else on Earth, will be familiar with the implicit argument in *Stormy Monday*. This is very simply that at some point towards the end of the so-called American century, our everyday common culture finally became truly, ubiquitously American. But while this major cultural shift was implicit throughout the world, in the Eighties North-East it had a huge, unavoidable and certainly explicit living metaphor in the form of the stupendous, stupefying Gateshead MetroCentre.

In many ways the signature building of the age, the MetroCentre was so in tune with the spirit of its time and place that – to borrow a phrase of the philosopher Walter Benjamin – it was evidence of a collective dream. When it opened in 1986, and for many years afterwards, the MetroCentre was the largest commercial mall of its kind in Europe. Its construction, on the site of a disused power station, was the brainchild of John Hall, a local property developer and arch-Thatcherite, who would later become chairman of the football club Newcastle United during their Nineties peak (of which more later on). Channelling a climate of northern boosterism, which lingered throughout the Thatcher years despite the devastating effects of mine, factory and shipyard closures on the region, the MetroCentre was much celebrated as an example of how northern areas might regenerate themselves after the final collapse of heavy industry. In an open letter to the people of the North-East published to coincide with the MetroCentre's opening, Margaret Thatcher herself praised the 'will-power, perseverance and sheer guts to make it a reality of concrete and glass'. Meanwhile, a local newspaper article covering the opening ceremony applauded the 'most exciting shopping complex Britain has ever seen', and noted that it said 'a great deal for the North-East that [John Hall's company] didn't have to look outside the region for the help they needed to create their shopping revolution'.

But while the MetroCentre may have been touted as an example of northern grit and ingenuity persisting after the end of the industrial era, it was in fact an embodiment of a totally new cultural moment. In the last few decades of the twentieth century, the North of England was the epicentre of a distinctive brand of late capitalist culture, which enthusiastically drew on American models while adding liberal helpings of northern energy and idealism to the mix. This was, for want of a better terminology, the pinnacle of the *postmodern era*. Ranging over various cultural examples from this period, it is remarkable to see how much of the basis of the postmodern movement – if it can be called that – emerged directly from the ruins of modernism and modernity to be found in places like the North-East.

Or perhaps it wasn't so remarkable. In the story of the development of northern culture in these years, a sequel and counterpart to the narrative of the earlier post-war period, we see the central dynamic that has shaped the North's history at work once again. On the one hand, the people of the North clearly embraced the new blend of consumerism and postmodernism which came to dominate in these years, perhaps as an extension of a much deeper and longer-running northern obsession with novelty and commercial glamour. But equally, there is a sense in which this cynical, synthetic, undoubtedly exciting era was just another instalment in the narrative of the North taking a giant leap forward, only to take several more back – and this certainly seems to be the main legacy of this period from the vantage point of the twenty-first century.

As we turn to look at the northern culture of the postmodern *fin de siècle*, there are a couple of urgent, interrelated questions we must ask ourselves. How did the modernist belief in the future come to die in the late twentieth-century North? And is there anything to be said for the new collective dream which replaced it?

Montagu Court, Newcastle (built early 1960s), setting for a climactic encounter between Melanie Griffith and Tommy Lee Jones in *Stormy Monday*

We must start, of course, by blaming Richard Hamilton. As we saw in the previous section, while the pop art project Hamilton pioneered in his Newcastle phase was a colourful assertion of everything new and forward-looking in the post-war world, it also tended to favour novelty and faddishness for their own sake. This was a drastic break with the more idealistic basis of earlier forms of modernist art. Hamilton's focus on the apparently cheap and ephemeral artefacts of the nuclear age – Western films, comic books, pop music, advertising billboards – had much to be said for it in creative terms. But equally, the surface-oriented ethos of pop marked a radical departure not only from the modernist tradition, but also from a much longer and deeper tendency in European culture, which saw art as a means of accelerating social change. If pop art was, as Hamilton had claimed in 1957, all about watchwords like 'Sexy, Gimmicky, Glamorous, Big business', then sooner or later those watchwords would come to define it above all else, and the wider movement would have to revoke its claim to being anything other than a service industry churning out endless carbon-copies of consumerist artefacts. Without any more daring social aspirations, an artistic tendency which starts as pure gimmick will pretty soon die as pure gimmick.

In fairness, Hamilton's own long and varied post-Sixties career always retained a store of political awareness. (See, for example, his satirical 2008 portrait *Shock and Awe*, which dressed hawkish British prime minister Tony Blair in a cowboy outfit and stood him in front of a bombed-out landscape in the Middle East.) But certain of Hamilton's students in the Fine Art Department at Newcastle University would be much less scrupulous.

Bryan Ferry would eventually become the lead singer and songwriter of the seminal Seventies glam-pop band Roxy Music. But prior to his rockstar apotheosis he spent two years studying fine art under Hamilton at Newcastle, during the mid-Sixties interlude which also bore witness to the composition of Bunting's *Briggflatts*, the construction of the Civic Centre, Hamilton's own relocation of Kurt Schwitters's *Merz Barn* wall to Newcastle, and his re-creation in the Fine Art Department of Marcel Duchamp's *Bride Stripped Bare*.

Unlike Hamilton, Ferry was very much a product of the North and its working-class culture (even if, in an ironic twist, Ferry would spend much of his adult life pretending to be – and then actually becoming – a sort of quintessential Home Counties gentleman). Born in Washington in the County Durham coalfield in 1945, Ferry was shaped in his early years by the ambiguous relationship between urban and rural which has always been one of the defining characteristics of northern life. In the later post-war years, Washington would be substantially redeveloped as a 'new town', a showpiece development in a major social-housing programme which brought together modernist design and social–democratic ideals to create a series of large new settlements throughout Britain. (Never one to let social optimism get the better of him, Basil Bunting would deride Washington New Town as a 'slave barracks designed by a team of lunatics', after he went to live in one of its council houses in the late Seventies.) But unlike the wholly original County Durham development of Peterlee – site of Victor Pasmore's visionary Apollo Pavilion and the incidental cause of T. Dan Smith's imprisonment in 1974 – Washington was already a town of sorts prior to its reimagining in the early Sixties. The ancestral home of the first US president George Washington (and hence the reason for Jimmy Carter's detour there when he visited Newcastle in 1977), the settlement was the hub of a typical County Durham coalmining district when Ferry was born there in the months following the Second World War. Located about halfway between the more overtly urban districts of Sunderland to the south-east and Gateshead to the north-west, it incorporated powerhouse collieries like Glebe and Usworth, as well as a good deal of open countryside which sustained more traditional rural forms of work. Ferry's family inheritance was a combination of the two: his father, Fred, was a farm labourer who would at times look after pit ponies – a suitably amphibious job in a typically northern locale that was equal parts pastoral and industrial.

But like almost everyone else in the strongly centralized North-East, Ferry felt the pull of urban Newcastle pretty strongly in his teenage years. In a premonition of his later adventures in high fashion, the adolescent Ferry would travel to Tyneside to work in a gentleman's tailor shop on Percy Street, just opposite the eventual site of the Civic Centre. As well as moulding him into exactly the sort of aesthete who would later be amenable to Richard Hamilton's glamorous pop sensibility (Hamilton's own favourite clothes shop, Marcus Price, was a few doors down from the teenage Ferry's employer on Percy Street), this formative experience of working in men's fashion was in another sense a logical continuation of an essential strand of the North's sartorial heritage.

As a port city, and one that was historically closely linked to London via a coal-carrying sea route which sustained the wealth of both cities for several centuries, Newcastle often had first dibs on the latest cosmopolitan fashions from the late Middle Ages on. Partly as a result, to this day the city shares with Liverpool (another northern port city) an often fanatical obsession with consumerist artifice. As in the case of the lazy media stereotype of the Scouse bimbo (and himbo), this has given rise to plenty of hateful caricatures of the largely working-class leisure culture of the North-East. (See, for example, the fake-tanned golems in the scripted 2010s MTV 'reality' show *Geordie Shore*.) But even allowing for the snarkiness of such media portrayals, there is absolutely no doubt that both Scousers and Geordies – the *beau idéal* of northern citizenry – love shopping, clothes and the trappings of weekend glamour to an extent that often borders on open mania. Crucially, this partiality is felt by all genders. In the 1994 article which first popularized the term 'metrosexual', the journalist Mark Simpson explicitly singled out young Newcastle men by way of example, claiming that they spent more money per head on clothes than anywhere else in Europe. In support of such notions, Bryan Ferry would later credit his 'more than average interest' in fashion with that fact that he grew up close to Newcastle, 'a very clothes-conscious place, a bit of a mod town really'.

As we can see, Ferry was an authentic product of the style-obsessed North-East – a proto-metrosexual if ever there was one. But it was only under Richard Hamilton's tutelage that this organic instinct would be channelled into a coherent aesthetic programme. Much has been made of the influence of Hamilton's experiments in pop gimmickry and Americana on the blockbuster consumerist project that was Roxy Music – the pop band Ferry founded after moving from Newcastle to London in 1970. Ferry himself has been open about his indebtedness to Hamilton's influence, and the evidence of Roxy songs like 'In Every Dream Home a Heartache' (a virtual paraphrase in its central theme of Hamilton's seminal 1956 collage *Just what is it that makes today's homes so different, so appealing?*), not to mention the title of Ferry's 1977 solo album *The Bride Stripped Bare*, tells its own story. As Michael Bracewell suggests in a long section on the post-war Newcastle art scene in his 2008 book *Re-Make/Re-Model: The Art School Roots of Roxy Music*, the essence of Roxy Music was a sort of mass-marketed precis of the ideas and influences swirling in the Fine Art Department of Newcastle University in the mid-Sixties. As Bracewell argues,

> while it would be perilous indeed to claim Richard Hamilton and Bryan Ferry to be in any sense generational reflections of one another, there was nonetheless a powerful constellation of ideas in Hamilton's art and teaching that would leave an imprint on aspects of Bryan Ferry's creation of Roxy Music. These would include: a connoisseur's appreciation of the rhetoric, signage and allure of popular culture; a particular interest in the conflation of warm, erotically romantic, often feminized imagery, and a colder, mechanistic, meticulously designed artistic representation; the concept and practice of drawing on a wide range of artistic potentialities and solutions, rather than remaining within one narrow approach; the blurring of 'high' and 'low', 'intellectual'

110

and 'mass cultural', 'popular' and 'esoteric' forms and ideas; an exploration of recreating and replicating existing works by either other artists or oneself; the perfecting of a work's surface – preferring the pristine and the polished (the machine fresh, so to speak) to the ragged edges demanded by self-conscious authenticity; and lastly the idea of being both artist and art director within the realisation of a work – perhaps the heaviest creative burden and challenge to undertake.

In Bracewell's view, as well as absorbing such nuanced precepts, the key lesson Ferry learned during his studentship with Hamilton was an understanding of how art might respond to the resurgence of technological advancement and mass culture in the immediate post-war years – a 'cuspate period between the trauma and ruination of the Second World War and a future which looked to space and the atom for both its salvation and its shadow'.

In spite of such evocative summaries, and for all the seminal influence of Roxy Music on multiple worthy late twentieth-century figures, it must be said that in practice the band's actual artistic output was rather less interesting. On the classic albums *For Your Pleasure* and *Stranded* (both released in 1973) there are several glorious moments, from the louche, Paris-salon rock of 'Beauty Queen', to the artsy funk of 'Amazona' – not to mention standout anthems such as 'Do the Strand' and avant-garde asides like 'In Every Dream Home a Heartache' (the last of which features synth and tape effects by original member Brian Eno, who would famously go on to mastermind far more modernistic fare, broadly in the Delia Derbyshire tradition, after his departure from the band). Elsewhere, a handful of notable singles – 'Virginia Plain', 'Love is the Drug' and 'All I Want Is You' – certainly lit up the otherwise stolid backdrop of early Seventies trad rock with their combination of neo-classical rectitude and occasional weirdness. But though the Roxy example and Ferry's solo output are often cited as shining examples of the British art school tradition conquering the mainstream of mass culture (and thus allowing Richard Hamilton's obsession with post-war consumerism to reach its natural endpoint), it is hard not to conclude that capitalism took far more from Ferry's commodification of late modernism than it ever gave back.

Bryan Ferry in Roxy Music, 1973

A large part of the problem with Roxy Music lay with Ferry's simplification of certain key ambivalences in Hamilton's pop vision. If Hamilton had sought to extend the blurring of 'intellectual' and 'mass' culture, which was ultimately a legacy of the Bauhausian practice of putting the applied and the fine arts on the same level, it is difficult to see how the 'intellectual' functioned in the Roxy project beyond Ferry's mildly eccentric vocals, occasional flashes of lyric complexity and the band's iconically stylized – if clearly misogynistic – album covers. Roxy's celebrated artwork and packaging, which typically centred on a coldly sexualized image of a young woman, has sometimes been interpreted as an ironic commentary on the exploitation of female subjects in late twentieth-century pop culture. As the critic Mark Fisher once commented of the Roxy project, Ferry's 'sheer coldness and distantiation [aloofness] cannot but draw our attention to the framing machines that make possible the emotions of which he sings'. In other words, perhaps Roxy artwork was implicitly encouraging consumers to be critical of the capitalist processes which had turned its cover starlets, and by extension the music behind them, into lifeless commodities. But in the final analysis this is a generous assessment of what is, for the most part, mere soft pornography. For all the much-feted 'artiness' of Roxy Music, they really represented a folding back of the pop-art aesthetic into the murky surface world of advertising and commerce, which Hamilton had managed to exploit and ironize – to far more subtle creative ends – in his best works.

Unlike that other celebrated avatar of glam-rock sophistication, David Bowie, who achieved a rather more successful blurring of the boundaries between pop and the avant-garde, it is difficult to see much in Bryan Ferry's biography either before, during or after Roxy's Seventies peak which speaks of a progressive – or even a faintly socially aware – view of the role of art in society. Musically, Ferry's life's project was good-time cabaret – valid on its own terms as dancefloor fodder or the soundtrack to teenage kicks, but emphatically not something with any civic or modernist leanings of the kind we have witnessed in previous chapters. Certainly, Ferry was not at all interested in offering any kind of meaningful practical or aesthetic suggestions about how the North might move forward in the wake of its industrial decline.

Indeed, while the youthful Ferry underwent an important sartorial and intellectual apprenticeship in post-war Newcastle, his superficial take on pop's parody of the big-business ethic would turn him into a sort of mass-media mannequin who embodied the shadowy sense of place at the heart of an increasingly globalized economy. On the one hand, Ferry's journey into international pop stardom represented the triumph of what Mark Fisher terms 'the deterritory of American-originated consumer culture' (yet another example, perhaps, of the enduring special relationship between the United States and the English North). But ironically, the one place-specific identity Ferry did come to embrace in these years was the polar opposite of the North and his roots there.

Throughout the Seventies and Eighties, Ferry would transform into a paragon of establishment Englishness, as he became a terrifyingly real impersonator of the rural southern *nouveau riche*. As time went on, and as his functioning creative life became a mostly distant memory, Ferry's existence would come to comprise little more than living in a stately home, mixing with the jet set, dressing in elegant tweeds, attending fashion shows, advocating fox hunting and endorsing the right-wing pressure group the Countryside Alliance. It should go without saying that, in coming to this pass, Ferry had decisively abandoned post-war Newcastle and its culture of progressive engagement with civic surroundings. To rephrase a standout lyric in one of the better Roxy tunes: from County Durham to Eldorado sure is a mighty long way.

The process embodied in the life and work of Bryan Ferry, which saw modernist dreams replaced by an uncritical willingness to embrace both American-led consumerism and much older forms of tradition, is perhaps best understood by way of the term *postmodernism*. This much-debated term is crucial to the history of the North in the later twentieth century, though it should be pointed out that it can mean many different, sometimes contradictory things depending on the context. In the twenty-first century, when almost no one is willing to champion the postmodern cause, it has come to refer very loosely to the apparently morally lax climate which persisted throughout the West towards the end of the twentieth century and into the new millennium. As such, right-wing commentators will bemoan the damaging effects of 'postmodernism' on education (by which they mean something like the move away from traditional academic subjects and towards a more diverse curriculum). Meanwhile, left-wing critics tend to equate 'postmodernity' (virtually a synonym in this context) with the vaguely apolitical mood which deepened following the fall of communism in Eastern Europe in the years around 1990 – and which provoked the economist Francis Fukuyama's famous claim that the human race had by this point reached a capitalist 'end of history'.

Venturing beyond debate about its broader definitions, it is useful to note that perhaps the best – and most historically grounded – examples of postmodernism are to be found in late twentieth-century architecture. Partly because the emergence of modernism's International Style in the first half of the century was so starkly embodied in the hard-edged buildings of Le Corbusier, Mies van der Rohe and their followers, it was relatively straightforward to start talking about a literally *post*-modernist tendency when certain architects started doing something radically different in the Sixties and Seventies. For a while, postmodernism in architecture was a marginal, pioneering style whose main representatives – Robert Venturi, James Stirling, Charles Moore – designed buildings that were often only slightly out of kilter with the lingering modernist orthodoxies of the Sixties and Seventies. But by the Eighties, as the reactionary turn in Western politics signalled by the rise of Ronald Reagan and Margaret Thatcher coincided with a wide-ranging rejection of the post-war era and its values, postmodern architecture had begun its astronomical rise in developed cities throughout the world.

In the context of British architecture, perhaps the foremost outright postmodernist was Terry Farrell. Farrell belonged to a slightly older generation than Bryan Ferry, having been born in 1938 in Sale, in what is now Greater Manchester. However, there were also a number of striking affinities between Farrell and Ferry. The most obvious was that both were shaped in their formative years by the civic atmosphere of post-war Tyneside. Like Ferry, Farrell grew up in a locale that was, as he put it, 'the edge of the edge' – a part of the already marginal North-East which epitomized the ambiguous class and place identities of northern culture.

Most typologies of class would place Farrell's upbringing somewhere in the lower-middle bracket: his father was a civil service clerk who relocated to Newcastle from Manchester after the Second World War in order to work at the Ministry of Pensions and National Insurance (now HM Revenue and Customs) headquarters in Longbenton. Farrell spent the conscious part of his childhood living in the Grange Estate, a social housing development of the immediate post-war years, which, though not overly affluent, was nonetheless located in the leafy, suburban sprawl that extends from Gosforth on the north side of Newcastle into rural Northumberland. (Aside from Farrell, the most famous former resident of the Grange Estate is the footballer Alan Shearer.) There were several coal mines in and around this area, many of which were still open in the Forties and Fifties. But this was – and is – a slightly more urbane, more culturally connected locale than Bryan Ferry's native County Durham coalfield.

Despite such nuances of northern geography, there is a sense in which Farrell and Ferry were kindred spirits – and they would come to shape the history of late twentieth-century British culture in parallel ways. In common with Ferry's formative educational experience of the mid-Sixties, the starting point of Farrell's creative biography was a subtle reshaping of modernist orthodoxies during his university years. These were also, perhaps not entirely coincidentally, spent at Newcastle University. Here, in 1956, Farrell enrolled in the School of Architecture, just as Richard Hamilton was starting his tenure in the Fine Art department. Though he had nothing like the backdrop of Hamilton's freewheeling, Bauhaus-influenced learning environment to surround and inspire him, Farrell's time at university allowed him to cultivate an already established spirit of determined individualism, which has obvious parallels with Ferry's slightly later embrace of American consumerism and its hysterical cult of the self.

Part of the motivation for both the Ferry and the Farrell forms of postmodern individualism seems to have sprung from what might be called the 'northern stowaway' impulse. We will explore this tendency in more detail in Chapter 11 by way of a series of examples from twentieth-century film, music and literature. But for now a simple definition will serve. A northern English version of a much wider global phenomenon, the stowaway impulse is found in the fierce desire to transcend a working- or lower-middle-class existence by rejecting its collective structures and systems (with the glamour of American culture often acting as a source of inspiration – even if relocation to London is often the ultimate outcome in the British example). For Farrell this escapist yearning was apparent in his attraction to the rugged, flamboyant architecture of the modern American tradition, which went hand in hand with a rejection of the more socialized doctrines of European modernism.

A passage in Farrell's autobiography makes clear that his architectural studies at Newcastle were guided by exactly this combination of class escapism and a developing pro-American, postmodern aesthetic:

I was separated from everything familiar due to the onward and upward personal march through levels of privilege, from sixth form on to university ... I felt I had to adopt a stance of becoming unbelievably motivated to justify my choice to my family, my peers and my old and new teachers. All this was based on a belief in myself. I did not know where it came from or where it would ultimately lead, but I knew I had to follow it. I focused on emulating major successful architects – absent 'mentors', as it were, like Frank Lloyd Wright, and eventually Buckminster Fuller, whom I discovered only in my final year. They were very independent architects away from the European traditions; we in the North were influenced more by Americans than Europeans – I was never a believer in the Bauhaus or Le Corbusier. Unwittingly I had been attracted by the much-admired stereotype of the 'creative individual manifesting his will in action', as described by Andrew Saint in his book *The Image of the Architect*. It was probably a result of my having had little contact with contradiction, competition or wider reality, which a broader base would no doubt have facilitated. The ideal mentor at this lonely stage in my life was the robust heroic individualist, much praised and idolised in America.

In a further illustration of the peculiar relationship outlined here between northern roots and the modern American sublime, Farrell's final-year design thesis centred on a high-tech geodesic dome inspired in equal measure by the work of the American architect Buckminster Fuller and the Blackpool Tower. Several disparate cultural strands were coming together in this blueprint for a distinctively northern form of postmodern art. One of the most striking was a reprocessing of the North's Victorian pre- or proto-modernist heritage, as seen in Farrell's interest in Blackpool's attempt to mimic Paris's Eiffel Tower for the sake of the 1890s Lancashire tourist trade. As technicolour civic schemes driven by private

118

money became the new normal after the decline of the Welfare State from the Eighties onwards, a revival of the entrepreneurialism and early consumerism of the Victorian era would increasingly take centre stage. In this context, it made a lot of sense to backtrack to the heroic capitalist structures of the *laissez-faire* nineteenth century, of which there were many obvious surrounding examples – from the Blackpool Tower to Newcastle Central Station – for architects like Farrell emerging from the post-industrial North.

The MI6 Building, London

Just as Bryan Ferry's commodification of pop art would help to pave the way for the style-obsessed Eighties (and the more lasting misfortune of 'celebrity culture' after that), so Farrell's architectural innovations helped to create the civic landscape we have inherited, for better or worse, from the final years of the twentieth century. Farrell's blockbuster works, such as Charing Cross Station (1990) and the MI6 Building (1994) in London, the Peak Tower in Hong Kong (1995) and the Beijingnan railway station in Beijing (2008), are notable for the way in which

119

they capture the *dynamism* of the era of radical globalization which unfurled around Fukuyama's end of history. Farrell buildings tend to incorporate the classic corporate-postmodern trademarks (monumentality, glazed façades, Americana, mild playfulness) which became ubiquitous throughout the world from the Eighties onwards, as cities like London and Beijing morphed into towering centres of global finance in a newly market-driven economy. But they are not, like certain other forms of postmodern architecture, conservative per se. Indeed, Farrell's best works showcase a kind of rambunctious, boomtime expansiveness, which seems to derive from his roots in the industrial North just as much as his reverence for Frank Lloyd Wright and Buckminster Fuller.

But for all that Farrell's northern postmodernism embodied the extrovert energy of *fin-de-siècle* capitalist progress (such as it was), it also had a slightly sinister aspect, which separated it from the more forthright civic modernism of the preceding era. This aspect of his work is highlighted in Patrick Keiller's 1994 film *London*, during a digression on the mysterious ongoing construction of the MI6 Building (mysterious partly because MI6 was not officially acknowledged by the UK government until after both film and building were made). In a sad, disembodied voice, the film's narrator, played by Paul Scofield, points out that six new hospitals might have been built with the money spent on Farrell's design, and alludes to the spiralling costs of an underground tunnel being dug to connect the new structure to the MI5 headquarters further along the Thames. Farrell can hardly be blamed for such dubious political subplots, which speak sorrowfully of the resurgence of a traditional, somewhat martial England amid the decline of the Welfare State. Nevertheless, judging his designs on their own terms, it is certainly true that his brand of postmodernism tended to combine individual forcefulness with a rather enigmatic air of introversion, which intentionally or not placed his buildings in alignment with their circumstances of production in the post-Thatcher economy. A typical Farrell building showcases the varied colour palette and occasional classical allusions which defined the whimsical, ironic side of postmodernism. But there is also something eerie and hieratic about his architectural style (and indeed postmodernism more generally), as if these puckish details have been put there to dissemble all the shadowy negotiations involving government agencies, private finance initiatives and other powerful interest groups which gave rise to the buildings' construction.

In spite of such quibbles, there are limits to the comparison between Ferry and Farrell, for all the startling similarities between these two flamboyant postmodernists of the post-war North. While Ferry ventured enthusiastically and irrevocably into the consumerist Eldorado first imagined in his music, Farrell's relationship with the world of power and money was, at the risk of stating the obvious, a largely inevitable by-product of his existence as an architect in need of regular commissions (unlike pop music, architecture has never had a really fully developed countercultural infrastructure to offer an alternative to the inducements of the market). What is more, if Farrell's aesthetic could at times suffer from a certain graceless egotism, there is no doubt that it was also focused on enriching the public sphere in concrete and lasting ways.

Nowhere was the civic dimension of Farrell's work more apparent than in his attempt to revive his home town throughout the Nineties. In a faint echo of the regeneration narrative of *Stormy Monday*, Farrell was responsible for the redevelopment of a large part of the Newcastle Quayside in these years. His masterplan for the eastern section of the Quayside was bankrolled by the Tyne and Wear Development Corporation, a quango formed at the behest of the Conservative minister Michael Heseltine, in order to expedite public–private development projects free from the Labour-controlled council (which had, of course, been the driving force of urban renewal throughout the T. Dan Smith era and its aftermath). Here at least, in spite of the conflicted political backdrop – a clear case of private money and the profit motive rushing into the gap left behind by the demise of the public sector – Farrell's northern postmodernism achieved a meaningful kind of social success.

Though it ultimately went way over budget, and though it created long-term problems for Newcastle's city centre by relocating office space to a peripheral site, it would be churlish to be too critical of Farrell's rousing, door-opening work on the banks of the River Tyne. His masterplan for the Quayside was the major catalyst for a timely regeneration of this ruined epicentre of the shipbuilding industry, which led ultimately to the construction of a new art gallery (BALTIC), a major concert hall (The Sage) and a sublime new feat of engineering linking Newcastle and Gateshead (the Millennium Bridge), one of the most invigorating structures of the millennium period. In an era otherwise obsessed with consumerist vulgarity and the restoration of old-school Englishness, here was an authentic modern northern rising worthy of the name.

Whatever happened to the dream of postmodern consumerist salvation? Over 30 years after Melanie Griffith tumbled headlong into Sean Bean in the opening scenes of *Stormy Monday*, the

Gateshead MetroCentre has lost all of its novelty and most of its glamour. In fact, it is hard to avoid the conclusion that this mercurial site is well on the way to becoming a wasteland once again.

At its opening, the MetroCentre was a model of individualist bravado. (Nothing to do with Terry Farrell himself, it was nonetheless designed by a fellow northern Frank Lloyd Wright disciple, the local architect Ronald Chipchase.) The outer building, described by Margaret Thatcher in rather workmanlike terms as a gritty northern 'reality of concrete and glass', was in fact merely the carapace for a dazzling indoor world of technicolour design and *Alice in Wonderland*-style fantasy – a series of wonderfully weird artificial cityscapes intended to offer an alternative to the high streets and marketplaces the MetroCentre was supposed to supplant. Even allowing for the tackiness of these dreamlike installations, perhaps there is some worth in channelling nostalgia to try to remember why they were such an exciting arrival in the socio-cultural desert of the Eighties North – and what this says more generally about the recent history of northern revival and failure.

When I first went there as a young child in the late Eighties – on day trips to the indoor theme park Metroland, or to watch films like *Back to the Future II* at the UCI cinema – it was the playful, even decadent qualities of the MetroCentre which most affected me. Wandering through this sprawling H-shaped complex was at once euphoric and disorienting. Around the edges of the glittering white arcades, there were forests of synthetic trees, giant chessboards, model hot-air balloons, fountains filled with real fish, a mock Roman forum, a Mediterranean village full of exotic eateries and an 'antique village square' complete with its own postbox, lamp posts and a surreal automated statue programmed to shout at shoppers as they passed by. For countless late twentieth-century children – and probably quite a few adults too – this parallel northern universe was nothing less than an abrupt realization of the world of fairy tale, made all the more astonishing by its emergence in Gateshead's industrial wilderness.

As well as acting as an epicentre of the chronic northern obsession with materialist glitz, which peaked so forcefully in the wake of postmodern cultural narratives like that of Bryan Ferry, the MetroCentre's interiors seem with hindsight to have been an expression of the surrounding political system and its deeper limitations. This plate-glass northern Shangri-La was radiantly evocative. But it was also excessively unreal almost to the point of melancholy. Its simulated fantasy of civic experience brought home the fact that this was probably the most far-reaching revival of the post-industrial wasteland that would ever emerge from scorched-earth consumerism. On the other side of this fleeting synthetic utopia, these transitory arcades seemed to say, wasn't there a better, more lasting way of rebuilding the North?

At the start of the 2020s, the MetroCentre is a shell of its former self. A symbol of the decline of physical shopping in an age of online retail, many of the shops have been boarded up and abandoned. The postmodern colour scheme has been exchanged for a drab palette of greys and whites. Meanwhile, rather uncannily for anyone who remembers their existence, the fountains, hot-air balloons and giant chess boards have been removed, and replaced with nothing very much at all. All of this seems like a final admission of defeat for the idea that places like Gateshead could be reborn through a heroic reclamation of the commercial culture of the nineteenth century. Indeed, it would seem a long shot that the MetroCentre will still be operating in the 2030s. If it was once evidence of a collective dream, one that viewed the glamorous trappings of consumer culture as a means of salvation for northern communities, the hollowed-out arcades of the present-day MetroCentre are evidence of a dream that has definitely now ended. It is high time for what Walter Benjamin would have called a historic awakening.

Crater on the site of a former mine, Baildon Moor, West Yorkshire

Hard Hats in the Heather

In the last months of 1986, a film crew gathered on Baildon Moor, slightly to the north of Bradford in West Yorkshire. Part of the eastern edge of the South Pennines (backdrop to countless northern sagas, from *The Tenant of Wildfell Hall* to the Moors murders), Baildon was the perfect setting for the film-makers' work in progress, a low-budget Channel 4 film called *Rita, Sue and Bob Too*. At the crux of a low, dishonest decade, in which the North often seemed to be collapsing in on itself, this sweeping landscape was a fitting frame for a comedy about two northern teenagers who find an odd kind of freedom amid the social turmoil of the 1980s.

Heralded by the PR tagline 'Thatcher's Britain with her knickers down', and widely acclaimed on its release, *Rita, Sue and Bob Too* was one of the defining northern art works of the decade. But though it was directed by perhaps the most renowned social-realist of its era, the Scouse auteur Alan Clarke, the film was largely the product of humbler origins closer to its South Pennines setting. A welding together of two earlier stage plays, *Rita, Sue and Bob Too* was in fact based on a simple but brilliantly outré script by Andrea Dunbar, a 25-year-old Bradford writer with a biography every bit as wild as any of her dramatic creations.

The basic narrative of *Rita, Sue and Bob Too* comprises a sort of madcap erotic tryst between its three title characters. After babysitting for a yuppyish Bradford family man (Bob),

Sue and Rita accept his offer of a lift home, which culminates in a fumbling sexual encounter in his car out on the moors. From this point on, all three are caught up in a risqué, exploitative, slightly improbable affair. Through a frenetic plot which ranges freely over the stock devices of post-war kitchen sink – council-estate gloom, domestic violence, interracial love – this peculiar film manages to transcend its generic roots by channelling a sort of rainbow-coloured abandon. Like countless visionary northern texts before and after, it does so largely by heightening and deepening the ecstatic impulses in the dream-lives of its characters. Drawing on Shelagh Delaney's *A Taste of Honey* as well as Emily Brontë's *Wuthering Heights* (in a fairly blatant nod to literary influence, one scene takes place in the Brontë Disneyworld that is Haworth), *Rita, Sue and Bob Too* uses the landscape of the South Pennines to embody the girls' deep yearning for mental and physical release. But unlike Brontë in *Wuthering Heights*, Dunbar does not, or does not only, present the moors as a symbol of gothic isolation. In this one-off masterpiece, the light-dappled hills which surround post-industrial Bradford act as a relatively straightforward metaphor for eagerly grasped erotic pleasure – and the brief escape from the shadows of late twentieth-century northern life it could bring.

I can remember there being a BASF VHS copy of *Rita, Sue and Bob Too* in my childhood home, which my parents probably recorded when it was first broadcast on Channel 4 in 1988. But of course, given the subject matter, I wasn't allowed to watch it until much later – not in fact until the early 2010s, long after my parents had died, when my partner Louise and I were living in East London and dreaming of northern vistas in exile. (Louise grew up on the edge of the Staffordshire Moorlands, at the opposite end of the Pennines from my native Roman Wall country.) When we discovered the film at this point in our late twenties – at the same

time as we were starting to plot a permanent move northwards –
we were utterly blown away by its off-the-wall take on a timeworn
tradition of Pennines escapism. But we were even more affected,
and frankly upset, when we did some Google research into Andrea
Dunbar's life story later on.

Andrea Dunbar, Bradford, late 1980s

The pathos of *Rita, Sue and Bob Too* is immensely deepened
for modern viewers when they discover the fate of its author. In
December 1990, barely three years after the release of her best-
known work, Andrea Dunbar died of a brain haemorrhage after
collapsing on the floor of the Beacon pub in the Buttershaw
estate, her long-time home, in south-west Bradford. Though
Dunbar was a shockingly young 29 when she died, there is a
sense in which she had endured an eternity of sadness before
coming to this pass. Much of her work was based on her
lived experience of growing up in the bleak environment of
Buttershaw – a Fifties council estate built on open moorland

on the edge of Bradford, which had become a byword for deprivation even prior to the social meltdown of the Thatcher years (like Dunbar's narrative more generally, Buttershaw is a necessary caution against over-idealizing the social-democratic Sixties and Seventies). Dunbar's first play, *The Arbor*, was a thinly veiled account of her own experience of giving birth to a stillborn baby at the age of 15, after a turbulent relationship with a Pakistani boyfriend marred by violence, addiction and racial prejudice. By the time she sprang to national attention in the mid-Eighties, Dunbar had given birth to three children, all with different fathers, and had spent long periods living in a Women's Aid refuge in nearby Keighley as a result of abusive relationships. Her early death in 1990 was almost certainly triggered by her chronic alcoholism, which accelerated to the point of no return after a local backlash against *Rita, Sue and Bob Too*. Dunbar's heavy drinking also led her to badly neglect her children. (As detailed in Clio Barnard's harrowing 2010 biopic *The Arbor*, Dunbar's eldest daughter, Samaya, was later imprisoned for manslaughter after her own daughter swallowed a fatal dose of methadone under her care.)

We have encountered several examples of failed northern dreams before now in this book, and we will encounter several more in the pages that follow. But it is difficult to imagine a more devastating case of northern failure than the fleetingly luminous narrative of Andrea Dunbar. After *Rita, Sue and Bob Too* was first broadcast in 1988, featuring several added scenes which Dunbar hated, and provoking deep resentment among her neighbours for its treatment of Buttershaw residents, she said that her 'dreams were all finished'. 'There were just one thing,' she explained: 'as a kid, I always thought, "One day, I'll be on telly." I was. And after that, it were gone.'

Andrea Dunbar's personal nightmare – a sort of shadowy underside to the Eighties *paradiso* glimpsed in the last chapter – is an extreme, exceptional case. Yet in one important sense her story is far from atypical of the North of England's inner self. Indeed, in its basic outline, Dunbar's life and work is a grim archetype of a collective trauma which disproportionately ravages northern homes.

Alcoholism is the great malady of the northern English people – an illustration of how the North's outward disadvantages are reinforced by a deeper, darker form of self-harm. Sadly, this is no parochial stereotype. The notion of an alcoholic North is unfortunately backed up by plenty of hard medical statistics, which place the region on a par with the other north-western portions of the islands – Ireland and Scotland – who suffer the same curse.* According to recent research, binge drinking and alcohol-related mortality rates are both substantially higher in the North-East, North-West and Yorkshire and Humber than in London and the South-East. (Oddly, the South-West has high consumption but low mortality rates, which further proves that it is a special case which complicates sweeping references to 'the South'.) To take this regional divide at its starkest, in 2020 there were 20 alcohol-related deaths per 100,000 people in the North-East, compared with only 9.9 in London – an astonishing and grisly differential of over 2 to 1. This is not the place to try to get to the bottom of the North's alcohol problem in any clear-cut scientific sense. But a brief sociological overview is probably in order as we try to work out how this fatal flaw in northern culture came about.

---

*For a range of reasons too complicated to speculate on here, the rates of alcoholism and alcohol-related fatality are slightly less severe in Wales (which isn't to dismiss the severity of the problem there, or indeed anywhere else).

Perhaps surprisingly, given its ancient pedigree, there is still very little consensus about the underlying causes of alcohol addiction as a global phenomenon. This has the knock-on effect of making its geographical variations also very hard to explain. There is some scant evidence that DNA influences drinking habits, which may have some relevance in the North of England, where long-term migration patterns have produced a fairly distinct genetic mix (one that is, perhaps tellingly, not unlike those in similarly blighted Scotland and Ireland). Climate is another important factor; indeed, the age-old curse of the northern English weather is probably more relevant in this context than easily misinterpreted genetic data. As in most other northern European regions and nations – such as the Scandinavian and Baltic countries, where rates of alcoholism are also very high – the North's long winters and dark nights offer copious incentives for excessive drinking, from the need to warm the body to the urge to stifle seasonal melancholy.

Cultural and historical factors almost certainly have a role to play here too. Historians seeking to offer sweeping, ancestral theories about the North's drinking culture have tended to emphasize the wildness of northern society before the Industrial Revolution, suggesting that the turbulence and scarcity of these years encouraged orgiastic bouts of indulgence (rather than the proverbial Sensible Social Drinking apparently more common in plusher climes). A more recent, more plausible explanation is that the rise of heavy industry in the long nineteenth century helped to foster a hardcore masculine drinking culture in the North. According to this theory, male workers in the surging mining, steel and shipbuilding trades turned increasingly and eagerly to alcohol outside of work hours (especially at weekends), through a simple mixture of physical thirst, mental desperation and the tribal desire to mingle with comrades in the half-utopic, half-nihilistic setting of the pub or club. This would certainly appear to explain the cultural stereotype embodied in Paul Morel's hard-drinking father in D. H. Lawrence's *Sons and Lovers*. But it does not shed much light on the fate of Andrea Dunbar, and many others.

Ultimately – and certainly in the context of the last few decades – the main cause of the North's alcohol epidemic is surely plain old socio-economic hardship. Culture and climate may have provided a strong historical foundation for a hard-drinking culture to develop in the North of England (and they probably make the difference in setting the region aside from other economically challenged corners of the globe, many of which do not suffer excessively from alcohol misuse). But more recently, and accelerating in the post-industrial era, the region's steep unemployment figures, civic decay and the various knock-on effects of these factors – from lower life-expectancy to alarmingly high suicide rates (13.3 per 100,000 in the North-East, compared with only 7 in London in 2020) – have almost certainly helped to create a breeding ground for alcohol misuse.

At the same time, it really hasn't helped that the boosterist side of post-industrial northern culture has tended to promote the region as a place of carnivalesque boozy hedonism, as the weekend escapism of areas like Liverpool's Cavern Quarter and Newcastle's Quayside has been thrust to the fore of successive post-Eighties regeneration campaigns. Meanwhile, the faded tourist capital of Blackpool, which has the highest rates of liver cirrhosis in England, offers a contrastingly bleak example of a once thriving northern town where service-industry boosterism seems to have failed on all counts. The gleeful stereotyping of the North as a playground for pleasure-seeking consumers can have a vaguely orientalist edge, as in the summary on the website of Hertfordshire-based 'Hen and Stag weekend specialists' Maximize, which states that 'the North of England is Stag Do heaven'. In tandem with such commercial ventures, TV shows like *Geordie Shore*, where the action is based almost entirely on alcoholic overkill, have entrenched the cliché that the North is a place where dreams of sensual gratification can be cheaply and fluidly fulfilled.

Whatever the intentions, the effect of these direct and indirect marketing campaigns has been to deepen the centrality of alcohol in the northern economy, at the same time as wider economic decline has created an ever stronger basis for the spread of addiction and drunken escapism. Between the budget hotels and gin bars of the tourist trade on the one hand, and a more native culture of determined episodic drunkenness on the other, it sometimes feels like the whole of northern civic life depends on what is poetically known in the North-East as *getting mortal*.

Given this wretched social backdrop, it is hardly surprising that alcoholism is one of the defining themes in the northern cultural imaginary. This may be a straightforward result of the sorts of hard sociological statistics outlined above. People living in the North are, quite simply, more likely than their southern counterparts to drink to the point of fatality (twice as likely in the North-East than in London), which makes it a basic scientific probability that notable northerners in politics, sport and the arts will frequently suffer from alcohol misuse. Away from the statistical picture, there are more speculative ways of understanding alcohol's prominent place in northern culture. Just possibly, the problem is in some way bound up with a sort of deeply embedded failed idealism, which sees northern romantics turning to drink after the inevitable collapse of their ambitions in a society that is – thanks to our old friend regional inequality – structurally rigged against their chances of success.

It is certainly true that many of the northern writers, musicians, sportspeople and politicians who have dreamed most fiercely about the North's rise – or maybe just their own salvation – have succumbed to some form of destruction brought on by heavy drinking. Aside from Andrea Dunbar, who felt empty and redundant after her dream of TV stardom collapsed in ruins, we might think of T. Dan Smith, who turned to Valium and Carlsberg Special Brew when his Brasilia of the North failed to materialize, the quixotic Teesside-born football manager Brian Clough, who continued to drink diabolically even after he achieved glittering success with Derby County and Nottingham Forest in the Seventies and Eighties, and Gateshead's Paul 'Gazza' Gascoigne, Clough's heir of sorts in British football lore, who threatened to become the world's greatest player before he starting drinking away the pain of a knee injury in the early Nineties (and seemingly never stopped). It is probably no coincidence that perhaps the most powerful cinematic treatment of alcoholism in recent times, the 1995 Hollywood film *Leaving Las Vegas*, was written and directed by a northerner (Newcastle native Mike Figgis). Even the title of this book was first dreamed up by a notoriously self-destructive northern alcoholic, the Manchester singer–songwriter Mark E. Smith. Smith's madly creative lyrics for his post-punk band the Fall – including 1987's 'Hit the North' and 1980's 'T.N.W.R.A.' ('The North Will Rise Again'), both of which combined pessimism about the North's future prospects with hints at its buried potential – were very often driven by his chronic dipsomania.

The distinctive northern mix of alcoholic waste and frustrated idealism has also made its presence felt in more traditional literary contexts – since at least as far back as the 1840s, when Branwell Brontë drank himself to death in West Yorkshire, shortly after his sister Anne had indirectly memorialized his struggle in *The Tenant of Wildfell Hall*. John Braine's 1957 novel *Room at the Top*, perhaps the noblest and darkest of all the post-war kitchen-sink narratives, is one of the foremost examples of a booze-fuelled northern tragedy (like *Rita, Sue and Bob Too*, it was written by a famous Bradford alcoholic).

On the surface, *Room at the Top* is a typical 'angry young man' narrative, in which a likely northern lad tries to rise through the English class system against the backdrop of an apparently grey and lifeless post-war Yorkshire town. But whatever else it may be, *Room at the Top* is also a work in which drink is at the heart of almost every chapter, from its hungover opening to a holiday episode in which 'each day [started] with strong tea and rum'. Tellingly, the novel ends with a description of the main character, Joe Lampton, hopelessly attempting to medicate a deep, multilayered trauma through alcoholic oblivion.

Along with Keith Waterhouse's *Billy Liar* and Alan Sillitoe's *Saturday Night and Sunday Morning* – both of which are heavily indebted to booze as either a central plot device or a creative stimulant – *Room at the Top* helped to lay down an enduring template for modern northern novels which rely on alcohol for their basic situational backdrop. Even in our own time, northern fiction is still dominated by the simple realist premise that drink is both a reflection and a reinforcement of the region's wider social malaise. Perhaps the finest novel to come out of the North in recent years – Jessica Andrews's 2019 debut *Saltwater* – proves that this dark archetype has not yet outlived its relevance. Among other things, Andrews's blunt portrait of her alter ego's struggle to cope with her father's alcoholism, which is set mainly in unregenerated modern Washington, is a sort of ironic proof that Bryan Ferry's postmodern shenanigans have done little to inspire and enliven even his own ultra-specific corner of the post-industrial North-East.

But the literary work which to my mind best embodies the relationship in northern culture between alcoholic nihilism and failed dreams of deliverance is far less well known than either the Fifties kitchen-sink novels or their recent successors. In fact, perhaps the most haunting piece of writing to be spun out of this theme is a relatively obscure publication from the extreme margins of British literary culture. This remarkable work is the 1995 poem sequence *Pearl*, by Barry MacSweeney, who began his career as a member of the dynamic modernist scene we encountered in our survey of Sixties Newcastle in Chapter 3. MacSweeney's life story epitomizes both the myth and the reality of northern alcoholic self-harm, so it is worth exploring in some detail.

On the mythic side, from the start of his writing career MacSweeney's self-image was defined by a series of familiar, even clichéd cultural models. As his fellow poet Andrew Crozier wrote in an obituary for the *Guardian* in May 2000: 'his notion of the artist was formed around a myth of exemplary failure and belated recognition.' MacSweeney's belief in exemplary failure arose mainly from his embrace of the Romantic *poète maudit* ('accursed poet') archetype, which he derived from literary forerunners such as the French symbolist Arthur Rimbaud and the doomed English boy-poet Thomas Chatterton. It was also inspired by a certain strand of the post-war counterculture, which found a special place in heaven for turbocharged renegades like Jack Kerouac, Jim Morrison and Anne Sexton (the last of whom supplied MacSweeney with a morbidly detailed blueprint for poetic suffering – as indeed it would, not so long after, for a teenage Steven Morrissey dreaming of subversive pop glory in Seventies Manchester).

But while these more distant touchstones helped to shape MacSweeney's poetic worldview, there is no doubt that his compulsion to romanticize his own, apparently inevitable downfall – and to use alcohol to accelerate the process – was also inspired by his direct lived experience of the collective psychodrama of the North of England. Here it was the more mundane side of his professional life that would make all the difference. After growing up in the down-at-heel West End of Newcastle, MacSweeney got a job at the city's *Evening*

Chronicle as a trainee reporter in the early Sixties, joining a long line of culturally important figures (including fellow poet Basil Bunting and future Dire Straits guitarist Mark Knopfler) who found gainful employment there at one time or another. Arriving at the *Chronicle* was arguably the most crucial development in MacSweeney's writing career. If growing up in the post-war North-East had given him an understanding of what post-industrial decline looked like in practice, his journalistic work would instil in him a sense of how the North's disadvantages were met with apathy by the region's intellectual elite – and ultimately used as the basis for a sort of semi-official collective anaesthesia.

At the *Chronicle*, MacSweeney seems to have been indoctrinated into a peculiar variety of northern fatalism, which combined a sort of shrugging acceptance of the North's bleak prospects with a cynical willingness to excuse – and sometimes collaborate with – local establishment corruption. Part of this professional mode involved turning a blind eye to various forms of dubious behaviour exhibited by local authority figures (of which there was plenty in the Sixties and Seventies, to go no further than the rather vanilla example of T. Dan Smith). But the ethos MacSweeney absorbed as a trainee journalist could also brutally compromise the act of writing itself. In the view of another notable *Chronicle* graduate, the Middle East expert Robert Fisk, the newspaper's docile approach to reporting seemed to act as a form of social and regional control. As Fisk would later recall:

> I had a suspicion that the language we were forced to write as trainee reporters ... had somehow imprisoned us, that we had been schooled to mould the world and ourselves in clichés, that for the most part this would define our lives, destroy our anger and imagination, make us loyal to our betters, to governments,

138

to authority. ... We reported the closure of Blyth's mines. But we rarely asked why the mines had to die. We watched Blyth decay. We reported its death. In my cub reporter days, we watched its last moments as a coal-and-ship city. But we didn't scratch the black, caked soot off the walls of Newcastle and ask why Britain's prime ministers allowed the centre of the Industrial Revolution to go to the grave.

In his *Guardian* obituary, Andrew Crozier suggested that employment at a series of local newspapers would lead MacSweeney to contract 'the journalist's industrial illness, alcohol dependency'. But as Fisk's summary of the *Chronicle*'s culture seems to show pretty clearly, there were processes of denial and forgetting already hard-wired into the basic structures of this pillar of the northern establishment. In a workplace where writers were actively encouraged to numb themselves to the effects of the managed regional decline they were witnessing at first hand, alcohol must have seemed like a fairly natural accessory. Somewhere in this tangle of political paralysis and mental stupefaction lies the ultimate source of the North's wasted sense of self-esteem, of which addiction is a mere side-effect.

The mind-forged manacles of post-war Newcastle and its journalistic Borstal were temporarily loosened when MacSweeney achieved a startling breakthrough into the technicolour poetry scene of the High Sixties. First of all, in the mid-Sixties, he became a regular attendee at the Morden Tower readings organized by Connie and Tom Pickard (and mentored by his sometime *Chronicle* colleague Basil Bunting). Then, slightly later in the decade, while studying journalism at Harlow Technical College in Essex, he made contact with the radically avant-garde 'Cambridge School' of poets (which comprised the likes of Crozier, J. H. Prynne,

Veronica Forrest-Thomson and Peter Riley). After receiving encouragement in his own literary endeavours from these two very different late modernist communities, MacSweeney published a psychedelic debut collection, *The Boy from the Green Cabaret Tells of His Mother*, in the first months of 1968. Later that same year, he became a national cause célèbre when his publisher nominated him to become the new Oxford Professor of Poetry, after the veteran war poet Edmund Blunden stepped down. From this point on, MacSweeney's poetic career would be firmly established along with his journalistic day job. At the same time, the manner of his literary debut would also help to instil in him an attitude of weariness and futility that would overshadow his later career.

In the judgement of the critic Paul Batchelor, MacSweeney's highly public failure in the Oxford election in 1968 was a sort of life-defining psychological trauma. According to this view, MacSweeney's literary debut and its aftermath cemented his self-image as an avatar of 'exemplary failure', at the same time as it permanently fixed his status as a marginal northern writer who would probably always be shunned by the English literary establishment. Receiving only two votes in the Oxford election (a country mile behind the stylistically conservative winner, Roy Fuller), MacSweeney was widely ridiculed as a joke figure, perhaps most notably by Kingsley Amis, who dismissed him as an 'anti-candidate' and a 'trendy hippie of no achievements'. Batchelor suggests that after the Oxford debacle 'a sense of exile and a siege-mentality never really left MacSweeney', but also that 'this exile was largely self-imposed', and that it led him to develop an unwavering 'poetics of opposition'.

On the one hand, MacSweeney's half-deliberate, half-enforced marginality would act as a source of creative empowerment. Ensconced in the North, and in the avant-garde haven of British late modernism for the last three decades of the twentieth century,

MacSweeney was able to produce a large body of work that was invariably forceful and innovative. Even more importantly, his poetry – which ranged over subjects from the history of British Miners' Strikes to the life of the Newcastle child murderer Mary Bell – was consistently politically honest in a way that the output of duller, Poet-Laureate-style figures from the same period never was (and never could have been). Crucially, in spite of his literary schooling in a modernist tradition which tended to view surrealism and abstraction as cardinal virtues, MacSweeney remained a fairly orthodox local journalist for most of his adult life, moving to the *Shields Gazette* in Tyneside and the *Telegraph and Argus* in Bradford after apprenticeships in Newcastle and Kent. (During his time in West Yorkshire he reported on the Bradford City stadium fire of 1985, a tragedy which underlines the tortuous reality of northern civic neglect in this period.) This backdrop of social realism helped to ensure that his verse was most often rooted in direct experience, for all its experimental nuances, and singularly powerful as a result.

Barry MacSweeney (far left) with Stuart Montgomery, Basil Bunting and Tony Harrison, Newcastle, 1970

But in the end MacSweeney's determination to inhabit and exhibit the northern periphery would contribute to his own annihilation. In the later Eighties, and into the Nineties, his poetry was published ever more sporadically, usually by small presses with small print runs. Far more seriously, he was repeatedly hospitalized as the century drew to a close, as his dependence on alcohol became increasingly life-threatening. Shortly after the arrival of the new millennium, in May 2000, MacSweeney succumbed to the hateful *poète maudit* archetype once and for all. In a final misfortune described by his partner Jackie Litherland as an 'alcoholic's death', he died by choking in his home in the West End of Newcastle, alone and very largely unacknowledged.

Despite the horrific conclusion to his narrative, a few years before he died MacSweeney managed to channel the agonies of his surroundings into one of the greatest and most moving of all northern poems. A series of 22 short-ish fragments, MacSweeney's *Pearl* sequence of 1995 was very loosely inspired by a Middle English dream poem, in which the subject laments the death of his 'perle' – a figure who then appears in the form of a beautiful maiden beckoning from across a stream towards images of a heavenly city. In MacSweeney's radical modernist reworking, the religious idealism of the medieval original is reconfigured in a modern Pearl. This angelic character, who is alternately speaker and addressee of the poems, is apparently based on MacSweeney's memories of a mute, illiterate young girl he taught to read on childhood visits to his aunt's home near Allenheads in the North Pennines.

No one quite knows whether MacSweeney's Pearl was a partially or wholly real person, or whether she is a multilayered metaphor (as indeed she is in the medieval poem) for a sort of lost but potentially recoverable form of spiritual salvation (for the North, for the socially marginalized more generally, or perhaps just for MacSweeney himself, fighting a losing battle in the Nineties against alcoholic self-erasure). But there is no doubting the remarkable pathos of Pearl's monologues, which are typically spoken against a backdrop of dreamlike northern desolation:

> When I stand on the top road and bow
> in sleet, knuckle-bunching cold, or
> slide over dead nettles on snow, do
> not mistake my flung out silhouetted
> limbs for distant arches and viaducts.
> I am not bringing you legendary feats
> of sophisticated engineering. I in
> worry eat my fist, soak my sandwich
> in saliva, chew my lip a thousand times
> without any bought impediment. Please
> believe me when my mind says and
> my eyes send telegraphs: I am Pearl.
> So low a nobody I am beneath the cowslip's
> shadow, next to the heifers' hooves.
> I have a roof over my head, but none
> in my mouth. All my words are homeless.

In this extract, and throughout the sequence as a whole, there is a surface tone of almost unbearable emotive innocence in the lines delivered by and about Pearl. Elsewhere we are told that she 'had the most amazing eyes in history', and that MacSweeney (if he is indeed the narrator) loved her 'absolutely and all of the time'. Meanwhile, Pearl herself says much more humbly that she would merely 'like a square meal daily / for me and my mam'. At one climactic moment of the poem, she implores someone – author or reader: 'Don't count on me for fun / among the towering cowslips, / but please don't crush my heart.' On one reading, then, *Pearl* is a work comprised of lucid, childlike and always acutely poignant fragments, which speak of themes of love, loss and the impossibility of recovering youthful happiness in simple terms.

But it is also clear that *Pearl* is a sort of indirect elegy, in which its doomed author comes to identify powerfully with a northern landscape that is also, like him – as MacSweeney puts it at one point – at the 'end of the road'. Away from the visionary glimpses of Pearl, we encounter fragments which evoke a desperate alcoholic existence full of accidental injuries and shabby bus journeys to run-down Tyne Valley pubs. While the news-headline imagery of the mostly joyless John Major years ('I lost my mind in Sarajevo', 'an adulterous prince', 'Strasbourg grants', 'fiery battleground of the sieged estate') intrudes to shatter the narrator's memories of an idealized post-war childhood, the abandoned backcountry of the North Pennines becomes a unifying symbol of everything that has gone so badly wrong for both MacSweeney and the North's inmost civic being in this crucial period.

Pearl is not, like certain other MacSweeney poems, a work which explicitly references the political struggles of the Thatcher years and their aftermath. Nevertheless, the ruined landscape of (parts of) northern England in the early Nineties – and the underlying cause of its socio-economic decay – is a permanent implied presence throughout the *Pearl* sequence:

> They –
> you call it government – are killing everything
> now. Hard hats abandoned in heather. Locked-up
> company huts
> useless to bird, beast or humankind. Tags
> in the rims: Ridley, Marshall,
> McKinnon and Smith. Deserted
> disconnected telephones, codes

and names I could not read.
Dead wires
left harping in the high wind ...

To be sure, it must be pointed out that areas like the lead-mining heartland of the North Pennines had been in economic decline for decades, long before Thatcher's Conservatives took a sledgehammer to the wider infrastructure of northern heavy industry in the Eighties. Nonetheless, the metaphorical treatment of mass regional despair in this period is essentially accurate. Indeed, as a figurative country of the heart and mind, which acts as a poetic shorthand for the human suffering caused by the 'broken / ovens of manufacture and employment' of these years, the bleak 'upland empire' MacSweeney conjures in *Pearl* has no rival – except, perhaps, for the evocative moorland vistas in Andrea Dunbar's *Rita, Sue and Bob Too*. Allowing for some fairly big differences in tone, there is a clear sense that both writers were trying to describe in art how their own failures – of which alcohol was surely both symptom and cause – were intertwined with the downslide of the North as a whole in the dying decades of the twentieth century.

Maybe texts like *Pearl* and *Rita, Sue and Bob Too* simply mean what they mean. On one level, they are great works of art because they are beautifully constructed, alternately funny and dark renderings of human emotion – and they don't necessarily have to signify anything more than this. At the same time, it is hard to resist the temptation to dig deeper. Standout works of northern literature like this can be appreciated for their beautiful surfaces. Yet there is also something about them which demands that we investigate their contextual nuances, which seem to

145

speak of both individual suffering and more widespread forms of communal pain.

In the absence of a hard scientific consensus about the causes of alcohol misuse (and indeed other forms of addiction), we will have to make do with guesswork and common sense as we try to work out how personal nightmares like Andrea Dunbar's and Barry MacSweeney's come about. As suggested above, genetic and climatic explanations probably go some way towards explaining the roots of problem drinking in the North, and indeed elsewhere. But there is surely a more straightforward environmental process, whereby individuals simply learn from the people around them how to deport themselves in life. This is what psychologists like to call 'learned behaviour'. In this context, the theory goes something like this: if, during childhood, your parents succumbed to a form of hopelessness which led ultimately to addiction, it seems pretty inevitable that you will be more likely to repeat this same psychological pattern later in life.

If this is true of individuals, then the same seems likely to apply to whole communities – and indeed whole countries and regions. Collective psychology is a notoriously difficult thing to speculate on, let alone prove. But it seems reasonable to suggest that learned behaviours might sometimes become embedded in the culture of particular places – and, therefore, that we should see some value in those sociological arguments which suggest that *learned helplessness* can take root en masse in areas where social decline is most pronounced. For all its local nuances, the North of England is a prime candidate for this sort of diagnosis. This is a place where long-term economic downturn has in the last few decades combined with a series of major sociological catastrophes – from the Miners' Strike (and its fallout) to the Austerity of the 2010s – to create a landscape ripe for endemic learned helplessness and the various forms of self-harm that follow from it.

As we have seen, socio-economic hardship is ultimately surely the best explanation for why alcohol addiction is a disproportionate problem in the North of England. But while economic factors are probably the main cause – and perhaps the only area in which the problem can ever be objectively tackled – there is another sense in which fatalism and fatality have become so deeply embedded in the collective psychology of northern society over the years, it is sometimes difficult to see how they can ever be meaningfully countered. This is one very important, very powerful reason why the future of the North must be radical or nothing at all. Without large-scale reform which empowers northern communities in concrete social and political ways, we will probably never exorcize the collective curse which makes us world leaders when it comes to self-inflicted agony. In the meantime, perhaps, all we can really do is try not to fall asleep in the hope of resurrection.

The Stone Roses in 1989

7

Flourishing

O, will you find me an acre of land,
Parsley, sage, rosemary and thyme;
Between the sea foam and the sea sand,
Or never be a true love of mine.
        — Anon., 'Scarborough Fair'

In spite of everything, there are always glitches in time, moments when the improbable happens, acres of land between the sea foam and the sea sand. Even in the Eighties and Nineties – in fact, *especially* in the Eighties and Nineties, when the bottom fell out of northern society, seemingly for ever – there were major pushbacks against decline. The denouement of the twentieth century witnessed a final flowering and ultimate defeat for the hope that the North might be rescued by its progressive culture, which enjoyed a last hurrah at this point through a series of vibrant artistic schemes. It may be true that the cultural exploits of this period – most of which centred on pop music and its offshoots – all failed in the end. But while we have to accept that culture alone cannot reverse deep-seated processes of socio-economic downturn, it is also true that even failed cultural dreams can survive in common memory to give a foretaste of collective awakening.

To get a sense of how northern culture peaked and then faded out in the late twentieth century, we could do a lot worse than look at how an old northern folk song was reimagined at the end of the Eighties – a decade that was, as we have seen, perhaps the most climactic in the North's modern history. The song was called 'Elizabeth My Dear', and it was recorded by the legendary Manchester band the Stone Roses. Though it has been endlessly retold, repackaged and reduced to cliché over the last three decades, the story of the Stone Roses remains a remarkable one, not least because it represented the high-water mark of a pivotal chapter in in the North's cultural biography.

It is no exaggeration to say that from the late Seventies to the mid-Nineties, the North of England was the setting for one of the great flowerings in the history of popular music. Throughout this period, against a backdrop of social disaster (and in the context of a heyday for British pop music more generally), a prodigious array of bands and artists emerged from northern areas to justify the notion that culture in general – and music in particular – might be the driving force of civic revival in the wake of deindustrialization.

The local variants of this musical golden age were rich and abundant. In the waning Steel City of Sheffield, a crystalline form of electronic pop was pioneered by Cabaret Voltaire, Heaven 17, ABC and the Human League (a prelude to the rise, in the late Eighties and early Nineties, of the granular techno of Warp Records and the literate art-pop of Jarvis Cocker's Pulp). Elsewhere, there were similarly vital fusions of punk, avant-garde and commercial pop styles. In West Yorkshire, Gang of Four, Delta 5 and the Mekons honed fiercely intellectual pop projects, which overran the mainstream of mass culture with varying degrees of success; The Cult and the Sisters of Mercy popularized goth rock; and Marc Almond and Robert Palmer (who moved from Batley to Scarborough as a teenager) offered two very different blueprints for full-on pop stardom. Further to the East, in Hull, the Housemartins and Everything but the Girl typified the crossover between chart pop and bookish whimsy in this peculiar interlude, while Throbbing Gristle developed a quintessentially northern version of a genre aptly labelled 'industrial'. Meanwhile, true to its post-war history, Liverpool nurtured a majestic new brand of psychedelia (Echo & the Bunnymen, The Teardrop Explodes), and also acted as a breeding ground for several shades of aberrant camp in the form of Dead or Alive and Frankie Goes to Hollywood (with Orchestral Manoeuvres in the Dark sitting somewhere between the two poles). Perhaps strangest of all, the North-East suddenly became a global capital of stadium rock and pop, as Trevor Horn, Sting, Mark Knopfler (Dire Straits), Dave Stewart (Eurythmics) and Neil Tennant (Pet Shop Boys) conspired to manufacture a large portion of the most bankable music of the MTV era.

But if the wider North was a place where socio-economic crisis was the foil for an almost hysterical boom in monumental pop music in this period, it was in Manchester that this model was refined to produce a truly authentic, even miraculous cultural renaissance.

Underlying Manchester's blossoming in these years was a project very much in keeping with the northern modernist tradition examined in this book so far. As detailed in multiple books, films and documentaries over the years, the initial spark for the stellar rise of Mancunian pop music in this period – and the main reason why it had such a strong sense of internal coherence between the late Seventies and the early Nineties – was the foundation of the independent label Factory Records on Palatine Road in Didsbury in 1978. A brashly intellectual affair, the main players of Factory (Tony Wilson, Alan Erasmus, Rob Gretton, Martin Hannett and Peter Saville) found varied forms of inspiration in the North's history of futurism, radical protest

151

and advanced engineering, as they sought to create a self-ruling enclave for pop idiosyncrasy. From the Factory stable came a disparate cohort of bands and artists (Joy Division, New Order, A Certain Ratio, the Durutti Column, the Happy Mondays), all of whom ultimately had a profound influence on late twentieth-century culture – even when they weren't instantly commercially successful.

Central to the Factory project was a belief that the energies of capitalist society could be co-opted by a creative avant-garde and used to promote the liberation of a civic homeland (in this case Manchester, and often, by extension, the North as a whole). As well as deriving inspiration from older modernist touchstones like Wyndham Lewis's *BLAST* and other early futurist salvos, Factory took its cue in this regard from the French situationism of the Fifties and Sixties. This radical grouping – personified above all by the Parisian Marxist theorist Guy Debord – had suggested that there was subversive potential in seizing control of advertising, the mass media and other paraphernalia of the modern city, in order to redirect and overturn their surface meanings and functions. As such, situationists like Debord recommended venturing into the lurid landscape of everyday capitalist life – its high streets, nightclubs, marketing agencies, newspaper offices, television studios and ordinary public spaces – as a way of uncovering revolutionary possibilities on the other side of the market-driven 'society of the spectacle'. Perhaps more than any more elaborate credo, a piece of graffiti daubed on numerous walls during the insurrectionary student protests which engulfed Paris in May 1968 – *Under the paving stones, the beach!* – summed up the utopianism of this continental movement, which served as a guidebook of sorts for Factory as it set about assaulting the barricades of the mainstream music industry from 1978 on.

With the more immediate countercultural platform of punk acting as a springboard, Factory translated French situationism into the context of Eighties Manchester – proclaiming that beaches might be lurking under the paving stones of the decaying post-industrial North. The main thrust of the Factory campaign was an attempt to take control of the structures of the post-Sixties music business, thereby redirecting its riches toward ordinary Mancunians at a time when the Thatcher government was overseeing the 'managed decline' of northern cities. At the centre of this project was the Haçienda nightclub in central Manchester, its name an overt homage to a 1953 situationist pamphlet which called for utopia to be built amid the rubble of the post-war city. Opening in 1982, the Haçienda eventually became an epicentre of the vibrant electronic dance scene – variously called 'rave' or 'acid house' – which exploded in the latter years of the decade, and hence a physical embodiment of the hope that radical artistic schemes could be used to regenerate ailing northern communities.

A fragment of dialogue about the Haçienda from *24 Hour Party People*, a 2001 biopic of the Factory story, gives a sense of how these ideas were given a specifically northern emphasis:

TONY WILSON: Buildings create synergy, they're a focus for creativity. When the Victorians built the railways, they didn't just put up Portakabins: they went to town. [...] Buildings change the way people think. That's how it happened it Renaissance Florence.

MARTIN HANNETT: Yeah, but this isn't Renaissance Florence. This is Dark Ages Manchester.

As both the Wilson and the Hannett comments here underline, the Factory campaign was based on the notion that the North was in serious trouble as it headed deeper into the Thatcher era. But Factory was also, paradoxically, suggesting that this moment of crisis might be the spark for a miraculous recovery that would put the North back on track with its latent technological heritage. As we have seen, this was really the key progressive idea at the heart of late twentieth-century northern revivalism.

With Factory as main driving force, the Manchester music scene of the Long Eighties shot off in myriad directions, to become one of the seminal traditions in post-Elvis popular music. Two bands Factory famously failed to sign – the Smiths and Oasis – put the situationist japery at the Haçienda into relief, by evolving alternately refined and raucous forms of pop classicism. In spite of their contrasting musical styles, these world-conquering bands were nonetheless united in their Mancunian–Irish roots, melodic emphasis and deeper commitment to postures of rebelliousness which often had an overtly oppositional, northern demeanour.

But it was the Stone Roses – another oversight on Factory's part – who most poetically embodied Manchester's musical flowering in these years. More pointedly, it was the Roses who helped to turn this narrative into a more lasting testament to the pathos of northern hope and failure.

Formed around the core songwriting duo of John Squire and Ian Brown – two Clash fans from Timperley, on the edge of south Manchester – the Roses took root in the fertile post-punk moment of the early Eighties. For several years, as they laboured sometimes farcically on the margins of the Manchester scene, their only major selling points were: first, their astonishingly talented drummer, Alan 'Reni' Wren; and second, their strikingly lyrical name, a tacit assertion of the Wordsworthian romanticism lying beneath the harsh topsoil of northern culture. Then, in the last years of the decade – as the Berlin Wall fell

154

and the Haçienda became the hub of a rave-induced 'Second Summer of Love' – everything suddenly clicked into place for the Roses. After the release of their eponymous debut album in the spring of 1989, they became one of the public faces of the last really large-scale countercultural upsurge in the late twentieth-century North (and arguably, Britain as a whole). Adjacent to rave and its utopic lifestyle, the 'Madchester' or 'baggy' scene personified by the Roses emerged at the exact moment when long-building countercultural opposition to Thatcherism climaxed in a technicolour explosion of hedonism, spontaneity and playful subversion – as youthful dissidents partied away the decade in jubilant spaces seemingly beyond establishment control.

Perhaps inevitably, the zenith of the Madchester scene the Stone Roses embodied was short-lived and ultimately lacking in lasting socio-political impact. By 1994, at the very latest, when the Roses were supplanted by their louder, less cerebral fellow citizens Oasis, Factory Records had filed for bankruptcy, the anarchic culture of rave had given way to an era of corporate nightclubs and government restrictions on mass gatherings, and so – largely as a result – Manchester's remarkable blossoming in the Long Eighties was basically over. But for all its brevity, there are compelling reasons for remembering the sheer beatific radicalism of the countercultural movement the Stone Roses set into legend.

Like Factory Records, the Roses project was partly an attempt to translate situationism into a northern English landscape where the streets had been made cold and lonely by socio-economic decline. Their debut album contained a song about the May 1968 student uprisings in Paris ('Bye Bye Badman'), while its cover art – one of several pastiches of Jackson Pollock's drip-paintings by artist-guitarist John Squire – featured a tricolour and a lemon, the latter a tribute to an anti-tear-gas treatment deployed by the French student rioters. Gestures of oppositional defiance abounded in the Roses' public pronouncements and private antics. Musically, they sought to blur the boundaries between post-Smiths guitar music and African–American funk (if not quite the new electronic dance music), while singing lyrics about the Messiah being a woman of colour and writing songs with spiritual subtexts like 'Love Spreads', 'Where Angels Play', 'Breaking into Heaven' and 'I am the Resurrection'. As an extension of such visionary messaging, the Roses were also stridently political, even if this aspect of their art was often hidden under layers of psychedelic poetry. As lead singer Ian Brown would later comment, every song on their debut album was deliberately intended to be 'a call to insurrection'.

The Roses were a progressive, internationalist northern project. (As Ian Brown once rebuked a crowd chanting pro-Manchester slogans in a concert: 'It's not where you're from: it's where you're at.') But it was a northern project nonetheless, albeit one which defied cosy regionalist clichés. The Roses' hybrid of modern avant-garde influences and an older northern language of radical Christianity and trade-union militancy was perhaps most evident on a short, pivotal track wedged in the middle of their eponymous 1989 debut album. Underpinning 'Elizabeth My Dear' was a melody usually associated with 'Scarborough Fair', an old northern ballad with variants deriving from locations throughout Yorkshire, County Durham and Northumberland. The melody was in fact collected by the radical Salford folklorist Ewan MacColl in 1947, who first heard it from the lips of Mark Anderson, a retired lead miner from Teesdale in County Durham (part of the Deep North backcountry explored in Chapter 4). In the Roses' adaptation, this ancient tune was plangently rephrased by way of a chiming acoustic guitar part played by John Squire

156

and a delicate vocal line which made the most of Ian Brown's distinctive Mancunian vowels.

And yet there was more going on here than mere melody. Looking closer at the lyrics Squire and Brown added to the 'Scarborough Fair' template, we get a powerful sense of the sort of insurrection they were attempting to achieve by way of their cosmic northern crusade:

Tear me apart and boil my bones
I'll not rest 'til she's lost her throne
My aim is true, my message is clear
It's curtains for you, Elizabeth my dear.

More than a mere countercultural daydream, the Stone Roses were the ideal expression of the enlightened civic tradition from which they emerged. As this quietly devastating lyric underlines, this was largely because they understood that northern revival would have to be radical or it would fail completely, and that real resurrection would only be possible when the English system – along with its staid, stifling monarchy – was one day utterly and finally overhauled.

In the early twenty-first century, I was part of a musical project which seemed to underline just how completely the dream of cultural renewal for the North failed after the heyday of the Stone Roses in the Eighties and Nineties. As we saw in Chapter 4, the deeper roots of this venture, the pop band Everything Everything, were in the millennial Deep North, where most of the founding members grew up. But the band actually materialized as a working proposition in Manchester, across a two-year period from the summer of 2007 to the autumn of

2009. By the end of this time, as we started to receive offers of record deals, I left to go back to university to study for a PhD – and ultimately, I suppose, become a writer.

To this day, I'm not quite sure of the extent to which Everything Everything should be regarded as a 'Manchester band'. None of the original members were from anywhere near Manchester, and though we formed and developed there, there's a sense in which we might have done so just as easily in any other large-ish global city. Two of the band's founding members studied at the University of Salford, on one of the new popular music courses which have changed the nature of British pop music, for better or worse, over the last quarter century. Perhaps Everything Everything should therefore be seen as a product of the new, business like Mancunian culture which comprises professional arts training-programmes like this. At any rate, it's certainly true that when we came together in 2007, we did so at the end of a long period during which Manchester's recent cultural history had been pretty thoroughly, and often very cynically, marketized.

After the great flowering of northern pop music drew to a close in the mid-Nineties, a posthumous branding of Manchester as England's 'Music City' began to pick up pace. This process was hugely accelerated by New Labour's 'urban renaissance' of the millennium years (a campaign discussed in more depth in the next chapter, with reference to its effects on urban Tyneside). As we will see through the example of the North-East, the urban renaissance attempted to regenerate post-industrial areas largely by way of culture – in essence taking the Factory Records model and making it more genteel and bureaucratic. In Manchester (or rather, Greater Manchester) the harnessing of music and media to create a sort of Blairite cultural Arcadia was if anything even more extravagant than on Tyneside (unsurprisingly, given that the city's Eighties counterculture had supplied a stronger foundation for arts-based revival than anywhere else in Britain). This whole movement climaxed in the mid-to-late Noughties, with the creation of MediaCityUK in Salford, on the north side of Manchester's city centre. This was a conversion of former dockland on the Manchester Ship Canal into a gargantuan 'mixed-use property development', ultimately the home of large parts of the BBC, ITV, the University of Salford and countless other cultural and business HQs.

The rise of MediaCityUK, Salford, 2008

Away from these developments, highly visible and even portentous in the late Noughties, Manchester played a relatively minor role in the formation of Everything Everything's identity in its early stages. We began rehearsing in the autumn of 2007, after we all moved into a terraced house on Burton Road in West Didsbury. (Though we didn't know it at the time, the house was just around the corner from the flat where John Squire and Ian Brown had written much of the Stone Roses' debut album in the late Eighties.) True to the careerism that was part of the band's make-up from day one, there was a record company A&R at our very first gig, at Night and Day in the Northern Quarter in October 2007 (and in fact, another A&R had already attended one of our basement rehearsals in Burton Road just prior to this point). After this rather formulaic beginning, over the next year or so we worked away at the Manchester live circuit (Retro Bar, Dry Bar, Ruby Lounge, Tiger Lounge, Joshua Brooks and so on), venturing further afield as time went on to venues all over the North, and then the country as a whole.

Throughout this whole time, Manchester existed for us as a largely incidental backdrop, perhaps in part because everywhere in Britain in the New Labour years had started to look more or less the same. I can't speak for the other members of the band, but I was frustrated that we never really embedded ourselves in the city's grassroots, and saddened that Manchester's spirit of place proved so elusive in the time I lived there. As an adolescent poring over Smiths and Stone Roses biographies in rural Northumberland, I had often fantasized about skiving off school, getting the train down to Manchester and just wandering around the city for a day or two. What I would have done there as an under-age stowaway with 25 quid in my Halifax Solo account, I have absolutely no idea. But it was significant that it was the alternative, northern 'capital', rather than more distant and dismal-seeming London, that was the subject of these teenage reveries. This will probably sound ridiculous to anyone who grew up in the city, but going by summaries of the Eighties scene in books and sleeve notes by Johnny Rogan, Mick Middles, John Harris, John Robb and Dave Haslam, the basic Mancunian topography of

Afflecks Palace, Piccadilly Gardens, Rusholme, Hulme and Levenshulme sounded to me like one of the most exotic places on earth.

Slightly later, as I became interested in books other than those about late twentieth-century pop, I would gravitate to Mancunian authors most often and most eagerly. Terry Eagleton's Catholic–Marxist critical theory, Paul Morley's postmodern fantasies about millennial music, Anthony Burgess's sci-fi dystopias and memoirs of life in interwar south Manchester – all of these seemed to point to the existence of a highly sophisticated modernist metropolis somewhere near the banks of the rivers Irwell and Mersey. Meanwhile, Russell T. Davies's seminal TV series *Queer as Folk*, first broadcast when I had just turned 15, portrayed Canal Street's Gay Village as a mecca of liberated excitement – highly enticing even to a mundane heterosexual like myself. Again, this might all seem slightly absurd, but from the vantage point of the socially barren Tyne Valley I imagined the built-up North-West to be a place of ineffable urban glamour, bohemian adventure and artistic energy.

This youthful idealism – partly a symptom of the rural northern isolation discussed elsewhere – was always going to collide head-on with the more banal realities of twenty-first-century Britain. But the disappointment I felt after embarking on my own musical adventure in Manchester in my early twenties was, I think, more than just a case of collapsing teenage dreams (though there were plenty of these too).

When I finally made it to Manchester in 2007, I looked in vain for traces of the earlier musical tradition which had meant so much to me growing up. South Manchester, where the Everything Everything project was based, seemed to be a sort of suburban scorched earth filled with young professionals, debt-ridden students and the scattered detritus of Eighties and

161

Nineties indie. This cultural landscape was shrewdly satirized by the 'Madchester denier' blog Fuc51 (a takedown of Fac51, the Haçienda's Factory catalogue number), which collated examples of clichéd Mancuniana to suggest that the city was stuck in a permanent retro stasis, where 'Mancs are still pretending it's 1988.' An opening statement on the blog was uncompromising as it ridiculed the heritage industry which had swallowed up the more organic counterculture of the late twentieth century:

> Manchester will have you believe it is a forward thinking city. A Northern Republic standing up against the tide of Londoncentric nonsense. However, what Manchester fails to realise is that it cannot ever move forward because it is so determined to rest on recent history. Manchester is a joke and has been irrelevant for too long.

The Fuc51 perspective was difficult to argue with then, and for all that Manchester's counterculture is far healthier now than it was in the late Noughties, it remains broadly applicable to the 2020s.* Despite the fact that money poured into Manchester more liberally than in any other northern city throughout the

---

*I think it's important to stress here that I haven't lived in Manchester for well over a decade, so I'm only able to comment on the city's more recent creative life in general ways – as an acolyte and consumer of its culture from afar (which is, of course, how I fell in love with the city in the first place). While it seems clear even from a bird's-eye view that Manchester is still – like every other British city – awaiting another truly transformative countercultural breakthrough, I should say that every time I have gone back to the city in recent years it has seemed more and more culturally vital – especially in the youthful political circles which found a focal point in the left-wing Momentum group of the late 2010s.

162

New Labour years (and continued to do so, in a more uneven and sinister way, in the 2010s), the notion of a one-time futurist capital 'resting on recent history' was and is a sadly pithy summary of a city that has struggled to move past nostalgia for its own pop folklore since the Nineties, for all the determined recent efforts of its canny, creative populace.

Wandering around south Manchester as a resident in the late Noughties, I would often pass the old Factory Records office in Didsbury, or do a double take when I saw Alan Erasmus or Vini Reilly from the Durutti Column walking down Lapwing Lane. But I think it's fair to say that by this point romantic Manchester was very largely dead and gone. On painfully long bus journeys back to Didsbury from my job as a barista at Bella Italia in the Arndale Centre, I would sometimes pass through Moss Side and see a large crater at Maine Road, where Manchester City used to play football – and where Oasis had marked the end of the city's great flowering with a huge homecoming gig in the spring of 1996. More tragically and symbolically, about a month after I arrived in Manchester, in the thick of the rainiest summer I have ever known, former Factory boss Tony Wilson died at the age of 57 while undergoing cancer treatment at the Christie Hospital – a stone's throw from the old Factory depot on Palatine Road, and not too far from our new home in West Didsbury.

Perhaps this is just a retrospective pipe dream, but I like to think that we would have got Wilson involved with the nascent project that was Everything Everything if he had managed to live for just a little longer. There were obvious affinities between his worldview and our own neo-modernist dreams, and I often think that something like the Factory model – an attempt to give the North strong cultural institutions at far remove from the London establishment – was the one thing really lacking in our story (and ultimately the reason why the band ended up becoming a rather blunted, industry-centric affair). Maybe a collaboration with Wilson wouldn't have come to anything. But in another glitch in time, it would certainly have been worth a try.

After a year or so of being embedded in Manchester, the band increasingly became a London-centric project in all but name. Through a combination of creative originality and the music-biz training other members had picked up at university and from elite backgrounds, we began to be seen as the coming men of British indie. Although our London-based manager advised us to foreground our status as a Manchester band, the final year of my time in Everything Everything was dominated by the capital and its industry networks (which are, by the way, every bit as shockingly amoral, absurd and predatory as everyone says they are). There was a messy, complicated period during which three members relocated for personal reasons to London and Oxford, at the same time as an obsession with the music of Michael Jackson started to dominate the band's self-image in ways I never quite understood. Then, in a final, painful phase, it became clear, to me at least, that we were going to get a record deal pretty imminently – but also that I had no interest in hanging around to see what might happen afterwards. This is probably not the place to go deep into the circumstances which led to this crossroads. But in brief, the reasons were in equal parts musical (I found the band's frantic math-rock bouts and rhythmic hyperactivity very hard to gel with), political (there seemed to be nothing left that was even faintly countercultural about the Noughties 'independent' music scene, which I found personally quite devastating) and personal (I lost all respect for my fellow band members, partly because of clashing views about careers and ideals, but also as a result of deeper, more complex friendship issues). I suppose there was also a more pragmatic inkling that bands on the old boy-meets-guitar model would seem increasingly outdated as a diverse new century continued to unfold.

All in all, the two years I spent in Everything Everything were not much fun, despite or because of the fact that we evolved so astronomically, going in the space of a few months from point zero to playing Reading Festival and being hyped by insufferable Radio 1 DJs, as record deal offers waited in the hallway. By this point my hope that Manchester might be a place of creative adventure had evaporated in the tired, aimless environment of Britain in the dying days of New Labour. When I think back to those two years in the city, my abiding memory (aside from agonizing experiences of public transport on the Wilmslow Road corridor) is of a sort of hazy, dishevelled anaesthesia. Shorn of all countercultural glamour, this time now comes to mind as an impressionistic blur of rainy days, rubbish-strewn yards in squalid terraced houses, peevish rehearsals in disused warehouses in Salford and Stockport, and lost nights muddied with wine or other sedatives when you would completely forget who you were and where your home even was.

In the end, fittingly, I said goodbye to my old school friends at Newcastle Central Station after a final gig down by the Newcastle Quayside in September 2009 – subsequently refusing all offers of financial compensation on point of principle. After this symbolic parting of ways in one of the capitals of northern modernity, I boarded a train bound for Oxford, where I now lived with my partner, Louise, and where a life of writing seemed to offer some faint prospect of the creative freedom and social purpose I had failed to find in the postmodern music industry. And so, for the most part, it has proved.

In the middle of my rather dim personal memoir of Everything Everything's foundation years, some stray moments of clarity stick out. One, in particular, speaks of the sorrow I felt on encountering Manchester in the early twenty-first century, at a time when the city's leftover cultural glories were dropping out of sight like the last sands in an hourglass.

In the summer of 2008, as Lehman Brothers trembled and the financial crisis spiralled, we were booked to play a live session on Channel M, a now defunct regional television station based in the Urbis museum (itself a short-lived project of the Blair years, which hosted tub-thumping exhibitions about local legends like Peter Saville, the Haçienda and the architect Will Alsop's plan for a northern 'SuperCity', before it was replaced by the National Football Museum in 2010). TV studios are strange places to be at the best of times, especially when you are not – as none of us was at this point – familiar with their 2D atmospherics, intensely bright lights and abrupt shifts in tone. Performing our two or three best songs was relatively straightforward: a slightly drier version of a live gig. But there were some bizarre moments in between, as we sat around taking part in various segues and mini-features, which, I would guess, probably ultimately ended up on the cutting-room floor. Most of these involved Channel M's resident celebrity Frank Sidebottom – in reality the local musician and comedian Chris Sievey, a comic persona with an oversized papier-mâché head and a complex identity.

Sidebottom had become a cult figure in the Eighties and Nineties, as a peripheral member of the Madchester scene and its spin-offs. Built into his persona was a kind of tacit admission that the dreams of the North and northerners would ultimately come to dust. Frank was ostensibly an aspiring pop star, whose act consisted mainly of farcical musical interludes and discussions of imagined celebrity encounters – with half-satirical, half-serious fragments of trad comedy and music-hall-ish antics thrown into the mix. On one level, there was a wonderfully warm, down-to-earth aspect to the Frank routine. It seemed to evoke an older northern structure of feeling from before the rise of postmodern irony – a world of variety shows, seaside cabaret and the gentler side of working men's clubs – which worked well in counterpoint with the more caustic values of the post-punk comedy scene Frank inhabited.

But there was an ocean of melancholy swirling beneath it all. In this respect, Frank was in step with a specific strain in northern comedy of the Long Eighties, which began with Victoria Wood and passed through Morrissey's lyrics into the less nuanced terrain of later shows like *Shooting Stars* and *Phoenix Nights*. In this post-kitchen-sink tradition, the underlying joke tended to derive ultimately from an implicit sense that northern hubris would almost always end in failure in a country where nine-tenths of the culture industry is based in London. While Frank talked eagerly about his dreams of stardom, there was deep pathos in the realization you had in watching him: beyond all the satire, you were always very conscious of the fact that he was a cipher for thousands of real-life performers in the marginal North who would almost certainly never amount to anything, and who would probably eke out their lives without ever being acknowledged, let alone acclaimed.

Now, in the late Noughties, as we sat around on brightly coloured sofas in the blazing lights of the Channel M studio, Frank tried to engage us in his syncopated banter. But we didn't have much interest in taking part, either because of shyness (in my case) or from cynicism about this gentle parody of northern hopelessness, who had himself become a slightly hopeless figure in the hollowed-out culture of Noughties Manchester. In the space of a few years, after I had left the band, the experiment in regional TV that was Channel M had ceased to exist. Meanwhile, after a short battle with cancer, Chris Sievey died in poverty in 2010 at the relatively young age of 54, taking his Frank Sidebottom alias with him to the grave.

Looking back, it's difficult to recall in any detail what Frank said to us on that day in the Channel M studio, in the slowly disintegrating summer of 2008. In fact, the whole, surreal

167

episode has the feeling of something that didn't really happen. I do vividly remember, though, that at some point during filming Frank paid us an immortal tribute, by announcing that he'd created a new musical outfit, and then proceeding to sing a ramshackle version of its debut single to jangling accompaniment on his tiny Casio keyboard.

The name Frank had given his imaginary new band was, of course, Nothing Nothing.

Frank Sidebottom memorial statue, Timperley, Greater Manchester

Part III

RUIN & REVIVAL

We take up the task eternal
The burden and the lesson
Pioneers! Oh! Pioneers!
— Chopwell Lodge miners' banner,
after Walt Whitman

Newcastle Quayside, with the Sage concert hall and BALTIC
art gallery in the background

The Great Betrayal

In the early hours of 17 July 2005, a long queue of mostly sober people began to grow steadily bigger on the newly regenerated banks of the Newcastle–Gateshead Quayside. By 3.30 a.m., as nightclubs emptied of their dazed patrons, the line of people was packing the riverside between the Tyne Bridge and its graceful new sibling, the Millennium Bridge, opened to much acclaim only five years earlier. Other new buildings gleamed in the background as dawn pierced the clouds. At the top end of the queue, kittiwakes nested on the cornicing of the BALTIC art gallery, and at its side the larval curves of the Sage music centre loomed like a great glass hillside. For a while, in the thick of this strange tableau, men with megaphones walked purposefully along the line of locals, barking instructions at them and handing out plastic carrier bags, instruction sheets and numbered tickets. Then, in a serene gesture of civic openness, everyone in the crowd suddenly began to take off their clothes. The public, we might say, revealed itself. Cameras filmed a swaying mass of pink and white and brown, 1,700 naked people spilling over bridges, round buildings and up medieval side-alleys – liberated citizens enacting the vision of the artist-provocateur who lay somewhere behind it all. For a fleeting moment, the sleeping city really was reborn.

As an expression of a popular moment, this curious art installation, *Naked City* (one of several similar projects by the New York photographer Spencer Tunick), could not have been more apt. It was brought into being at a time of great optimism and unbuttoning for the North of England, at the height of a long and dynamic period of civic growth in wider millennial Britain. These were years when it really did seem like the North might renew itself. However, as we have already seen – and as we will continue to see in our final chapters – this turned out to be a short-lived, mostly rather superficial dream.

The late Nineties and Noughties were a distinct, heady and hubristic era in modern northern history. At the centre of the narrative of these years is the totemic figure of the British prime minister Tony Blair, who came to power in a landslide victory at the 1997 general election. Over the next few years, Blair and his New Labour government would talk at intervals about the rejuvenation of the party's urban heartlands, most of which lay in the post-industrial North. Much of this levelling-up agenda was set by another key figure in the New Labour story: the deputy prime minister, John Prescott. In many ways Blair's polar opposite – and still a mostly unsung northern hero – Prescott and his regional disciples put a great deal of energy in these years into a concerted, impassioned and multilayered New Labour strategy, which sought to drastically boost the North's prosperity, empowerment and underlying sense of self-esteem.

By 2005 this campaign appeared to be bearing fruit in places like Tyneside, site of Spencer Tunick's strange experiment in *au naturel* community art. As we saw in the previous section, Terry Farrell's postmodern masterplan for the Newcastle-Gateshead Quayside helped to kickstart its regeneration in the late Eighties (echoing similar quango-led schemes in Manchester–Salford, Merseyside, Leeds, Sheffield and Teesside, all of which imitated the pioneering Thatcherite redevelopment of the Docklands area in East London). As such, there is a meaningful debate to be had about whether showpiece northern projects like BALTIC, Sage Gateshead and the Millennium Bridge, all of which were first conceived in the Thatcher and Major years, should be associated with the Blair government at all – even if all were completed, and boastfully opened, after the 1997 landslide. Likewise, the magisterial *Angel of the North* sculpture designed by Antony Gormley, which finally arose in Gateshead in 1998 to provide an enduring symbol of the optimism of these years, had in fact been commissioned under John Major and championed by the Conservative peer and Arts Council chairman Grey Gowrie. As the key dates in this timeline prove, the Blair years were a *culmination* of long-term developments rather than a sudden golden age. Even if they have rarely been successful, it is always important to remember that *every* government of the last half century – bar none – has paid some form of lip service to the idea of northern regeneration.

Nonetheless, there is no doubt that New Labour continued and accelerated an unusually vigorous revival for northern urban areas in the millennial period – often aided, or at least in some way inspired, by John Prescott's pro-North patronage. This was perhaps the last – and certainly the most vivid – episode in living memory when the possibility of equality for England's regions seemed genuinely within reach. Culturally, this was a time when economic growth gave rise to widespread feelings of exuberance and expansionism in northern areas, as new art galleries, football stadiums, coffee shops, chain restaurants, music venues, office buildings and apartment blocks sprouted throughout the region's cities and towns.

More pointedly, it was also a moment of breakthrough and ultimate failure for the cause of regional devolution – and the impact of this movement's collapse on England's internal politics and geography is still being powerfully felt nearly two decades later. The defeat of the 2004 referendum on the creation of a North-East regional assembly was perhaps the single most important event in the modern political history of the North. As well as its immediate outcome – the cancellation of plans for regional assemblies throughout Britain – the triumph of the No campaign in 2004 (partly masterminded by a young Dominic Cummings) mostly shut down the wider regionalist movement for a generation, offering an apparently black-and-white example of why devolution in England would never work. In the long term, crucially, it helped to ensure that the moderate economic and cultural boom the North experienced either side of the millennium was not underpinned by any more permanent political reforms.

As a result, and in the context of a wider failure of the Blair government to engineer anything other than a temporary, boomtime *atmosphere* of positive change (aside from a handful of more meaningful achievements), this period seems in retrospect to have been a mere reprieve rather than a genuine northern revival. Because of New Labour's inability or unwillingness to change the internal power structures of England in lasting ways, the Nineties and Noughties now seem like a false dawn: a brief moment of respite before the economic and human catastrophe of the 2010s – in many ways, as well shall see, the most abject decade for the North since the Second World War (even allowing for the nightmare of the Thatcher years). The narrative of this period, and the central story of how the North's relationship with its avatar the Labour Party was fatally dislocated, is crucial to understanding how the region got into its present mess. This is the cul-de-sac we must think around and beyond if we are ever going to restore the hope of a radically reformed northern future.

For all its nuances, the story of New Labour is at heart a classic, even mundane one about what happens when soul and identity are sacrificed for the sake of power. And bearing in mind the history of the Labour Party, it was predictable that much of this narrative of sell-out in the millennium period would revolve around the North of England.

To understand what happened to the North in these years, we must first understand the historical basis of its relationship with the Labour Party. Labour was, in its origins, less a political party than a collection of communities – very often, though not always, northern English ones. In the territorial pattern which guided Labour's formation in the late nineteenth and early twentieth centuries, local associations would spring up in industrial areas to empower groups of workers and their families. As time wore on, these local units gradually merged into a national network of disparate factions, united by a simple, empirical sense that, for all its ideological diversity, it always embodied the cause of *labour*. The English North played a starring role in this narrative. From the foundation of the Trades Union Congress (TUC) in Manchester in 1868, to the rash of local organizations in places like Colne Valley and Salford that would join together to form the Independent Labour Party (formally founded in Bradford in 1893), and finally to the historic proposal in 1900 by a Doncaster railway worker that a conference should be held to allow the TUC to establish a parliamentary front in the form of the Labour Representation Committee, Labour was in its early years very much an outgrowth of northern industrial consciousness.

The rise of the tiny, maverick Northern Independence Party in the early 2020s is discussed elsewhere in this book. But we should note that for much of the twentieth century an explicitly northern party of this kind was simply not necessary, because the Labour Party was viewed by most working-class northern voters as their vanguard, mouthpiece and birthright. Without discounting the pivotal role of Scottish, Welsh, Midlands and southern English areas (especially London) in Labour's development, and allowing for the significant Tory presence in certain northern districts (especially non-industrial rural ones), it is important to grasp that the democratic socialist project in England was predominantly an outgrowth of the northern landscape. In the 1906 general election, when Labour won its first tranche of parliamentary seats, two-thirds were in the North of England. In 1923, when Labour finally broke through to power, around half of Labour's MPs represented constituencies in the North or the North–Midlands borderland (Derby, Nottingham, Stoke etc.) – and this proportion would be replicated in every subsequent election where Labour did not substantially cross over into traditional Conservative territory in the South. More crucially, in the vast majority of post-war elections, Labour won a majority of seats in the North, usually by a fairly significant margin. Historically, Labour was *the* party of the North in all but name.

However, after it became a governing party in the 1920s, Labour soon got into the habit of disappointing, exploiting and ignoring its northern heartlands, as it sought to cosy up to – and increasingly become part of – the Westminster establishment. Because it was for the most part a fragile progressive faction in the overwhelmingly conservative and traditionalist British constitutional system, even at times when it seemed to have the upper hand – such as in the late Forties and mid-Sixties – Labour was always only one step away from political irrelevance and long exile. Due to this basic vulnerability, the party's chariness in trying to win large-scale, long-term reforms for its working-class voting base, and its projection of an image of anti-radical respectability for much of the twentieth century, were somewhat predictable.

Harold Wilson visiting a retirement home in Washington, late 1960s

Nevertheless, despite major betrayals like the party leadership wiping its hands of the Jarrow Crusade in 1936, and Neil Kinnock's calculated refusal to support the Miners' Strike in 1984–5, the rise to power of Tony Blair and his New Labour regime in the mid-1990s, which depended on a pretty wanton electoral double-crossing of the North, was something more momentous than the usual story of compromised principles, careerism and realpolitik. In fact, Blair's overall strategy as party leader, and then prime minister, would undermine Labour's relationship with its northern working-class base in ways that would eventually threaten the party's very existence. For all the tawdriness of earlier treacheries, indeed, there is a strong

179

case for saying that New Labour's let-down of the North in the millennial period is by some distance the most shameful, most damaging episode in the long history of the Labour Party.

There was a biblical aspect to the narrative, which derived in part from the fact that Blair was – at least on the surface – a northerner of sorts. Indeed, like many of the key architects of New Labour (Peter Mandelson, Alan Milburn, Stephen Byers, David Miliband, John Hutton), Blair had an intimate connection with the North-East of England, which was, by the late twentieth century, perhaps the most neglected, underdeveloped corner of the region (and the country) as a whole.

Despite some equally tangled Scottish roots, Blair spent much of his childhood in the North-East, and he would often in later life lay claim to various forms of kinship with the area. From the age of five, after his father acquired a lecturing job at the city's Oxbridge-imitating university, Blair lived in Durham – in many ways an appropriate starting point for his biography. A small cathedral city mostly populated by academics and students from private and grammar schools in more affluent parts of the country, Durham was both right at the heart of, and hermetically sealed from, Labour's traditional working-class homeland in the surrounding Great Northern Coalfield. This ambivalent dynamic would set the tone of Blair's relationship with the movement he would one day come to lead. Whether or not Blair ever attended the Durham Miners' Gala as a child or adolescent (as the Gala dominates its host city on the second Saturday in July, this seems highly likely), he certainly had plenty of North-East credentials that would be stored up for deployment in his future political career. However, it must be said that when Blair spoke of them, he had the air of someone who was straining to remember an authentic northern upbringing he had in fact experienced at second hand.

In later interviews, for example, Blair reportedly claimed that his support for Newcastle United football club began in early childhood, when he sat in the Gallowgate End at St James's Park to watch legendary striker Jackie Milburn play. This was probably a misquotation: as the Gallowgate End had no seats at this point, and as Blair was living abroad throughout Milburn's last years at the club, one would certainly hope so. But whatever the truth of such half-memories, Blair's attachment to the football history of his childhood home would play a key role in his man-of-the-people PR campaign after he became Labour leader in the mid-Nineties. After assuming the leadership in 1994, Blair arranged for a photo shoot with Newcastle United manager Kevin Keegan, wrote a sentimental foreword for the club's official history, *United: The First 100 Years*, and generally played up his attachment to the football culture of the North-East (allegedly also claiming some form of affection for Newcastle's rivals on the other side of the Tyne–Wear conurbation, Sunderland AFC). In his contribution to *United*, the historical timespan of which coincided very nearly with that of the Labour Party itself, he was at pains to point out that, 'as someone who was brought up in the North-East', he understood 'how important it is to *our* community that we have success in sport' (my italics). It seems improbable that Blair would have worn an Adidas Newcastle replica shirt while holding a phone conversation with Elizabeth II in the aftermath of Diana Spencer's death in September 1997, as wryly suggested in Stephen Frears's 2006 film *The Queen*. But it is, at the very least, a poetically resonant image.

Though Blair would return to Durham outside of term time while attending private school in Edinburgh and then university in Oxford, after he began a legal career in the late Seventies he would spend the vast majority of his time in London. Nevertheless, the North-East would re-enter his story – and that of the Labour Party he would soon rebrand – at a crucial moment as his political career began in earnest. In the run-up to the 1983 general election, Blair won the nomination to stand as Labour Party candidate for the Sedgefield constituency in County

Durham, duly becoming its MP when the results came through in the early hours of 10 June. A sprawling, largely rural seat comprising much of the southern Durham coalfield, Sedgefield is an archetypal 'Red Wall' area. This sort of constituency would prove decisive in the 2019 general election, when, as we have seen, the capture of a tranche of former Labour seats in the North and Midlands helped to guarantee a landslide victory for Boris Johnson's Conservatives, effectively ending Labour's age-old claim to be a party of and for the North (although it is important to point out that, even in 2019, Labour held a clear majority of northern seats).

In this much later moment, helped along by an opportunistic Tory victory rally in Sedgefield two days after the election, the seat's switch from red to blue was framed in countless election summaries as the climactic collapse of a former Labour stronghold with close ties to its last electorally successful leader. Highlighting the irony of the occasion, *The Times* reported that the Conservative campaign office in Sedgefield had cheekily blasted out the New Labour anthem of 1997, D:Ream's 'Things Can Only Get Better', as news of the result came through on election night. Meanwhile, *The Observer* surveyed the 'surreal spectacle' of Blair's 'symbolic home' falling to the Tories, and claimed that 'to rewrite the electoral history of this particular place was perhaps beyond [Johnson's] imagining'.

There is something to be said for this sort of analysis, which speaks of a sudden, historic, even unlikely defeat for Labour in Blair's old stamping ground. But there is another, deeper sense in which this catastrophe had been decades in the making. In order to understand what happened to the so-called Red Wall in 2019, and indeed what has happened to the political make-up of the North more generally in recent decades, we should be clear about exactly what kind of place Sedgefield was – and wasn't – back in 1983, when Blair returned to County Durham to claim his political seniority after wanderings in Edinburgh, Oxford and London.

If there is an essential sociological fact about the North over the last half century, it is that this period has been defined by the transition from a time when northern coal mines were already being closed to a present moment in which the vast majority exist only as a distant memory (and only then in the minds of people above or approaching retirement age). Though the Miners' Strike of 1984–5 was of great symbolic importance as a marker of the final collapse of the North's mining industry and culture, it is useful to bear in mind that northern pits had been shutting down at a rapid rate even prior to the Eighties, when a Thatcherite government committed to irrevocable neoliberal reform of the British economy foisted a merciless form of deindustrialization on the region. In County Durham, to take a representative example, an astonishing 118 collieries were wound down or merged between 1947 and 1979, with almost half (56) closing their doors under Harold Wilson's Labour government of 1964–70. Meanwhile, only 14 closed in Durham during Thatcher's 11-year premiership, with a further six following under John Major in 1990–97.

There are important caveats to this statistical overview. Post-war governments before Thatcher tended to close (or merge) mines at times when alternative employment was more plentiful and the safety net of the Welfare State more robust, which mitigated the impact of resulting job losses. Wilson's mine closures were often the result of tortuous, many-sided negotiations between government, the unions and the National Coal Board, in stark contrast to Thatcher's preferred method of all-out (sometimes literally militarized) confrontation, leading to a scorched earth of devastated communities. And it's probably fair to say that earlier Tory prime ministers such as Harold

Macmillan and Ted Heath would never have dared to demonize striking workers as 'the enemy within', as Thatcher famously and symbolically did in 1984 at the height of the Miners' Strike. Nevertheless, the crucial point is that in places like Sedgefield – which acquired the Red Wall label at the end of the 2010s, supposedly because of its status as a 'former mining area' – most of the mines had been boarded up long before Thatcher even came to power over 40 years earlier. Indeed, when Blair arrived in Sedgefield back in 1983, there were no collieries at all left in his constituency; Fishburn, the last remaining pit, having shut its doors in 1973.

Deindustrialization was, then, an inescapable fact which Blair inherited, though he would make plenty of conscious choices as he sought to respond to its legacy. At the heart of Blair's political narrative is a double-sided process, whereby the new reality of a post-industrial, post-mining North was used as an excuse for a more deliberate and wholesale uprooting of Labour's communitarian bedrock in places like County Durham. Though he bought a relatively seldom inhabited family home in Trimdon Colliery after being elected as MP for Sedgefield (apparently recognizable in the village as 'the house with two chimneys'), and in spite of his professional Newcastle United fan routine, Blair's strategy as the figurehead of New Labour was, pretty blatantly, to rely on the electoral support of Labour's northern heartlands, while ultimately doing very little to alter the political and economic underpinning of the North's long-term malaise.

In the 1997 general election, Labour's near-total dominance of the North paralleled its conquest of similar heartland areas in Scotland and Wales. Labour won almost every seat in the sprawling M62 corridor, all seats in South Yorkshire, most seats in Cumbria and all but two of 29 seats in the North-East (with Hexham, the only Tory seat in the region, morphing from a true-blue stronghold into an ultra-marginal, which Labour lost by scarcely 200 votes). Out of around 160 constituencies in the North, the Tories held barely a dozen in 1997 (by 2019 it would be nearly 60), mostly in their own northern heartland of north and east Yorkshire (though even here Labour took Scarborough and Whitby for the first time since its creation in 1918). Every single seat in County Durham was held by Labour, all with majorities of more than 10,000. The Labour majority in Easington, where toe-tapping Miners' Strike movie *Billy Elliot* would soon be filmed, and where several pits had stayed open long into the Nineties, was over 30,000.

As these statistics underline, Blair's rise to power was overwhelmingly based on the loyalty of heartland Labour voters (and as ever, its core regions in Scotland and Wales shared the glory with the English North). However, once in power, New Labour continued a habit, begun prior to the 1997 landslide, of orienting policy largely around the imagined desires of voters in a small number of a suburban swing seats, most of which lay in the English South. At the 1996 Labour Conference, Blair asserted that the party should appeal to an archetypal 'man polishing his Ford Sierra' on an 'ordinary suburban estate'. Although this small-C conservative rallying cry was apparently based on a real encounter with a voter somewhere in the Midlands, it justifiably came to form the basis of claims that New Labour had, in 'Mondeo man', discovered its own version of the 'Essex man' median voter theorized by the Conservatives in the Eighties and Nineties, as they sought to explain the appeal of Thatcherism outside of their traditional base. In the midst of an electoral strategy oriented around a handful of bell-wether southern seats with large numbers of affluent voters, the northern heartlands could apparently be taken for granted. Indeed, in the view of Peter Mandelson – the absentee Labour MP for Hartlepool in County Durham and Blair's chief spin doctor in the early days of government – spending too much time worrying about working-class voters was 'wrong', because they had 'nowhere else to go'. According to Mandelson and his ilk, Labour's working-class northern heartlands were an electoral shoo-in. Far better to focus instead on more mercurial voters in southern marginals like Crawley and Gravesham.

In fairness to Blair, he seems to have genuinely believed that the British public were 'all middle-class now', to quote another famous claim made in the run-up to the 1997 landslide – and importantly, that this new mega-bourgeoisie was a cross-regional phenomenon not just confined to the South. With this assumption somewhere in mind, Blair would talk about Sedgefield in surprisingly nuanced ways in a key passage in his 2011 autobiography, *A Journey*:

> Sedgefield was a 'northern working-class' constituency, except that when you scratched even a little beneath the surface, the definitions didn't quite fit. Yes, of course you could go into any of the old mining villages – the Trimdons, Fishburn, Ferryhill, Chilton and so on – and find the stereotype if you looked for it, but increasingly it wasn't like that. The new estates were private estates of three- and four-bedroomed houses, and while the people who lived there couldn't be described as 'middle class', neither were they 'working class' in the sense of Andy Capp. They drank beer; they also drank wine. They went to the chippy; they also went to restaurants. They were taking one, two or even three holidays abroad a year, and not all of them in Benidorm.

On the one hand, and ignoring Blair's snooty references (Andy Capp, Benidorm), this is a not inaccurate portrait of the changing class bias of (parts of) the North in recent decades. As we saw earlier, although they still lag far behind their southern counterparts on a range of socio-economic measures,

Red Wall seats like Sedgefield, where the mines closed relatively early in the timeline of post-war deindustrialization, have latterly become standard rural areas, with large elderly, financially stable (if not quite affluent) homeowning populations. In this sense, they have indeed relinquished their 'northern working-class' status in favour of a generic, less region-specific English-bourgeois identity. If we make allowance for the major caveat of age (the changing class character of places like Sedgefield has depended largely on economic benefits accrued by people born before circa 1980, with younger Red Wall residents locked out of the process and often forced to migrate elsewhere), Blair's comments provide a decent overview of what happens to 'former mining areas' when the socio-cultural hub of the colliery has become a long-forgotten ruin. Unsurprisingly, they tend to become like rural and semi-rural seats everywhere else in England, almost all of which are staunch Tory strongholds.

However, while we should note the ways in which deindustrialization has complicated the class underpinnings of the North–South divide, it would be a big mistake to think that New Labour built its governing mission around a new median voter – an ultra-privileged, shiraz-quaffing 'Sedgefield man'. In fact, and as Labour's headlong decline in popularity in northern areas even during Blair's time in office showed quite clearly, the phenomenon that would later be billed as the 'collapse of the Red Wall' – that is, the fatal severing of Labour's ties to its heartland areas in the North – would occur because northern areas continued for the most part to be passed over by Westminster, even as many baby-boomers in places like Sedgefield benefited in certain key fiscal ways from the combination of Thatcherism and watered-down social democracy at the heart of the New Labour project.

Much of Labour's collapse in northern areas over the last decade or so – discounting short-term triggers like its opposition to Brexit and the highly effective media demonization of its leader Jeremy Corbyn – was a direct consequence of the party's conduct under the leadership of Tony Blair and his successor Gordon Brown. Between 1997 and 2010 the party of the North finally had, for the first real time in its history, a long, mostly unchallenged spell in government. And sadly, when it came to long-lasting northern reforms – if you will permit the colloquialism – they totally fluffed it.

To be sure, in the early years of the New Labour regime, up to and including the mid-Noughties moment which bore witness to Spencer Tunick's jubilant disrobing exercise on the Newcastle Quayside, there was much optimism about the possibility of renewal in the North after 17 years of Tory misrule. Especially in the major northern conurbations (Greater Manchester, West Yorkshire, South Yorkshire, Merseyside and Tyneside) there was a rash of government investment in the millennium years, which at the very least briefly and markedly changed the tenor of northern urban life for the better.

Much of this followed from the 'urban renaissance' campaign spearheaded by John Prescott, who offered a gutsier, more soulful New Labour alternative to the calculating 'nowhere else to go' approach favoured by Peter Mandelson. A token 'left-winger' (of sorts) in the Blair government, Prescott was MP for Hull East, and had childhood roots in both South Yorkshire and Merseyside. Such impeccable trans-Pennine credentials may or may not have contributed to the fact that Prescott was one of the few major New Labour figures to make a determined effort to champion root-and-branch reforms of northern society. Prescott's campaign for the North began with a forceful, overarching plan for its revival. In 1998 Prescott commissioned a report – the modernistic 'Towards an Urban Renaissance' – which announced its determination to 'identify causes of urban decline in England and recommend practical solutions to bring people back into our cities, towns and urban neighbourhoods'. According to the summary of its overseer Richard Rogers, a superstar architect in a vaguely similar mould to Terry Farrell, the report 'marked a major shift in thinking and practice in urban policy', setting out 'a vision of sustainable regeneration of our towns and cities through making them compact, multi-centred, live/work [*sic*], socially mixed, well designed and connected, and environmentally sustainable'.

With Prescott's enthusiasm (and Treasury money) behind him, Rogers's organization Urban Task Force determined that many urban areas in the North of England were 'stuck in a spiral of market failure', and that only a revival of the modernizing ambitions of the post-war years would be capable of halting the region's long-term decline. In opposition (at least nominally) to the spirit of deregulation, private enterprise and postmodern eclecticism which held sway in the Thatcher and Major years, Rogers argued passionately that local and national governments would have to take back control of their civic environments if they were to have any hope at all of levelling out the inequalities which had deepened in the preceding era:

> Urban design and planning can manage the dynamism of towns and cities to tackle social problems and achieve social inclusion. However paternalistic and narrow the approach may have been in the past, and however disastrous some of its results through a focus on quantity at the expense of quality, spatial planning remains a vital tool for creating cities for people and a better quality of life for all citizens, through improving the physical environment and in particular creating the public realm that is our shared space.

Not since the post-war era had this sort of civic idealism been expressed with quite such confidence. To riff on a common historical meme of the period, if a pop band like Oasis were the Beatles of the Nineties, and Tony Blair a sort of Harold Wilson tribute act for the millennium, then the urban renaissance was among other things an attempt to recapture the reforming, modernist zeal which had once driven a figure like T. Dan Smith to try to transform Sixties Newcastle into 'a city in the image of Athens and Florence and Rome'.

The problems with Labour's campaign to revive the North were, however, manifold. For the most part, they arose from the short-sighted, money-minded default setting of New Labour, which tended to look for solutions based on sudden injections of boomtime cash, rather than establishing a more permanent strategy for tackling regional inequality. Instead of looking closely at how the North's economy and culture had been torn apart in places like County Durham – where a landscape of struggling small towns and villages was the legacy of the now departed mining industry – the urban renaissance was (predictably given its name and remit) focused on large cities. In places like the Salford Quays in Greater Manchester and the Newcastle-Gateshead Quayside, ritzy set-pieces which brought together cultural venues and private housing offered an ostentatious *spectacle* of revival. But they did little to reverse the long-term decline of their wider regions, where poor transport links meant that residents of places like Sedgefield were, in any case, unlikely to visit a new art gallery in central Newcastle. While a select group of inner-city areas reaped the benefits of regeneration, much of the post-industrial heart of the North – from the former mill towns of Lancashire to the former mining villages of South Yorkshire – was relatively ignored by New Labour, and at a time when sustained economic growth provided little excuse for such inaction. It is therefore no surprise that these rural and exurban areas formed the core of the Red Wall which finally crumbled so dramatically at the end of the 2010s.

Tony Blair in 2001

But even inside the big northern conurbations, New Labour's short-termism meant that the mood of renewal which dominated in the millennial North would not last long. For all their flaws, T. Dan Smith's schemes for the post-war North-East had at least been based on the notion that regional renewal would have to depend on a comprehensive new infrastructure – a Metro train system, a new Education Precinct, a Civic Centre to house local government and, most ambitiously of all, a determined social housing programme to provide long-term security (in theory) for the city's working-class populace. In contrast, the Blair government did comparatively little to renovate the deeper civic structures of the North. What it did achieve in this area was drastically compromised by the interference of private finance, not to mention the party's near-pathological fear of radical reforms (notably rail renationalization) which, it ceaselessly worried, would damage its newly won pro-business reputation.

There are several major infrastructural failures that epitomize New Labour's inability to level out regional and class inequalities during its time in office, from its utterly

191

abysmal record on social housing and its reluctance to challenge private utility companies to the increasing outsourcing of healthcare provision to private suppliers. All of this, in combination with a failure to find meaningful replacements for the North's vanished manufacturing base, and a rather relaxed approach to growing income inequality, would lay the ground for the social immiseration of the more radically austere, anti-statist 2010s, from which northerners would suffer disproportionately (as of course they had done during the original neoliberal onslaught of the Eighties). But New Labour's failure was perhaps most shocking and symptomatic in the key area of transport. It will cut a long political history short if we focus – in this condensed overview – on just this one textbook example of Blairite failure.

As the means by which the North is connected both to itself and to the rest of the world – not to mention a symbol of its momentous technological heritage – its public transport system acts as a kind of litmus test for any government's plans for reform of the region. With a handful of important exceptions, New Labour spectacularly flunked this test. While T. Dan Smith had expended much energy in laying the ground for works like the Tyne and Wear Metro, and while Sheffield City Council (at the time led by future arch-Blairite David Blunkett) had introduced heavily subsidized public bus fares in the so-called People's Republic of South Yorkshire as late as the early Eighties, the Blair government's main contribution to the history of the northern transport system was to continue the privatization initiatives of the Thatcher and Major years. Rail fares rose steeply during New Labour's time in office. Meanwhile, the national rail network continued to fracture into unwieldy, inefficient and of course profit-driven private operating companies, of which Richard Branson's Virgin was perhaps the most visible (and visibly money-motivated).

True to form, John Prescott made significant headway with transport infrastructure in his role as head of the newly created Department for Environment, Transport and the Regions. A personal advocate of rail renationalization, Prescott labelled privatization a 'national disgrace' at the 1998 Labour conference, to rapturous applause from the party's still rather radically inclined membership (and, one suspects, the nervous smiles of more right-wing Blairites in government, who were far more in tune with Richard Branson's way of doing things). With a prescient grasp of environmental concerns, Prescott cancelled some of the road-widening schemes devised by the previous Tory government, gave the go-ahead for local authorities to introduce congestion charges, sponsored park-and-ride schemes and announced a series of ambitious tram-building projects in places like Manchester, Sunderland, Nottingham and Leeds.

However, in spite of such modest successes, for the most part the North was still appallingly served by its transport system by the time New Labour left office. In keeping with the Blair government's economic worldview, which tended to see Britain's future in a mostly London-based *mise-en-scène* of corporate derring-do and the razzamatazz of the financial services, the really big rail infrastructure projects announced in the Blair years (the Overground, the Elizabeth Line, improvements to the Eurostar hub at St Pancras International) continued to build up London's status as one of the mega-cities of the global neoliberal empire. Meanwhile, northern cities lagged far behind. Despite his tough talk in the wake of the 1997 landslide, Prescott ultimately took a rather mild-mannered approach to rail regulation, which should have provided scope for a movement towards reintegration of the North's terminally divided transport infrastructure. Plans for a Leeds Supertram system were cancelled in 2005 (echoing a more general failure to extend tram and light rail systems into further flung parts of the North), and again, deepening privatization – for example, of Sheffield's Supertram network in 1997 – continued to prevent integration of bus, train and tram in a way that might prioritize regional connectivity over shareholder profit. Car use increased dramatically in parallel with train ticket prices throughout the millennium years, hardly helped, from a PR perspective, by the fact that Prescott himself acquired the epithet 'Two Jags', because of his fondness for publicly funded commutes in his chauffeur-driven Jaguar (supplemented by another, privately owned version of the same model).

In the end, in spite of the best efforts of Prescott and his delegates in local government, the overall northern experience of transport in the millennium years was a dismal one. These were years dominated by the rise of cheap, ecologically damaging budget airline flights both within and without Britain, absurdly expensive inter-city train journeys in crowded carriages with broken air-conditioning and, in much if not all of the North – especially outside of the major conurbations – immense difficulty and hardship in getting from A to B when accessing basic amenities like hospitals, colleges, cultural venues and restaurants.

In a shocking indictment of New Labour's transport policy – and indeed its overall record when it came to northern infrastructure – many parts of the North emerged from the Blair years without having benefited from a significant revamp of travel links since the Beeching axe had annihilated large swathes of the rail network half a century earlier. In Blyth, a former mining town on the Northumberland coast with a population of 37,000, there was no train station at all in 1997, when New Labour came to power (a legacy of its Beeching-era closure in 1964). There was still no station when Labour left government in 2010. Was it therefore surprising that voters in this long-time

194

Labour bastion – many of whom had hoped across many decades that a long period of Labour government would reverse the town's post-industrial decline – would desert the party in large numbers in 2019 to ensure a Tory victory?

All in all, there is no other way to describe the recent history these voters were responding to, which saw a powerful, boomtime Labour administration mostly fail to provide lasting structural reforms for its loyal northern heartlands, than to say that these were the years of a great betrayal.

Wark Forest, Northumberland, planted in the mid-twentieth century
partly to provide work for unemployed northern miners

9

Wark Forest with the
Geordie Mafia

I think it's important to make clear, at this point, that this book about the fate of the North has a basic political argument at its core, aside from all its personal and cultural examples. This is very simply that England does not work well for its constituent regions.

Part of the problem is that the overall framework for English nationhood is so confused and confusing. Far more than is normal in other countries, the disparate half-country that is England has very little in the way of a cohesive common culture to define its sense of self. Perhaps more to the point, beyond insecure England itself, the actual nation of which the North of England is a region – the United Kingdom of Great Britain and Northern Ireland – is for the most part a post-imperial fudge of increasingly fragmented territories, with no written constitution and no clear sense of shared identity. Because of this, it seems pretty obvious to me, and to many others, that the UK's political geography will have to be firmly overhauled – rather than just cautiously reformed – if inequalities of place are ever going to seriously decrease on these islands.

To their credit, in the immediate wake of the 1997 general election, the leading lights of New Labour seemed to grasp this basic constitutional reality, as they set about enabling long-overdue processes of structural reform in Scotland, Wales and Northern Ireland. In this area at least, in stark contrast to the monumental failures of infrastructure reform described in the last chapter, New Labour achieved some lasting successes. Most crucially, the momentous Good Friday Agreement of 1998 brokered by the Blair government created a window of opportunity for future Irish reunification, stipulating that there should be a referendum on the question 'if at any time it appears likely ... that a majority of those voting would express a wish that Northern Ireland should cease to be part of the United Kingdom and form part of a united Ireland'. In the same timeframe, the devolution referendums New Labour waved through in Scotland and Wales within months of coming to power – both of which resulted in Yes votes and produced parliamentary bodies in Edinburgh and Cardiff – represented the most radical uprooting of the UK's political architecture since the Irish Revolution. There is a lesson to be gleaned from the timing of these events, and it is a vital one for those of us who look forward to a time of greater autonomy, if not outright independence, for the English North. In the sluggish British system, paralysed for most of its history by conservative interests who tend to obstruct constitutional change, major reforms must arrive hard and early in the first days of a dynamic reformist government. Otherwise, they will almost certainly not happen at all.

And so it proved when New Labour attempted to replicate the success of its devolutionary campaigns in Scotland and Wales throughout England's regions. The roots of the millennial push for regional devolution lay in the Thatcherite Eighties, when rapid deindustrialization (and the Tory government's brutal response to it) created a viciously polarized electoral geography in Britain. While the resurgent

South of England voted in increasingly large numbers for a Tory Party which served its economic interests pretty well, staunchly Labour areas in post-industrial Scotland, Wales and northern England were effectively disenfranchised for the best part of two decades, as their needs were scarcely if ever taken into account by an imperious Conservative majority. It was in this context that support for devolution in Scotland and Wales began to take precedence in Labour circles over the party's traditional belief that it would be, at best, a diversion from class empowerment, at worst right-wing nationalism. The case of the North was more complicated, as it did not bring along with it any deeper historical tradition of nationalist agitation. Nevertheless, the North's recent socio-economic history had been very similar to that of Scotland and Wales, so it was logically incumbent on New Labour to tackle the Northern Question after it came to power and gave the green light to referendums on the Scottish Parliament and Welsh Assembly.

Fatefully, however, the Blair government's first move towards northern devolution was rather slow to arrive. In its first term, New Labour divided England up into Regional Development Agencies (RDAs) with the aim of furthering the regeneration schemes begun under Thatcher and Major. But otherwise it did very little to address the question of constitutional reform within England, such that the regionalist academic John Tomaney could opine in 2000 that 'the Labour government has said it will legislate for English regional government when there is demand for it but is doing notably little itself to stimulate such demand'. This all changed in 2003, when John Prescott presented the Regional Assemblies (Preparations) Act to parliament – a document which paved the way for referendums throughout England to provide a mandate for regional government.

Unfortunately, the reformist energy New Labour had mustered in the wake of the 1997 landslide had largely dissipated by this point. The Blair government had managed to get Scottish and Welsh devolution over the line in an early *Blitzkrieg*, which capitalized on the popular euphoria of the so-called Cool Britannia moment of the late Nineties, and which left little time for wrong-footed conservative business and media interests to mount a meaningful counter offensive. But the atmosphere of New Labour's compromised, highly controversial second term (2001–5) was starkly different. The more principled, even radical, wing of Blairism – faintly audible in the voices of Robin Cook and John Prescott – had always struggled to make itself heard above the clamour for centre-right compromise; but by 2003 the morale of the soft left had been pretty well gutted by a combination of the Iraq War and the corrupting torpor of governmental power. This was not a period in which a comprehensive overhaul of the British constitutional system was likely to be met with much enthusiasm, by either a weary electorate or a Blairite top echelon which had by now settled down into a reflex mode of privatization and triangulation – with an eye on simply clinging onto power whatever the cost.

Given Labour's historic roots in the English North, the campaign for regional devolution in the millennium years was in a sense a battle for the soul of the party, centring on its conflicted relationship with its original and biggest heartland. Here again, at the risk of over-simplification, we might see this as a struggle embodied in the contrast between the party's two diametrically opposed northern protagonists, Tony Blair and John Prescott. While Blair thought that devolution in England was 'stupid', doubtless because it was a genuinely radical initiative, Prescott became the public face and ideological champion of the cause. Blair had a tenuous connection to his Sedgefield constituency, and his deeper relationship with the North in reality consisted of little more than a handful of carefully chosen PR tidbits about Newcastle United. In stark contrast, Prescott's signature campaign as deputy Prime Minister, announced in 2004, was the so-called Northern Way, a genuinely bold initiative which brought together the three northern Regional Development Agencies (Northwest Development Agency, One NorthEast and Yorkshire Forward) to advocate for pan-North co-operation in promoting the region's socio-economic interests. If Blair's attitude to the North was often blatantly superficial, Prescott deserves great credit for at least trying to reform the structural basis of regional inequality – even as the right-wing press lumbered him with a public persona in which familiar 'northern oaf' stereotypes merged seamlessly with folk memories of T. Dan Smith's private-plated Jaguar.

To be sure, Prescott was not sent to jail and permanently cancelled from public life, as happened to his more controversial predecessor. But his attempt at sparking a northern renaissance would suffer a similar fate to Smith's dream of creating a shining modern city-state on the edge of a greater northern super-region. After Prescott's Regional Assemblies (Preparations) Act had made its way through parliament, the North-East was identified as the most auspicious site for the first – and at the time of writing still the only – referendum ever held on devolution in England, which was duly scheduled for 4 November 2004. In 2002 a nationwide survey had shown support for the idea riding high in the North-East, at 72 per cent (a figure exactly matched in North-West and Yorkshire and the Humber samples). But as the 2004 campaign unfolded, it became increasingly clear that the North-East referendum – and by extension Prescott's wider vision for a devolved North – was not going to win a democratic mandate for reform. When the ballots were finally

201

counted, the No campaign had triumphed in a landslide, with 78 per cent of the vote, and a majority in every council area in the North-East. By the following Monday, a deflated-looking Prescott announced that no further referendums would take place, effectively killing dead the Regional Assemblies Act and its underlying blueprint for northern regional empowerment.

How to explain the dramatic collapse of New Labour's regionalist campaign? There is, in fact, a sense in which plans for devolution in the North-East – and therefore the wider North – were defeated by two hoary auld enemies: intra-regional rivalry and self-directed bitterness. While Prescott's Northern Way consciously attempted to bring the three major sub-regions (North-East, North-West and Yorkshire and the Humber) together, and while he would later advocate the creation of a 'super-region' to solidify pan-North co-operation, the North-East referendum was hampered by tensions arising from its internal geographies. The No vote was notably higher in areas like Teesside and south Durham, which were both at far remove from urban Newcastle (the proposed assembly capital). In a sense, this was an early premonition of the collapse of the Red Wall in the 2019 general election, which was partly caused by voters outside of the really big northern conurbations giving vent to long-harboured feelings of resentment against adjacent larger cities (where the local political establishment was, and still is, almost always a Blairite Labour one). As such, this was another case of pointless territorial squabbles based on fine-grained differences in accent and identity getting in the way of a united push for northern revival. Looking to the future, this is one of the major hurdles the North will have to get beyond if it is to have any hope at all of levelling itself up.

And yet, we might also view the decisive rejection of the North-East Assembly as the first really major sign of a popular backlash against New Labour's failure to provide a meaningful renewal of civic life in the North. Despite his much-trumpeted North-East connections, Tony Blair scarcely bothered to appear in the region in support of the Yes campaign in the autumn of 2004. Perhaps it was just as well. From the other side, in his role as strategic adviser to the North-East Says No organization (Nesno), County Durham native Dominic Cummings put much effort into framing the referendum as an opportunity to reject the apparently costly and superfluous manoeuvrings of an out-of-touch political elite. During the course of the campaign, Cummings devised the pointed anti-Assembly slogan 'Politicians talk, we pay' (an obvious precursor in style and content to the 'Take Back Control' meme he would propel into the 2016 Brexit referendum campaign with lethal effect). Cummings was also responsible for one of Nesno's most memorable PR stunts: a giant, inflatable white elephant, which was wheeled out at speaking events and photocalls to provide a rather crass visual metaphor for the No campaign's main argument.

Cummings's approach was cannily mindful of a much deeper and wider movement in liberal democracies in the early twenty-first century, which saw electorates grow increasingly distrustful and resentful of the detached, managerial political class which had come to dominate Western governments in the apparently 'post-ideological' neoliberal period – and which would later lead to the destabilizing shocks of the 2010s (most notably, Trump and Brexit). But there is no doubt that his cynical harnessing of the North's age-old spirit of anti-establishment populism was, in the context of the North-East in 2004, directly framed as a chance to take revenge on a New Labour government which had failed to help the North move closer to economic and cultural parity with the South. Why should referendum voters believe that this new 'white elephant' would succeed where a government led by northern MPs had conspicuously failed throughout seven years of comfortable majority rule?

Nesno's 'white elephant' by the Tees Transporter Bridge, 2004

At the height of the referendum campaign, Cummings worked up a monologue for the opening of a Nesno political broadcast. It capitalized on a peculiar variety of northern fatalism which is ancient, even if it acquired a new emphasis in this early twenty-first-century context:

[Geordie man in his seventies:] I've been a member of the Labour Party for 25 year, right, and I am absolutely becoming disillusioned now, really disillusioned.

[Narrator speaking over a montage featuring images of Tony Blair, Alastair Campbell and Peter Mandelson:] The North-East has been let down by politicians for years. Remember 1997? We were told that things can only get better. But politicians have failed us. Now politicians want even more power for themselves, by creating a Regional Assembly made up of more full-time, professional politicians. It's time to say No.

The people of the North-East accepted Cummings's recommendation, and from this moment on, John Prescott's millennial Northern Way would rapidly run out of track. Despite its historic identity as the political superego of a clear majority of northern voters, the Labour Party had once again – and this time with some finality – failed to give the North a chance to rise. On the other side of this broken dream of political deliverance, things could only get worse.

The giddy rise and abject failure of the Blair government were among the main formative influences on my life, and on the lives of my millennial contemporaries. Partly because my generation has not, at the time of writing, secured a meaningful stake in the political mainstream (even as many of us enter middle age), we are still unable to move on from the boxed-in progressive schemes of the millennium years. As in the case of the failed North-East Assembly campaign, the partial success and ultimate evaporation of the Blairite dream has come to act as a cautionary tale told by centrist and conservative elders, who argue that the modest achievements and tough compromises of this period are the best we and the North can ever hope for. In the North, as in the country as a whole, real change seems likely to arrive only when this variety of pragmatism-cum-fatalism gives way to the more hopeful energies of a youthful vanguard in the first flush of political breakthrough.

As well as being psychologically shaped by this rather limiting historical context, like most members of my generation I also had some more direct encounters with the New Labour project. In fact, because I grew up in the North-East – coreland of the Blairite soul (or rather, the lack of it) – the lamentable tragedy of Tony Blair, his deeds and companions always seemed to be unfolding somewhere just upstage in my later childhood and adolescence. One example in particular shows how my story and the story of New Labour's northern breakdown overlapped.

In 1991 my dad said goodbye to Newcastle Polytechnic, leaving the lecturing job which had first brought him to the North-East back in 1977. As it turned out, he moved just a few hundred yards away, to the Dental School at Newcastle University, where he took on a cumbersome 'behavioural sciences' role in the ever more market-driven world of modern academia – an unhappy posting that would ultimately demoralize him with tragic consequences, as he began to succumb to the alcoholism that would eventually kill him. In a poetic contrast which says much about the trajectory of modern British professional life, when he left his office at the Poly (mere months before its transformation into the sleeker, more sellable brand Northumbria University), two enterprising lecturers from the law department moved onto his former corridor as part of a restructuring exercise. Fatefully enough, both of these men would soon transpire to be coming men in the New Labour insurgency of the mid-Nineties.

One of the new office occupants, Stephen Byers, had come to Newcastle to work at the Poly in 1977 – the same year as my dad. On arriving in the North-East he quickly became a key figure in Tyneside Labour circles. As deputy leader of North Tyneside council in the Eighties, Byers flirted with the radicalism of the far-left Militant group. But by the start of the Nineties he had swung firmly behind the centrist tendency in Labour. Elected as MP for Wallsend in the 1992 general election, Byers would soon become a key figure in the so-called Geordie Mafia – an influential centre-right clique that would act as Tony Blair's Praetorian Guard during his rise to power (and for some time afterwards). In reality a pan-North-East affair, with dominion far beyond Tyneside itself, this 'Geordie' faction also included key New Labour courtiers like Alan Milburn (another once radical Newcastle Labourite, who became MP for Darlington in 1992), Peter Mandelson (parachuted into the Hartlepool constituency in County Durham in 1992) and Mo Mowlam (a Newcastle University politics lecturer elected as MP for Redcar in Teesside in 1992). In a crowded field, Byers would become the most controversial member of this grouping. Nicknamed the 'Blairite's Blairite', he provoked outrage in September 1996, when he told journalists that Blair would 'break [Labour's] links with the unions altogether' if forced to deal with too many industrial disputes (so much, it would seem, for the historic roots of the party of organized labour). Byers's name would eventually become a byword for Blairite decadence when, in the last days of New Labour, he was embroiled in the 2009 Expenses Scandal, after securing £125,000 of public money for his partner's London flat. He was also, it transpired, a self-described 'cab for hire', who touted fast-track links between the business world and the New Labour high command (Byers was finally exposed in the 'Cash for Influence' scandal of 2010).

Byers's neighbour on my dad's former corridor at the Poly was another member of Blair's Geordie Mafia. John Hutton was a close friend of Blairite *pasionarias* Byers and Alan Milburn, and indeed Blair himself. Elected as MP for the Cumbrian industrial port town of Barrow-in-Furness in the 1992 general election (which Labour lost nationally, despite having led in almost all prior polling), Hutton would become a key junior minister in the New Labour government, eventually entering Blair's cabinet as Chancellor of the Duchy of Lancaster in 2005, and work and pensions secretary shortly after. To be crystal clear, Hutton would not feature in any of the scandals which so compromised the later reputation of his former Newcastle

Polytechnic colleague Stephen Byers. He would, however, become an enduring example of just how far Blairism managed to push the political centre – and the nominally democratic–socialist Labour Party – into traditional Conservative territory in the millennium years. After standing down as Barrow MP in 2010, Hutton would hold a series of roles in the nuclear power industry. Perhaps more notably – and ironically, given his former career in state education – Hutton would, in 2010, lead a major review into pension reform at the behest of Tory chancellor George Osborne. Published shortly after its author was elevated to the House of Lords as Baron Hutton of Furness, the Hutton Review recommended a massive downgrading of public sector pensions, very much in line with the Austerity policies of the moment (and of course, Thatcherite principles more generally).

But for me, John Hutton was more than a mere cipher for New Labour and its pro-business, anti-state crusade. In fact, by the time he moved onto my dad's recently vacated corridor at the Poly, John was already fairly well known to me and to my family.

This was because of a fairly arbitrary crossing of paths, albeit one which spoke of the final dissolution of the leftist counter-culture of the twentieth century. In 1990 my mother and other of her teacher friends had set up a Tyne Valley branch of the Woodcraft Folk. Very little to do with carpentry per se, this national youth group had begun in the 1920s, as a spin-off of the pacifist Kindred of the Kibbo Kift movement led by the utopian eccentric John Hargrave. Breaking from the single-sex militarism of Robert Baden-Powell's Boy Scouts (of which he had been a leading member), Hargave founded the Kibbo Kift as a way of promoting a Scouts-style regimen of camping, hiking and handicraft – but with a far more progressive commitment to 'world peace and brotherhood'. The Woodcraft Folk (at first a sort of youth version of the Kibbo Kift, founded in 1925 by breakaway member Leslie Paul) spent much of the interwar years as a loose affiliate of the co-operative, feminist and trade union movements, with a power base largely in working-class industrial areas. But in the decades after the Second World War it mingled with the folksy wing of the hippy counterculture, whose Rousseauian values it shared, and by the Eighties it had won many converts among middle-class radicals like my parents. Though it would never really recover from a decision by New Labour Children's Minister Margaret Hodge to axe its government funding in 2005 in the wake of the Iraq War (which it had vocally opposed), the Woodcraft Folk was a valuable pan-left, grass-roots organization. It achieved the noble feat of uniting the children of Labour-voting professionals in more affluent areas with those of diehard trade unionists from places like Stanley in the Durham coalfield (a cross-class experiment which, I can clearly recall, sparked mini culture wars at the biennial regional camp at Barnard Castle, which often centred on the merits or otherwise of vegetarian food).

In keeping with the still skewed gender bias of the late twentieth century, the Tyne Valley Woodcraft group founded in 1990 was a largely female-led affair, with games and exercises mostly organized by my mother's posse of off-duty teachers, creative types and youth workers. But all parents were encouraged, if not quite expected, to help out at some point with group activities. This was very much in line with the collectivist ethos of the organization, which looked to a humane (if stereotyped) ideal of Native American culture – and to the socialist and co-operative tradition more generally – as it sought to create a nurturing space for learning and play. At the centre of this quasi-tribal convocation, John Hutton's vivacious partner, Rosemary – and their four immensely likeable children – were major, even dominant, presences in the weekly Woodcraft meetings. These tended to revolve around games of tag, arts and crafts, parachute games and the like. There was also an opening exercise at each session – almost unimaginable in the anxiously safeguarded twenty-first century – during which the whole group would sit in a circle and share noteworthy stories from private goings on in the past week. These experiments in communal existence were hugely worthwhile, though they could also mean that you learned a little too much about the home lives of your fellow group members.

Despite these exercises in over-sharing, I should stress that I know almost nothing about the nuances of the Hutton family story. But I think it's fair to say that even going by the public face of things, it was clear to all of us that John Hutton was in the early Nineties headed in a completely different direction to the Woodcraft Folk and their gentle, utopian culture, dedicated – as a William Morris quotation in its promotional literature affirmed – 'to the fashioning of a new world'. Even so, nobody could have predicted at the time quite how far away John and his colleagues would drag both the Labour Party and the country as a whole, as they sought to bury the radical communal dreams of the twentieth century once and for all.

If the Nineties were a decade when surface was depth, there were plenty of external markers of the contrast between Old and New Labour which John Hutton seemed to embody. While most of the parents at Woodcraft meetings tended to wear some variation of the standard, left-ish baby-boomer uniform (floral dresses for the mums; woolly jumpers, jeans and stray bits of sportswear for both mums and dads), John was always dressed very tidily in an expensive-looking suit. He drove a smart car (whereas our family owned a second-hand Ford Fiesta). He often wore shades, which he would perch on top of a neat, slightly curled, slightly mulleted head of hair (whereas most of the other dads got by with a beard and no discernible hairstyle whatever). Basically, he looked very much like his friend and fellow lawyer Tony Blair does in photos from the late Eighties and early Nineties – though not perhaps so radiantly smug.

In keeping with the gender politics of the time (hugely unequal even on the supposedly feminist left), like most of the other dads, including mine, John would not often turn up to the regular Woodcraft meetings, which took place in the dusty former Victorian hotel in Hexham that would later provide the backdrop to my high school education. He would, however, occasionally come along to the camps and outdoor activities. One of these occasions has somehow stuck in my mind, even though it must have been in early 1991, when I was only six or seven years old.

It was a weekend in winter, and the Hexham Woodcraft group had ventured to Wark Forest for one of our habitual 'nature trails' (a precursor, I suppose, to the more widespread recent craze that is the Forest School). Then, as now, Wark Forest formed the southernmost border of the vast Kielder plantation in North Tynedale, the point at which the Pennines – in the form of their final offshoot, the Cheviot Hills – begin to say goodbye to the North of England, as they head towards the kindred but discrete kingdom of Scotland's Southern Uplands. Once a depopulated grouse moorland like much of north Northumberland, the Kielder area experienced pocketed forms of regeneration in the twentieth century. This was partly due to the creation of a large reservoir, Kielder Water, which would eventually harbour 99 per cent of the North-East's water supply. A more large-scale project was the plantation of the Kielder and Wark forestland (the largest man-made woodland in England), which originally provided work for thousands of former northern miners and shipbuilders in the wake of mid-twentieth-century deindustrialization.

However, by the early Nineties the instructional centres and purpose-built villages established by Forestry England half a century earlier to serve the plantation had mostly ceased to be hubs of activity. And so, once again, North Tynedale had become a mostly remote and beautiful wilderness. It was on this terrain that we Woodcraft children and our parents found ourselves wandering in the late winter of 1991, as we hunted for pine cones and mini-beasts to sketch in the name of something or other (ecological awareness, most likely). Somehow, at some point, I found myself lost amid the Sitka spruces and Douglas firs of the plantation. Cold and scared, I started to cry, went to the toilet on the mossy forest floor and began to feel that no one would ever find me in this endless maze of bristling conifers. Eventually, after what seemed like hours, a lone adult came walking along the dirt track towards me, asked if I was OK and gave me some tissue paper to clean myself with.

Perhaps it is the element of mild trauma in this incident which means that I can still remember it so clearly over 30 years later. But there was also something more deeply memorable, even slightly shocking, in this encounter with the future Baron Hutton of Furness – and this is surely part of the reason why I have never forgotten it. More than mere awkwardness at being alone in the middle of nowhere with a sobbing child, and more than the bumbling ineptitude the other Woodcraft dads tended to show in these situations, John seemed almost desperately ill at ease as he tried to comfort me amid the man-made groves of Wark Forest. Even to my childish eyes, it was pretty clear to me that he wanted to be somewhere else – and certainly, I would say with hindsight, far away from this remote corner of the North Country, where the eccentric ideals of the doomed left survived in marginal oases, and where sensible men of ambition had probably always seemed absurdly out of place. Whatever community my family and I belonged to, it was somehow glaringly clear to me, even then, that John Hutton formed no part of it.

After he won the Barrow seat in the 1992 general election, defeating the Tory incumbent by some 3,000 votes in a turnaround which foreshadowed the much more dramatic swing to Labour in the 1997 landslide, my mother took me with her to the Hutton house in Hexham to drop off a bunch of symbolic red roses. On the attached card she had written a simple note: *Thank you John for a single ray of light on a dark night.* After knocking on the door for a while, we realized there was no one at home, so we left the flowers and the card on the doorstep and went on our way.

Sycamore Gap on Hadrian's Wall, Northumberland

Going Home

The throes of a sort of moral earthquake were felt
heaving under the hills of the northern counties.
But, as is usual in such cases, nobody took
much notice.
— Charlotte Brontë, *Shirley*

In the autumn of 2015, after over ten years of exile, I finally made it back to the North-East. Throughout a long decade of mostly living, working and studying in the South of England, I had longed to get back to the North – sometimes with an almost unbearable, visceral intensity. But when this ambition was eventually realized, what I found on returning to my childhood home was not quite what I had expected.

When we were about seven or eight, my best friend Will Lee and I were obsessed for a while with the just released Hollywood blockbuster *Robin Hood: Prince of Thieves*. This was partly because one of its opening scenes had been shot at Sycamore Gap on Hadrian's Wall, a five-minute drive from where we lived in Settlingstones and Fourstones. Of course we were also, as fairly typical kids of our age, drawn to the film's send-up of chivalric heroism, which supplied plenty of raw material for juvenile playground dreams. For much of 1992, we would both wake up at 6 a.m. in our separate homes and try to watch the whole of the VHS of *Prince of Thieves* before meeting for lessons in our tiny village school in Newbrough. Later on in the day, teaming up at breaktime and lunchtime, we would recite huge chunks of the dialogue to each other, then go back to posing as Paul Gascoigne in crude games of football played under a distant Pennine skyline.

Partly because of these formative experiences – and also, perhaps, because Robin Hood is one of the key foundation myths of northern culture – when I returned to the North in 2015 after a long period of exile I kept thinking about the opening scenes of *Prince of Thieves*. In the central plot, Kevin Costner's Robin finally returns to England after many years of fighting in the Third Crusade with Richard the Lionheart. Back in his ancestral lands, he and his Moorish companion Azeem inspire the outlaws of Sherwood Forest to build a sort of treetop northern Free State and defeat the Satan-worshipping Sheriff of Nottingham (artfully rendered by Alan Rickman, in a performance which makes a virtue of the many comic anachronisms in the script). There is a dramatic scene at the start of the film, when Robin first reaches English soil. As he leaps out of the boat which has just brought him across the Channel to the south coast, a soaring, symphonic score begins to swell majestically in the background; Robin then throws himself onto the shore, kisses the sand, thanks God and starts laughingly shouting 'I'm home! I'm home!' again and again, to Azeem's stony bemusement.

The fact that I was able to return to the North-East at all in the 2010s felt like a God-given miracle on a par with Robin's delirious physical embrace of his homeland in *Prince of Thieves*. Partly, this was because of what had happened after I travelled South to start university in the mid-Noughties. I had been through a fair bit since then. As well as getting into the usual millennial scrapes, both my parents had died within weeks of each other in late 2005, when I was 21 and still in most respects a teenager.

My mother was unlucky enough to develop an aggressive form of breast cancer shortly after I left home. Meanwhile, as her illness became terminal, after two optimistically sober years, my father retreated into the alcoholic void which ruins so many northern lives – and with such self-destructive force that his liver started to shut down for good in the unbearable days after my mother's funeral.

There are, of course, worse things that could have happened to me and my sister. But the aftermath of this uncommon, uncanny tragedy was bad enough. On top of dealing with a large dose of emotional turmoil, we had to arrange funerals and burials, decide what to do with our deserted home in Fourstones (eventually sold at the low point of the recession), range over a jumbled hoard of heirlooms and begin to pick apart the cat's cradle of our parents' personal and financial affairs. Finally, most bewildering of all, we then had to make our way through young adulthood in a thoroughly individualistic society, without any elder voice to ask for advice, comfort or aid.

As a result of all this, my sister and I acquired a certain inner stoicism. We also learned, earlier than most, a fundamental truth about human identity and its relationship with home and homeland. Our ordeal made us realize that if anything is likely to deepen your attachment to a landscape, it is the cold, untranslatable shock of leaving your last remaining parent forever in its soil.

In Wales, the North of England's cultural cousin, the deep longing for home has a specific and beautiful name: *hiraeth*. Because it is also, like Wales, a part of the British Isles at far remove from the centre of economic and cultural power that is London, the North tends to instil in its people an especially strong form of *hiraeth* – even if we do not yet have a language of our own to put a name to it. In the long tradition of North–South

217

economic migration – one of the cornerstones of northern identity, and a key point of difference with the typical experience of early adult life in the South-East – young northerners are fairly routinely forced into far-flung exile from their homes and families in search of education and work. As in other peripheral parts of the islands (Scotland, Wales, Ireland and indeed the remoter parts of the South-West), if northerners want to pursue their professional interests above a certain level – or even just secure a basic, steady job – they are statistically overwhelmingly more likely than their southern counterparts to have to uproot and relocate somewhere far from home, usually London and its satellites.

Sometimes people brought up in the North may actively want to do this, of course, and often their lives are enlightened and enriched by the experience of moving to wealthier, more culturally powerful areas. On rare occasions – this may sound crazy, but it's true – some northerners may even grow to *genuinely like* the dreaded South. But in all seriousness, I think it's fair to say that many northerners would prefer to stay closer to home if employment prospects allowed. And even those who have willingly left will likely feel some ambivalence about the fact that they have, effectively, been offered a devil's choice between retaining the support structures of their local community and the prospect of gaining more material socio-economic rewards.

The experience of being exiled in one's own country can be difficult enough in itself. But it is made even more complicated by what might be called the *problem of return*. This is a scaled-down version of the classic migrant dilemma. Having relocated to an unfamiliar area, and having made new friends and acclimatized to new ways of life in the meantime, what happens when an exile finally gets the chance to return home?

As well as its romantic themes and northern locations, *Robin Hood: Prince of Thieves* was much in my thoughts when I moved

back to the North-East because of its allegorical treatment of
the problem of return. In the early moments of the film, after
he has kissed the beach on the south coast (and taken Azeem
on a miraculous detour to Sycamore Gap), Robin eventually
wanders back to his father's castle in Nottinghamshire. On
arriving there, he finds that, as he puts it, his world has been
turned upside down. Following a raid by the Sheriff and his
satanic companions, Robin's native Locksley Castle has been
reduced to a fire-ravaged ruin, putting an end to his family
inheritance and ultimately forcing him to seek the life of an
outlaw – a Prince of Thieves in fact – in Sherwood Forest.
Even more harrowingly, as Robin wanders around the burned
wreckage of his childhood home, he hears a macabre creaking
noise. It turns out to be the sound of his father's gibbeted corpse
swaying in the wind.

Robin Hood and Guy of Gisborne (1832) by the Northumbrian
radical engraver Thomas Bewick

The problem of return I faced on coming back to the North in 2015 had both personal and political sides, which faintly and absurdly seemed to recall the narrative of *Prince of Thieves* (absurd partly because I am clearly not Robin Hood, nor was meant to be). On the one hand, there were obvious subjective reasons why a story about dying parents and a lost family home would spring to mind at this point. But it was also difficult to avoid a more objective comparison with the film's treatment of the Robin Hood legend, which is ultimately derived from Yorkshire and Nottinghamshire ballads about popular resistance to the oppressive feudal system of the Middle Ages. Just as Robin's personal tragedy in *Prince of Thieves* (and in many versions of the legend) occurs in the thick of a reign of terror by the ruthless Sheriff of Nottingham, my return home in the mid-2010s occurred at a time when much of the North was suffering from the effects of a political regime with a visibly devastating impact on local communities.

Allowing for certain obvious contextual differences, I do not think that a broad comparison between the basic premise of Robin Hood and the political narrative of the early 2010s is at all far-fetched. In both stories, the central villain is a punitive economic system. First introduced by the Conservative/Liberal Democrat coalition government in 2010, the fiscal programme which became known as 'Austerity' was ostensibly a response to the Global Financial Crisis of 2007–8 – and the so-called Great Recession which followed in its wake. Proponents of Austerity, such as George Osborne, the Conservative chancellor of the exchequer from 2010 to 2016, argued that the only way to 'balance the books' of the UK economy in the severe downturn was to drastically curtail government spending. In practice, this meant radical cuts to public services, from hospitals and schools to transport and social services. In an area like the North-East – which is heavily reliant on public sector employment, as well as being historically disadvantaged in countless ways, as we have seen – the effects of Austerity were disastrous. When I left the North-East in the mid-Noughties, it was a superficially flourishing place, even though the cultural improvements of the Nineties and Noughties were papering over the cracks of a worrying lack of structural renewal after the deindustrialization of the late twentieth century. But while the narrative of New Labour in the North was a tragic combination of well-meaning attempts at revival by some and a more general attitude of indifference from the Blairite head office, the Coalition government's treatment of northern areas in the 2010s was of a far more one-sided and merciless kind.

In the years I had been away from the North-East, the push for recovery half-heartedly attempted by New Labour had ground to a halt, at the same time as Austerity had completely undone the modest progress of the Blair years and demolished much of the remaining infrastructure of the twentieth century. Austerity was, quite simply, a civic scorched earth project, as the United Nations special rapporteur on extreme poverty and human rights made plain in a chilling summary written at the end of the 2010s:

> The UK is the world's fifth largest economy, it contains many areas of immense wealth, its capital is a leading centre of global finance, its entrepreneurs are innovative and agile, and despite the current political turmoil, it has a system of government that rightly remains the envy of much of the world. It thus seems patently unjust and contrary to British values that so many people are living in poverty. This is obvious to anyone who opens their eyes to see the immense growth in foodbanks and the queues waiting outside them, the people sleeping rough in the streets, the growth of homelessness, the sense of deep despair that leads even the Government to appoint a Minister for suicide

THE NORTH WILL RISE AGAIN

prevention and civil society to report in depth on unheard of levels of loneliness and isolation. And local authorities, especially in England, which perform vital roles in providing a real social safety net have been gutted by a series of government policies. Libraries have closed in record numbers, community and youth centres have been shrunk and underfunded, public spaces and buildings including parks and recreation centres have been sold off.

While the effects of Austerity were felt across all regions – notably in deprived areas of London – there is no doubt that the bleak picture painted here of a civic landscape 'gutted' by the government policies of the 2010s was most accurate as a rendering of the cities and towns of the North of England. Another report from the end of the decade, this time by the Centre for Cities, is fairly unequivocal on this point:

> Cities in the north of England were much harder hit [by Austerity] than those elsewhere in Britain. Seven of the 10 cities with the largest cuts [were] in the North East, North West or Yorkshire,* and on average northern cities saw a cut of 20 per cent to their spending. This contrasted to a cut of 9 per cent for cities in the East, South East and South West (excluding London).

Austerity's leading architect, George Osborne, was fond of talking about an ambitious-sounding 'Northern Powerhouse'

---

*In fact, the six very worst-hit cities/large towns – Barnsley, Liverpool, Doncaster, Wakefield, Blackburn and Newcastle – were all in the North. (The seventh, Stoke, was a borderline case, with Gloucester, Glasgow and Hull completing a dismal bottom ten.)

project, which promised to return northern cities to their nineteenth-century status as sparkling centres of 'Victorian confidence'. But in reality such schemes were almost comically specious – far more so indeed than the partially effective regeneration campaigns of the Blair, Major and even Thatcher governments. To put it bluntly, there was absolutely no giving with one hand and taking away with the other in the Coalition government's brutal programme. There was only taking away.

The politics of the 2010s can now be seen with hindsight as a fairly knowing attempt by right-wing politicians to shore up the ailing British economy by encouraging the revival of the housing market (always overwhelmingly focused on the South-East) and the mostly London-based finance and service industries. This strategy unfolded in a political climate that was radically neglectful of the North and its people. In the years between the downfall of New Labour in 2010 and the sudden scramble to account for the 'left behind' which followed from the 2016 Brexit referendum, the mainstream of British politics was verifiably more South-centric than at any point since the Eighties (some might say the Thirties). While average cuts to northern areas were often double their southern equivalents, the governance of the country was dominated by an elite which seemed unable to imagine a world beyond its native heartland of Eton, Oxford and the City of London – and by a radically centralized Westminster system that was often fighting an open war with local authorities (disproportionately, as we have seen, northern ones). Meanwhile, even as the working-class residents of the capital joined their northern cousins on several of the most gruesome metrics of poverty, what economic resurgences did occur after the Great Recession – always highly partial and painfully brief – were almost all skewed towards London and the South-East.

Derelict bars and cafés in the Bigg Market, Newcastle, 2019

As a result of all this, the North of England drifted inexorably into one of the darkest phases of its modern history. Like many northerners, I couldn't help but feel this final regional collapse as a kind of personal tragedy. The results of Austerity had often been painfully apparent to me on northward visits in the early 2010s, when they seemed to differ from examples of poverty I had seen in the South in their sheer unbroken extent and sweeping civic impact. But when I moved home for good in 2015, they provoked a new kind of anger. If post-Eighties Thatcherite and New Labour governments had poured money into cultural projects which buoyed up the social life of the North-East, while failing to do much to tackle its more serious transport, employment and housing problems, the Coalition and Conservative governments of the 2010s seemed determined to attend to neither. The results of this civic cut-and-run were everywhere to be seen, as harsh statistics melted into a more tangible communal tragedy. Throughout the

224

2010s an estimated £300 million was slashed from Newcastle City Council's budget (to take the example closest to home), leading to the total elimination of its arts provision, the closure of libraries and swimming pools, the near-extinction of its lollipop men and women, a dramatic rise in homelessness and foodbanks and the transformation of many of the city's historic landmarks (perhaps most infamously, the iconic Tyne Bridge) into flaking, dilapidated shells of their former selves.

This was the landscape I discovered on finally making it back to the North in my early thirties: a region that had simply stopped growing – and started to decay – in the time I'd been away. Here, if you like, were the smouldering ruins of Locksley Castle.

And this, more or less, is where we find ourselves in the present. Though not totally dead – indeed, far from it – in the 2020s the North finds itself in the unenviable position of retaining its historic status as England's unheeded unconscious, at the same time as the various modernist, modernizing dreams of the last half-century appear to have come to dust. Where, we must finally ask ourselves, do we go from here?

In fact, over the last few years, in the wake of the civic cataclysm of Austerity, the North has already begun to experience a revival of sorts, though its long-term prospects look rather bleak. Ironically, given the source of the policies which devastated northern areas in the early 2010s (not to mention, further back, the Thatcherite liquidation of the northern economy in the Eighties), this tendency has mostly marched under the banner of a new, post-Austerity brand of North-focused conservatism.

Though its deeper significance has often been exaggerated by figures across the political spectrum, there is no doubt that the victory of the Leave vote in the 2016 Brexit referendum marked a watershed moment in how the cultural and political establishment *perceived* the North. The actual statistical breakdown of support for Leave tells a rather nuanced story; in fact, all the English regions bar London voted to reject EU membership, putting paid to the idea of a clear-cut North–South divide on the issue. Nonetheless, perhaps because of a more visible contrast between the political and media HQ of the capital (where Remain won nearly 60 per cent of the vote) and several of the most marginalized post-industrial areas in the North (for example, Hartlepool, Doncaster and Barnsley, all of which returned a Leave vote of nearly 70 per cent), the narrative of a growing gulf between the London metropolis and the forgotten enclaves of the English periphery became dominant in the later years of the decade. Suddenly, after years of being forgotten and 'left behind' (an overused but broadly accurate term), the North had once again risen to prominence in national debates.

In one sense, the aftermath of the Brexit vote was a case of *plus ça change*. While the fact that many of the most ardent Leave-voting areas were in the South-East was often forgotten, relatively well-worn clichés about northerners being lumpen xenophobes were wheeled out by establishment commentators desperate to find a scapegoat for a referendum result they had not entertained, let alone predicted. In the main, this was a familiar tale of regional prejudice – or perhaps just casual condescension – on the part of pro-Remain voices (and some pro-Leave ones) in the cultural centre, most of whom knew very little about the North. Aside from anything else, this perspective glossed over the many nuances of the northern Leave vote (at least one of which was an entirely rational expression of anger at years of neglect by successive Westminster governments), as well as ignoring the complexity of the electoral statistics. However, as time went on, it became clear that the Brexit vote had indeed been the canary in the coal mine for a more deep-seated change in the socio-political terrain of the North. As I suggested at the start of this book, this all became startlingly apparent at the time of the 2019 general election.

In roaring home to a comfortable majority in December 2019 – a few months after he had taken over from Theresa May's rather hapless late Austerity ministry – Boris Johnson was able to capitalize on a broadly new political trend with a clear northern emphasis. As we have seen, the defection to the Conservatives in 2019 of a tranche of once solid Labour seats in the North and Midlands – the so-called 'Red Wall', another loose-fitting term – was mainly the result of a long-running process which saw the staunchly pro-Labour culture of post-industrial areas gradually and inevitably disappear over several decades. But the decisive Tory victory in 2019 was important in the short term because it brought together this long-term trend and developments uncovered by the lifted rock of the Brexit vote, to suggest the existence of an authentically new political moment. With a large number of northern constituencies now represented in government for the first time since the New Labour years, there was a sense that some form of overdue acknowledgment of the North's travails – and just maybe, a revival of the regeneration schemes largely put on hold since the Global Financial Crisis – might finally be forthcoming.

The result of all this was 'levelling up', one of the main buzzwords of the early 2020s, and the first major contemporary idea we have to consider as we try to assess the prospects for northern revival after the post-industrial 'end of history' that was Austerity.

At the time of writing, barely three years after the 2019 general election, there is a sense in which it is still too early to say whether the levelling-up revolution promised by the current Conservative government will lead to any substantial improvements for the North. In ordinary circumstances, new administrations tend to waste no time in embarking on their most radical reforms (witness the Thatcher government's introduction of monetarist policies in 1979-80, the Blair government holding referendums for Scottish and Welsh devolution in 1997 and the Coalition's lightning imposition of Austerity in 2010). But the arrival of the Coronavirus pandemic within weeks of the Tory victory in late 2019 put obvious major obstacles in the way of a large-scale reformist programme. For a start, the succession of lockdowns which took up much of 2020 and 2021 made the planning and implementation of big infrastructural works practically difficult, if not impossible. More deeply, while the Tory pledges of regional empowerment which followed from the collapse of the Red Wall went hand in hand with an apparent turn away from hardline Austerity, and towards a more statist approach (with NHS budget rises apparently the prelude to windfalls for other areas of the public sector), the brutal economic effects of the pandemic have withdrawn much of the material base that previously made levelling up seem feasible.

But despite its prolonged infancy, I think we can already get some sense of the likely fate of levelling up. Unfortunately, if perhaps predictably, it does not look too promising, to put it mildly. There have, it is true, been some headline northern *grands projets* announcements since the 2019 general election, which have offered some faint suggestion that 2020s Toryism understands the need for hard institutional empowerment of the North, rather than more temporary forms of investment (the stumbling block of almost every northern revival project of the last half century). In early 2020, for example, Boris Johnson announced that he was pushing for the House of Lords to relocate to York – centre of the long-time Tory northern heartland of North Yorkshire. However, this was subsequently downgraded to a suggestion that officials devising plans for the restoration of the Palace of Westminster should 'consider' York as a temporary home for the Lords and Commons during repair works (and finally, even this recommendation gave way to plans for construction of a modest 'government hub' behind York railway station). Another, more serious proposal – which also suggested the rise of a new Tory super-heartland centring on North Yorkshire and southern and western County Durham – was the relocation of a part of the UK Treasury to Darlington. Apparently the brainchild of Johnson's Chancellor Rishi Sunak, Darlington's new Treasury North is at least a positive *attempt* to combat the radical centralization of the British economy and its citadels.

However, it must be said that beyond these rather meagre blueprints the prospects for a lasting reduction in regional inequality under the present Tory government seem remote. Again, as with New Labour's doomed attempt to empower the North, it is the historic, symbolic northern bloodstream of the transport system which most clearly shows up the hollowness of levelling up. Transport infrastructure is both the quintessence of the North's modernist heritage and the practical means by which it will achieve meaningful civic revival. However, by the start of the 2020s, it had become a symbol of the abject failure of successive governments to commit to substantial reconstruction of northern areas after the collapse of heavy industry. As in so many other areas, Austerity was the *ne plus ultra* of this long-running narrative. In the decade following the Global Financial Crisis, per capita government spending on transport was on average 2.4 times greater in London than in the North.

This shocking statistic is not even the most extreme of its kind. Even after the arrival of the apparently Austerity-sceptic Johnson government in the summer of 2019, projected per capita transport investment was nearly three times higher in London than in the North as a whole – and a scarcely believable *seven* times higher in the capital than in the North-East and

Yorkshire. Unfortunately, these projections from the start of the Johnson government's lifespan look like they will be followed by deeper, more lasting failures to rebuild the North's transport infrastructure. While the Conservatives announced a handful of minor improvements in the wake of the 2019 general election – such as, symbolically, the reopening of the Northumberland line connecting Newcastle to Ashington and Blyth – their overall approach to northern transport was probably exposed once and for all by the announcement, in late 2021, that plans for the HS2 rail network to reach Leeds were to be scrapped outright. This much-vaunted high-speed line will now serve mainly to bolster an already fairly well-established trans-Midland route between London, Birmingham and Manchester. Meanwhile, the so-called Northern Powerhouse Rail scheme (NPR or HS3), which promised to improve notably poor intra-North connections between Liverpool, Leeds and Manchester (idealistically, and unusually, NPR also remembered the existence of the North-East), was shelved along with the HS2 Leeds extension in late 2021. Tellingly, at the centre of this now sadly familiar story of civic treachery, the cancelled plans meant that Andrea Dunbar's Bradford – a large, diverse, still staunchly Labour urban area – is destined to retain its long-running status as the worst-connected city in Britain.

On the whole, and taking transport as the most visible symptom of a much wider malaise, it seems highly unlikely at the time of writing that levelling up will achieve very much more than its farcical 2010s predecessor, the Northern Powerhouse. In the short term, as mentioned, the economic fallout from Covid-19 has greatly diminished the potential for large-scale public works projects for governments who must always work within the anti-statist parameters of neoliberal economics. The publication in February 2022 of the long-awaited white paper 'Levelling Up the United Kingdom' seemed to confirm that where grand ambitions for infrastructure do form part of Tory plans for the North, they are almost never backed up by concrete funding commitments. (And indeed the absence of the former buzzword 'levelling up' from the government's economic rhetoric throughout the rest of 2022 suggested to some that neoliberal 'hawks' in the Cabinet had managed to persuade Johnson to forget the idea once and for all.)

But even if 2020s Conservatives were willing to go so far as to meaningfully reject neoliberalism along with its killer variant Austerity, there are more fundamental reasons why a truly impactful Conservative solution to regional inequality is unlikely to materialize. Despite the collapse of the Red Wall (almost certainly not a permanent electoral development), the Tory power base is still overwhelmingly centred on the South of England, both in terms of popular support and parliamentary arithmetic. For all that it has found itself in the unusual position of relying on a tranche of post-industrial northern seats to flesh out its parliamentary majority, the modern Tory Party is still at heart the political superego of the rural South – and its deep historic, personal and ideological ties to this part of Britain are unlikely to be frayed, let alone severed, this side of a vast and unprecedented overhaul of England's socio-economic make-up. Contemporary commentators may have detected a mild and partial leftward shift in parts of the suburban South in recent years, as put-upon millennial voters flee London's Darwinian housing economy for its more affordable outskirts. But reports of the demise of the Tory southern heartlands – the so-called 'Blue Wall' phenomenon – have in fact been greatly exaggerated.

When all is said and done, the English Conservatives are by definition the party of *the way things have been*, not as they might or could or should be. And the way things have been in this country – for several decades, if not several hundred years – is that power, wealth and resources have been deliberately concentrated in one part of the country at the expense of others. This is why, at bottom, a Conservative solution to regional inequality is a contradiction in terms, and why the latest right-wing attempt to doctor the North's deep socio-economic wounds is already revealing itself to be at best a feeble sticking plaster, at worst a cynical quack cure.

As should be pretty clear by now, this is at heart a book about the cultural and imaginative life of the North – in spite of its many political digressions. With this in mind, in the concluding sections we will explore some basic notions about what northern identity means in the twenty-first century, and how attending to northern traditions of imaginative escape and civic idealism is probably the best way to recover the North's forward momentum at this stage. Indeed, given the rather fenced-in political moment we find ourselves in – with seemingly little appetite for radical reform among any of the major parties, and a host of more ominous global narratives in the works – there is an important sense in which imaginative liberation is all we can realistically do at this point. One of the main arguments driving this book is that in order to get anywhere at all, northerners must first of all embrace their regional unity and commonality, and then try to recover and celebrate the basic, historic northern belief that an energetically reconstituted future for their region is both desirable and possible. It is this mental leap of faith, far more than any ingenious political scheme, that will ultimately lead the way to northern revival.

But while it is difficult to advance a single, brilliant solution to the North's many and complex historic problems, the examples of failed regional renewal we have encountered before now – especially those occurring in the last 40 years or so – do at least offer us some clues about how we might begin to build better, more successful models for tackling England's deep regional divides. In searching for a viable way forward for the North, we have to try to heed to the lessons of history and consider the practical possibilities for civic reform, even if we also have to accept that a detailed picture of an improved northern future is probably unattainable.

The first, most fundamental point to make here is that northern revival must be a radical, even revolutionary project. If the lessons of the last 40 years prove anything beyond doubt, it is that greater regional equality cannot be lastingly achieved by way of short-term spending increases (as we saw in the first decades of the twenty-first century, when the moderate northern revival of the New Labour years was immediately cancelled out – and indeed portrayed as an example of wasteful spending which called for the corrective of Austerity – by the subsequent Coalition government). Neither does it seem at all likely that England's jagged regional divides will be diminished by largely cosmetic initiatives like the Northern Powerhouse or the Urban Renaissance, which have tended to resemble elaborate marketing campaigns backed up by ad hoc, usually business-led, regeneration schemes focusing on civic microcosms (typically the bigger city centres) rather than the northern region taken as a whole.

Instead, it seems fairly obvious, from even a casual glance at recent British history, that the empowerment of the North must have a powerful constitutional – or at the very least institutional – basis. The most radical option here would be to use the North's country-within-a-country status to argue for full-on independence. Conjecturally, this would probably look something like the projected forms of Scottish independence devised by campaigners north of the Cheviots. As this is another constitutional future which has not yet come into being (though it may do so sooner rather than later), there is no single existing model to draw on here – and venturing back into history to examine, say, the unique and complex example of Irish independence in the early twentieth century, is also problematic for a host of reasons. However, all attempts to follow Scottish (and Irish) independence movements would inevitably have to involve some notion of the North breaking away, once and for all, from the Westminster-centred United Kingdom – for example, by becoming a fully autonomous, sovereign nation state.

Northern Independence Party poster, 2021

As a thought experiment, if nothing else, this idea is certainly worth considering. And indeed, at the start of the 2020s, the option of full independence for the North has entered the mainstream of debate, in the form of the Northern Independence Party (NIP) – a registered political party founded by the academic and activist Philip Proudfoot in 2020. In the chaotic, crisis-ridden atmosphere of the last few years, NIP has quickly built up a sizeable membership and a much bigger media profile, and begun to stand candidates in local elections and parliamentary by-elections. As such, it is a serious project, the particulars of which demand to be taken seriously. As we will see in the next chapter, there is a significant sense in which NIP is a playful, provocative tendency, largely dedicated to the imaginative liberation of northern citizens. But it does, nonetheless, incorporate a more pragmatic side, which has been cogently articulated in the form of its manifesto and social media pronouncements.

The outline of an independent northern English nation state which emerges from NIP's proclamations is a country of some 16 million people, provisionally called 'Northumbria', after the Anglo-Saxon kingdom which extended over almost all of what is now the North of England. There are – understandably – some unanswered questions in the NIP manifesto about exactly how independence would hypothetically be achieved. The main constitutional features of Northumbria would apparently be decided post-independence by popular vote: NIP promises referendums on whether the monarchy would retain a role in the Northumbrian state, where exactly the borders would be (with 'constituencies immediately south [of the three current northern sub-regions] offered the chance to join'), where the capital would be (with ideas touted for a 'mobile capital' or multiple capitals, to avoid London-style centralization) and whether or not Northumbria would seek membership of the EU. Underlying all this is an admirable ethical creed based on equality, respect for difference and democratic empowerment, as can be seen from the following extracts from the NIP manifesto:

> The Northern economy has been neglected for decades and our industries splintered or destroyed. Northerners have been made poorer and less healthy, are given fewer educational opportunities, and live shorter lives than our southern counterparts. We recognize that the 'United' Kingdom filters people, resources, and jobs to the South. We will end these disparities, reducing the gap between rich and poor to increase the quality of life of every Northerner. We will restore dignity to all and create a just and fair society. We demand lives worth living ...

> The North is vibrant and diverse. We recognize the many cultures across the North, and we want to celebrate the diversity of our people. We are proud of our distinct local histories, dialects, and traditions, which we will fight to protect and preserve ...

> We reject bigotry and all ideologies of hatred. The North was, is, and will remain international. Everyone who identifies as Northern is Northern, and so we welcome refugees who seek safety and security in the North ...

The basic righteousness of such sentiments – and indeed the vast majority of the NIP manifesto – is hard to dispute.

But for all the worthiness of the NIP cause, and for all that the idea of full northern independence should not be dismissed as an eccentric delusion (as it has been by many patronizing establishment figures), there are some major limitations to the idea of a Northumbrian nation state. I am personally firmly of the belief that it is important to go

236

big or go home when it comes to large-scale questions of nationhood and identity. However, it must be said that full independence for the North will be practically very difficult to achieve, even with the aid of a radical outlook. This is largely because – unlike Scotland, Wales and Ireland – the North of England has absolutely no ancient or modern tradition of nationhood per se. (Even the antique example of Northumbria was a loose regional 'kingdom' rather than anything resembling a nation in the modern sense.) As such, conjuring a northern nationalism out of thin air seems like an extraordinarily big ask. A more serious, related problem is the deeper *desirability* of full northern independence as a response to regional inequality. If the fundamental goal of northern reformism is to redistribute economic and political power evenly throughout the British Isles, then it is questionable whether this will be achieved by declaring an autonomous Northumbrian nation state. In fact, it seems likely that this would merely accelerate the existing divide between the English North and South, by enabling a cut-loose South of England to consolidate the enormous economic and infrastructural advantage it has built up over other parts of Britain since the Eighties, and long beforehand.

A subtler, more effective variation on the NIP model would be to work out a way for the North to *reclaim* the power and wealth which have been ceded to the South in recent decades (and much further back), rather than angling for an unlikely – and perhaps undesirable – cut-and-run strategy. In this vein, we are faced with the prospect of some form of regional devolution – and again, as with the full independence proposed by NIP, this is an idea which has in fact become prominent – even unavoidable – in the political debates of the early 2020s.

At its weakest, the idea has been expressed by both Conservative and Labour figures in terms of rather vague commitments to 'English devolution'. More often than not, such calls for English devolution tend not to have a solely northern focus, and indeed they are often articulated in the context of debates about Scottish independence – with regional devolution viewed as either a sort of English nationalist response to the so-called 'West Lothian Question' (which revolves around the notion that Scottish citizens have disproportionate power over English affairs), or else a counter-revolutionary way of stifling the Scottish independence movement by offering moderate forms of de-centralization in the current United Kingdom. Hence the 2019 Tory manifesto promised a white paper on English devolution in 2020 (subsequently and predictably cancelled to make way for the broader programme of levelling up). Meanwhile, the current Labour leader, Keir Starmer, has talked yet more vaguely about guaranteeing 'real and lasting economic and political devolution across our towns, communities and to people across the country', apparently as a way of renewing 'our United Kingdom for the 2020s and 2030s'.

At the time of writing, it remains to be seen how such talk will translate into concrete proposals, as we await the findings of a 'constitutional commission' led by the former Labour prime minister Gordon Brown. But there are sound historical reasons for being sceptical that a sufficiently radical plan for the North will emerge from such initiatives, not least because of their underlying anti-Scottish-nationalist motivation. Indeed, there would seem to be a good chance that the meagre institutional reforms of Tory levelling up – such as the building of Treasury North in Darlington – will ultimately prove to be the high-water mark of mainstream political fulminations about regional devolution in the early 2020s.

What can we set against such watered-down forms of regionalism, to offer the outline of a more thoroughly renovated future for the North? As a cultural critic and ordinary northern citizen, I do not pretend to have a simple answer to this question in the form of a comprehensive masterplan for creating a devolved northern polity. But as I hope this book has shown, I do know that there is only one thing likely to achieve a meaningful and durable northern revival. It is really quite simple. A more effective, radical plan for regional devolution will only transpire when vague talk about 'empowering local communities' and 'speaking beyond Westminster' makes way for a hard, uncompromising constitutional settlement based on the hard, uncompromising idea of a broad, inclusive, capital-letter North.

If full independence does not seem quite right for the North of England, it will take something almost as radical to break the back of English centralization and regional inequality. Some form of federalization for the English regions – whether along German, Swiss, American, Australian or Brazilian lines – is one plausible solution, given the size of England's population and the diversity of its territories. To an extent, this would represent a revival of the New Labour model of regional devolution, which was putatively based on delegating power to the major sub-regions (the North-West, Yorkshire and the Humber, and the North-East) with government based in a regional 'capital' – though of course, as the plan was not implemented following the 2004 referendum in the North-East, its full constitutional implications were left undeveloped.

Rather than New Labour's chaotic, half-baked strategy for breaking England up into devolved component parts, it seems fairly obvious that we would need a much more vigorous plan for root-and-branch reform of Britain's constitutional framework for regional government to have even a fighting chance of success. The move away from centralization would – paradoxically but also logically – have to be taken at central level, probably by a newly elected reformist government, with an overarching plan for England (and perhaps Britain) as a whole outlined in manifesto form, in place of scattered referendums driven by disparate local interest groups. Similarly, when it comes to deciding on the parameters of regional governance – in the North as elsewhere – a principle of bigger-is-better will be infinitely preferable to the emphasis on hyper-localism which dominated the 2010s (in the form of George Osborne's 'metro mayoralties' for a somewhat random array of newly invented domains such as 'North of Tyne'), and which is still the default setting in discussions of English devolution. (See, for example, Keir Starmer's announcement in late 2020 that Labour's constitutional commission would 'consider how power, wealth and opportunity can be devolved to the most local level'.)

Instead of focusing on 'the most local level' (which is in fact ultimately the individual and the nuclear family), a truly meaningful strategy for regional civic empowerment would have to look beyond intra-communal hair-splitting based on minuscule nuances of accent, county history and sporting rivalry, in order to discover a viable, large-scale alternative to South-East-centric English nationalism. In the North, this would mean putting aside micro-regional differences, perhaps in order to create large, devolved sub-regions – but certainly with some institutional basis for an overarching Greater North. As a certain tendency in the devolution debates of the last ten years has repeatedly asserted (see, for example, John Prescott's more recent public pronouncements and multiple reports by the IPPR North think-tank), pan-northern co-operation must be the alpha and omega of any truly serious plan for revival of the North. In the context of the civic landscape of the twenty-first century, it does not particularly matter that Gateshead was kept separate from Newcastle in the sixteenth century because of its Protestant credentials, or that Liverpool and Manchester have often squabbled over everything from the construction of the Manchester Ship Canal to the supremacy of their world-beating football teams. What matters more than anything else is that the North *as a whole* is disadvantaged in a United Kingdom overwhelmingly centred on Westminster. In order to beat the monopoly of this system, the North will have to come together to offer a formidable and powerful alternative.

It may be that devolved or federalized sub-regions will be enough to offer a counterweight to London's institutional hegemony. But the lessons of the last half century teach us that something grander may be required. Something like a northern *Landtag*, along the lines of the German state parliaments, or else some new constitutional innovation such as a Great North Assembly, is perhaps the only way to bypass intra-regional difference and create a truly cogent civic focal point for the North of England's 16 million inhabitants (this would probably imply a northern English polity resembling – in some but not all respects – Bavaria or North Rhine–Westphalia, the most populous of the German federal states). Such a radical innovation would, from the outset, have to accept and somehow sublimate debates about intra-regional bias – for example, by establishing a geographically inclusive capital. York would be an obvious choice, given current transport links. But a modernized, high-speed northern rail system for the twenty-first century might suggest other locations, perhaps on hitherto undeveloped land.

A northern state parliament or Great North Assembly would also, of course, need to establish a workable relationship with both smaller and larger national and civic structures, and this is one of the reasons why the constitutional corrective to regional inequality will succeed only if it is truly radical.* The designers of a pan-North centre of governance would have to find some way of working out how several disparate – and often divergent – major conurbations (not to mention their rural hinterlands) would be equitably served by the overarching structure. But in reality the inter-city rivalries so often cited as an obstacle to regional devolution are not the main problem. A far more significant question to address is how a devolved or federalized northern government would relate to the wider constitutional structures of the United Kingdom (or whatever replaces it). Indeed it is this issue, more than anything else, which has been at the root of the failure of successive attempts at regional devolution over the last few decades (as in the case of the proposed North-East Assembly, which was successfully – and not altogether unreasonably – portrayed as a 'white elephant' with no clear *raison d'être* amid the existing political bureaucracy of the UK).

A truly viable, autonomous northern polity can only hope to succeed when the South-East-based English Establishment is torn up at the roots. The truth of this assertion has – I hope – been illustrated by the various cultural examples explored in this book, many of which underline the negative, even terminal mass-psychological effects of a national society in

---

*There is an interesting – and paradoxically, arch-traditionalist – model for the administrative division of England's northern and southern halves in the ancient constitution of the Anglican church. In the Church of England, the 'provinces' of Canterbury (the South) and York (the North, including most of Nottinghamshire but minus most of Derbyshire and Lincolnshire) are quite separate and autonomous entities. There is perhaps some potential for an arrangement broadly on these lines – subject, of course, to necessary nuanced adjustments – to act as inspiration for a reimagining of England's national and regional governance.

which cultural institutions, cultural capital and media influence are overwhelmingly hoarded in London, to the detriment of the North and other parts of the British Isles. Yet – and this is a crucial point – it is not through cultural initiatives like the regeneration schemes of the Eighties, Nineties and Noughties that a fairer, brighter future for the North will ultimately be achieved. In reality, the North cannot hope to rise again until the United Kingdom's antiquated, neo-feudal political system, with its monarchy, House of Lords, Oxbridge and Home Counties public schools, is replaced with a truly democratic written constitution, which pays heed to the diversity of Britain or England, and to the need to create robust structures for the civic empowerment of its several parts. At a bare minimum, real constitutional reform capable of reviving the North will have to involve some form of major adjustment to the Westminster system, with the medieval relic of the House of Lords replaced with a second chamber based on principles of federalism or its cognates, to ensure that this country does not end the twenty-first century as the most inept and dilapidated has-been nation in the developed world.

Whatever the risks, the costs of letting the English periphery fall back into its pre-industrial state of underdeveloped marginality are infinitely greater. As we enter a period of history even more chaotic and potentially destructive than the now faraway Industrial Revolution, do we really want to live in a land where the traditions, rituals and power structures of a time before the invention of the railways still dominate our collective existence? Or do we dare to think about how power might be distributed equally across the British Isles when the decaying, outmoded United Kingdom finally gives up the ghost? In the end, it is a choice between standing still and moving forwards – or, if you like, between staying put and staying alive.

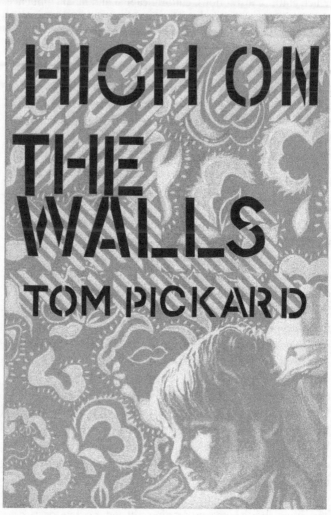

The cover of Tom Pickard's *High on the Walls* (1967),
designed by a pre-Blockheads Ian Dury

Acid Northumbria

I think we should just restart England. We should go back to the
old Roman idea ... We'll pick Hadrian's Wall up and just push
it down south, slam it down around Nottingham.

— Sam Fender

In the last days of the Sixties, Alan Hull was working nightshifts
at St Nicholas Hospital in Gosforth, on the north side of
Newcastle. An aspiring singer–songwriter from the city's West
End, Hull had taken a job on the psychiatric ward at St Nick's to
make money while he waited for his band, Lindisfarne (named
after the tidal 'holy island' off the north Northumberland coast),
to get a record deal. Perhaps with this career plan in mind, Hull
was not in the habit of behaving much like the other nurses at
the hospital. Behind the pale, ivy-covered walls of this decaying
Victorian building – called the Newcastle upon Tyne City
Lunatic Asylum before a progressive name change in 1948 –
Hull would treat the patients more like friends than medical
charges, playing card games with them and arranging trips to
the local pub for a pint. In the later recollection of one of Hull's
Lindisfarne bandmates: 'He saw things through their eyes that
other people wouldn't see.'

There were other, less conventional gestures of empathy.
Sometimes, according to some accounts, the alcoholics on
Hull's ward would be given medication with psychedelic

side effects – to alleviate their withdrawal symptoms, or perhaps just dangle the possibility of imaginative escape. At other times, according to some accounts, Hull would split the dosage, joining his patients in this questionable medical venture, unimaginable at any other time save the radical, anti-psychiatric Sixties.

Even though this all happened many years before I was born, a strand of my family history makes it seem echoingly familiar. At exactly this point in history, down South, my dad was studying for an undergraduate degree in psychology at North-East London Polytechnic, the prelude to an academic career that would eventually – after he died – lumber my sister and I with an inherited library of odd, yellowing books like *The Radical Therapist*, R. D. Laing's *The Divided Self* and multiple volumes by Sigmund Freud and Carl Jung. Meanwhile, up in Newcastle, at the peak of this pop-intellectual era, Alan Hull was also getting an education in modern psychology, though in a more informal, self-taught context. In between looking after his patients at St Nick's, Hull would spend his spare moments devouring multiple works by Freud and Jung, reading long into the night if circumstances allowed. In contrast with our own rather mentally hemmed-in era, the legacy passed down to us from the Sixties suggests evocatively that this was a time of far-reaching literacy and far-out cerebral inquiry.

As well as the classics of psychoanalysis, Hull would also find time to read and re-read the gothic tales of his favourite author, Edgar Allan Poe. Poe's 1839 short story 'The Fall of the House of Usher' was a particular favourite. In this magnificent prose work – perhaps Poe's masterpiece – the narrator journeys to the family home of his old friend Roderick Usher. Subsequently, as the plot progresses, the crumbling House of Usher reveals itself as the central motif in a story woven out of themes of inherited psychosis, psychic imprisonment and the divided self. The house's role as a symbol of troubled human mental states is first established in a famously evocative opening description:

> I looked upon the scene before me – upon the mere house, and the simple landscape features of the domain – upon the bleak walls – upon the vacant eye-like windows – upon a few rank sedges – and upon a few white trunks of decayed trees – with an utter depression of soul which I can compare to no earthly sensation more properly than to the after-dream of the reveller upon opium – the bitter lapse into every-day life – the hideous dropping off of the veil.

Just as this haunting backdrop offered Poe a poetic portal for the central themes in his story – which tells how Roderick and his sister Madeline are tormented by mental illness prior to their deaths amid the final destruction of their native home – it's tempting to think that Alan Hull would have identified profoundly with these descriptions of the House of Usher's 'vacant eye-like windows', 'bleak walls' and 'rank sedges'. As he found himself holed up in a dilapidated Victorian Lunatic Asylum in the rapidly deindustrializing North, Poe's overpowering physical metaphor for depression, decay and confinement must have seemed uncannily apt.

But it was the psychedelic aspect of Poe's opium dream imagery that would ultimately have the biggest impact on Hull's life and art. Shortly after dropping one of the doses meant for his patients (according to some accounts), Hull would embark on a prodigious writing spree. During this inspired interlude, he would dream-up several of the songs which eventually made Lindisfarne one of the best-known pop bands of the early Seventies – notably 'Clear White Light', 'We Can Swing

247

Together' and 'Fog on the Tyne'.* Most remarkable of all, whatever chemical assistance he may or may not have enjoyed, as Hull achieved sudden creative release from the bitter lapses into everyday life he endured in a psychiatric hospital in Sixties Newcastle, he would manage to craft his own warped adaptation of Poe's great tale of mental incarceration.

'Lady Eleanor' – loosely named after Poe's character Madeline, and ultimately the first song on Lindisfarne's 1970 debut album *Nicely Out of Tune* – was a genuinely visionary feat of pop songwriting. Through its trance-like musical effects, and more directly through its raw, psych-ward lyrics, it translated Poe's original into the context of post-war Britain, a place where dreams of escape from settings like St Nick's were being widely licensed by the weird, liberating pop culture of the period. This was a song which reached number 3 in the UK charts with an opening rhyme about a 'banshee playing magician sitting lotus on the floor', and a 'belly dancing beauty with a power-driven saw'. As Hull himself admitted to *Sounds* magazine in the summer of 1972, just as 'Lady Eleanor' was worming its way into millions of British homes: 'I'm worried about the 17- and 16-year-old girls and boys who buy it.'

But beneath its nightmarish images, there was also a subtle kind of radicalism in the haunting, ambiguous things 'Lady Eleanor' had to say about northern English existence. Along with the literary and drug experiences said to have inspired it, this extraordinary piece of music also allowed its author to break through to an otherwise inaccessible realm of northern consciousness: an exotic world of artistic freedom above and

---

*When we think of the curious backdrop to its composition, not to mention its surreally alliterated lyrics, the last of these works reveals itself as a far stranger, more ethereal work than the familiar stereotype of a comic Geordie drinking song.

beyond an often hopeless state of mind that will always – without reform – be in some sense imprisoned by the structures and strictures of the South-centric United Kingdom.

On the other hand, rather poignantly, in counterpoint with its dreams of escape, 'Lady Eleanor' was also, in its crucial moments, yearning for headlong retreat into an even more powerful imaginative space – an ideal homeland of the heart and mind which countless northerners, including Alan Hull, have never really wanted to leave:

> She gazed with loving beauty like a mother to a son
> Like living, dying, seeing, being all rolled into one
> Then all at once I heard some music playing in my bones
> The same old song I'd heard for years reminding me of home.

Away and back, escape and return, exile and home. In enough cases to prove the rule, these are the deep emotional aches of the northern English mind.

———

After having weighed up several possibilities for northern reform and revival in this book up to now – and their many, major limitations – it's tempting to say at last that civic life in the North of England often feels like being trapped inside a bad acid trip (or at least a kind of endlessly repeating psychodrama). As is true for English people more generally, but arguably to a greater extent, to be northern is to be a *subject* rather than a *citizen* – someone imprisoned inside certain dominant national, cultural and political structures, which don't have very much to do with your immediate reality, and which always seem as though they are being decided on elsewhere, far away and out of sight.

Given this enduring malaise, it's hardly surprising that northern culture has often been defined by dreams of escape which are by turns absurd, fantastic and forlorn. We might think here of the classic kitchen-sink narrative that is Keith Waterhouse's 1959 novel *Billy Liar*, and its 1963 film adaption starring Tom Courtenay and Julie Christie. In both novel and film, the protagonist Billy Fisher spends his time wandering around the grey landscape of post-war Bradford, indulging in surreal, often violent fantasies of ruling over a sort of fictional northern utopia called Ambrosia. After several sequences in which these totalitarian daydreams alternate with comic capers in Billy's personal life – always shot through with melancholy and menace – the escapist sub-plot reaches a moving conclusion in the narrative's final moments. In the film version, broadly similar to the book, after being reunited with his ex-girlfriend Liz (played here by a luminescent Christie), Billy joins her on a train bound for London, where it seems that he will seek his fortune as a scriptwriter. But then, at the last minute, he makes his excuses and steps off the train. As Liz's carriage glides out of Bradford, Billy watches her pitying face recede into the distance. Finally, as he walks home, Billy retreats once again into the twisted fantasy of political empowerment that is Ambrosia – this time, it would seem, for good.

With its ambiguous, fatalistic ending, *Billy Liar* is one of the most evocative and best-known examples of what might be called the northern stowaway tradition. This key tendency in northern literature, music and film tends to revolve around a protagonist who must make a painful choice: between remaining in a safe but suffocating home town, and venturing to a distant land (usually London) in search of the upwardly mobile option of probably permanent exile. Historically, the rise of this sort of narrative coincided roughly with the political empowerment of northern working-class subjects around the time of the First World War – just as the Labour Party was starting to become a party of government, and momentum was gathering behind a range of parliamentary reforms. Embodying the new spirit of opportunity which came along with such democratic breakthroughs, and giving a northern twist to a nineteenth-century literary tradition typified by novels like Thomas Hardy's *Jude the Obscure* and Charles Dickens's *Great Expectations*, the stowaway genre came into its own with works like D. H. Lawrence's *Sons and Lovers* and Arnold Bennett's *The Old Wives' Tale*. (The latter, incidentally, was an all-time favourite novel of the utopian German philosopher Walter Benjamin.)

While Bennett's 1908 text explored themes of elopement and staying put, by contrasting the lives of two sisters from Stoke-on-Trent, Lawrence's great 1913 novel used the semi-autobiographical method that would become crucial to literary modernism to narrate the formative years of the son of a Nottinghamshire miner. Enormously influential right up to the late twentieth century, *Sons and Lovers* was the first really confident and successful text by a northern writer to lay down the archetype of the protagonist who is simultaneously desirous of exile, and unable – mentally or physically – to move beyond the confines of a home environment portrayed as being only slightly less gloomy than the mind-prison of Poe's House of Usher.

From this point on, stowaway narratives would become the gold standard for writers from the British and Irish margins who wanted to pay tribute to their origins, while also achieving a career-enabling breakthrough into England's radically centralized literary culture. A more complicated, more claustrophobic version of a dilemma which confronts migrant subjects throughout the world – with some basic similarities as

251

well as some key differences – the northern English nightmare-dream of escape has been one of the central motifs in its cultural imaginary ever since, from the post-war kitchen-sink writers who consciously drew on Lawrence's influence, to more recent coming-of-age narratives like Jeanette Winterson's *Oranges Are Not the Only Fruit*, Alan Bennett's *The History Boys* and Lee Hall's *Billy Elliot*.

Yet while the literary examples of the stowaway tradition almost always took it for granted that moving outwards and southwards was the only possible way to move upwards and onwards, there have also been some subtler, more hopeful varieties of northern escapism over the last several decades. In fact, it was post-Fifties pop music that would most often try to find a way of reconciling the desire to cut and run from a northern homeland with a more transcendental suggestion that doing so might not, after all, be absolutely necessary.

The most succinct lyric statement of the desire to break free from northern origins is surely the 1965 song 'We Gotta Get Out of This Place', by the Newcastle band the Animals. Like the Animals' other signature tunes, 'The House of the Rising Sun', 'Don't Let Me Be Misunderstood' and 'It's My Life', this anthem of the High Sixties was not written by the band members themselves, who tended to perform covers or bespoke songs written by hit factories rather than original works. In fact, 'We Gotta Get Out of This Place' started out as a relatively mild-mannered love song composed by the New York songwriting duo Barry Mann and Cynthia Weil, originally intended for the Righteous Brothers. But crucially, the opening section of the final version of the song – with its graphic depiction of a dirty part of the city where sunlight doesn't reach, and where the singer's girlfriend and father are doomed to die miserable early deaths – was reworked during recording to emphasize the Animals' origins in working-class

Tyneside. As a result, the song ultimately came to life as a recognizably northern English anthem – a febrile musical update of the Fifties kitchen-sink tradition embodied in novels and films like *Billy Liar*. The chorus refrain of 'We Gotta Get Out of This Place', which states the title lyric and glosses it as a last-chance, do-or-die imperative, could scarcely have been more emphatic. In common with millions of northerners down the ages, the Animals wanted to get out of their home town once and for all, even if it killed them.

Of course, given that 'We Gotta Get Out of This Place' was written in New York and eventually became a hit record throughout the world, its sentiments were much more universal than specifically northern English ones. However, I think it's fair to say that in a rock 'n' roll context, the particular variety of escapist fantasy the song showcases has often been, as it were, enunciated in a northern accent. A certain strand of the later Manchester indie tradition, for instance, was always defined by a yearning to get as far away from a rain-soaked humdrum town as possible – as seen most powerfully in the songs of early Oasis ('Rock 'n' Roll Star', 'Live Forever' and 'Half the World Away' especially) and the plangent, monochromatic vignettes Morrissey intoned on the first few Smiths albums (and here again, it was the post-war kitchen-sink tradition, embodied in the work of writers like the Salford-born Shelagh Delaney, which supplied the main source of influence, especially on songs like 'William, It Was Really Nothing', 'Back to the Old House' and 'Still Ill').

But rather intriguingly, as the message of 'We Gotta Get Out of This Place' spread and ramified through the landscape of global pop in the late twentieth century, it would also develop a more ambivalent side. Indeed, as the Sixties pop songs of the provincial North were exported to the world throughout this period, they would be mimicked and modified in intriguing ways when they landed in kindred post-industrial areas.

A native of the proletarian New Jersey coastal region which is often viewed to be nearly synonymous with northern English areas like Tyneside (see, for example, the translation of US 'reality' TV series *Jersey Shore* into its British equivalent *Geordie Shore*), Bruce Springsteen has been fairly open about the influence the Animals had on his development as a songwriter. In a 2012 interview, after citing the influence of 'Liverpool wharf rats' the Beatles, Springsteen commented:

> For some they were just another one of the really good beat
> groups that came out of the Sixties, but to me the Animals were
> a revelation. [Theirs] were the first records with full-blown
> class consciousness that I'd ever heard. ['We Gotta Get Out
> of This Place'] is every song I've ever written. That's 'Born
> to Run', 'Born in the USA', everything I've done for the past
> 40 years. That struck me so deep: it was the first time I felt
> something come across the radio that mirrored my home life,
> my childhood ...

It would seem therefore that 'We Gotta Get Out of This Place' was a foundational influence on Springsteen's musical style, a fact apparently confirmed by the pinnacle of pop escapism that was 'Born to Run' – a 1975 masterpiece narrating a 'runaway American dream' of flight from a small-town 'death trap' (which, we can fairly confidently assume, was supposed to be coastal New Jersey in the Seventies). This was, if you like, the northern English stowaway tradition, but with a stars-and-stripes backdrop.

However, crucially, the flipside of Springsteen's dream of departure on records like 'Born to Run' was an aesthetic and public persona that was based largely on his status as a fairly grounded ambassador of the places he would, at times, present as suffocating post-industrial prisons. As the main architect and avatar of 'heartland rock' – a pop genre defined by its rootsy fidelity to blue-collar experience – Springsteen and his supporting E Street Band (almost all of whom hailed from Jersey or neighbouring parts of rustbelt America) were *champions* of their homeland at the same time as being its staunchest critics. As such, a classic Springsteen song like 'Born in the USA' – the lyrics of which are in reality a savage critique of life in a 'dead man's town' – has also to be understood as a slanted declaration of pride in its author's origins. For all its bleak subtexts, that is to say, the title refrain of 'Born in the USA' is most often heard and sung in a popular setting as a relatively heartfelt affirmation of American home.

The crucial point is that the democratic folk tradition of late twentieth-century pop culture – and pop music especially – has often suggested that it might be possible to achieve forms of escape while staying at home, and that seeking exile from one's family and friends in order to become a free and empowered citizen is neither inevitable nor essential. Clearly, in the case of Bruce Springsteen and others, the ability to transcend one's birthplace while making it a central part of the image you are selling to the world is at least partly enabled by immense privilege and wealth. But that does not mean that we should dismiss the central idea implicit in Springsteen's critical celebration of homeland. This is that the best manifestations of pop culture have the potential to enliven and emancipate our civic lives in profound ways, by showing us how to see infinity in a grain of sand without having to travel to distant shores.

In the context of the North of England, which, as we have seen, contributed disproportionately to the pop music of the late twentieth century (especially in the Long Eighties), the notion that an imaginative countercultural sensibility might hold the key to social liberation has been a fairly common one. We might describe this approach as an 'acid Northumbrian' one, with Northumbria viewed here in the broadest sense as the whole of northern England (and with due respect to the late cultural theorist Mark Fisher, who coined the term 'acid communism' to describe the political potential in remembering the freeing countercultural adventures of the Sixties and Seventies).* Of course, in trying to define acid Northumbria, we must look first of all to the Liverpudlian Beatles, and their popularization of psychedelic experimentation from around 1965. For our purposes, the really important thing about the Lennon–McCartney acid experiment – endlessly documented in countless books, documentaries and sleeve notes over the years – is that it allowed Liverpool to rise to the surface of the Beatles' music, where previously it had only been evident in the accents and mannerisms of the band members in public appearances.

To be sure, the first Beatles' songs written after their initial encounters with LSD are best viewed on a purely aesthetic level, as part of their famous sonic evolution across the major albums of the mid-Sixties. This trajectory is mapped by the mild psychedelia of 'Nowhere Man', 'Day Tripper' and 'Norwegian Wood' on 1965's *Rubber Soul* and its outtakes, and then by the more vigorously modernist 'She Said She Said' and 'Tomorrow Never Knows' on *Revolver*. But by late 1966, after Paul McCartney had joined his bandmates in the acid adventure,

---

*It is also important to emphasize that this 'psychedelic' mode is based mainly – like Fisher's definition of acid communism – on a premise of radical imaginative freedom. It does not – or does not necessarily – derive from the actual experience of taking specific substances.

there was a clear turn inwards and backwards on those Beatles' works which were most directly influenced by LSD. Recorded in the last weeks of 1966 but released in February 1967, the double A-side 'Strawberry Fields Forever'/'Penny Lane' was, among other things, a historic breakthrough in northern English art – and a foundation moment of sorts for acid Northumbria. This was largely because of the manner in which its two lead tracks suggested that the backstreets of the apparently provincial North could be a repository of infinite imaginative potential.

The idea was implicit on Lennon's lyrically chaotic 'Strawberry Fields' – partly in its title, which nodded at a neo-Gothic mansion near Lennon's childhood home in Liverpool (a counterpart to Alan Hull's St Nick's), and, more forcefully, in its musical arrangement, which arrayed a series of dazzling sonic irruptions emerging out of the 'trip' down into this real and imagined Liverpudlian location. But it was made yet more explicit on McCartney's 'Penny Lane', a staggeringly lucid celebration of northern civic life, which depicted the euphoric, liberating side of the acid experience in brilliant psychedelic colours. McCartney's initial reluctance to take LSD was a response to second-hand reports that it led to a kind of permanent exile from origins; as he later commented: '[We'd heard that LSD] alters your life and you never think the same again. I was rather frightened by that prospect ... [to] never get back home again.' But on 'Penny Lane' it became evident that McCartney had managed to use acid to reimagine a street from his Liverpool childhood as a literally utopic space – a place where everyone says hello to each other and youthful laughter is heard everywhere. Nonetheless, there is a sense of strangeness and transcendence on every corner (the nurse who feels she is in a play, the fireman who rushes in from the rain) to offset any sense of cosy northern parochialism.

In the wake of the Beatles' acid Northumbrian experiment, late twentieth-century pop would repeatedly try to find creative ways of uncovering the psychedelic colours lying beneath the monochrome surfaces of the deindustrializing North. As we have already seen in glimpses, the great flowering of the Manchester pop tradition in the Long Eighties was nothing if not such an endeavour. From the spacey sonic backdrop Martin Hannett painted behind Joy Division's austere post-punk soliloquies, to the bedroom psychedelia of the Happy Mondays and the flower-pop of the Jackson-Pollock-spattered Stone Roses, Manchester's catholic drugs culture would recurrently provide inspiration for musical daydreaming amid cold and lonely streets.

But away from such recreational diversions, it is clear that the acid Northumbrian approach could also act as a means of imagining concrete social and political structures outside of the psychic prison of ancient England. As we have seen, the Factory project, for instance, was really a dope-addled (and later hard-drug-hindered) campaign to create a cultural base for the growth of a northern renaissance city. To serve this end, the label enthusiastically embraced a strategy of wilful surrealism (by way of situationism) – 50/50 record contracts written in blood, elaborate artwork which subverted the clichés of consumer capitalism, a world-famous nightclub which didn't make any money and so on. But while these strategies have sometimes been viewed as little more than postmodern high jinks, the underlying intention was always to foster a strong infrastructure for cultural production outside of London's imperious music industry establishment.

For Factory, and for the whole of what I have been calling the acid Northumbrian tendency, broadly conceived, the implicit argument was that northern people should have the right to remain where they were, and yet still access the freeing energies of other psychological realms. But more deeply, and concretely, it also came along with a suggestion that escapist fantasies – and a related ethic of subversive, anarchic playfulness – were the means by which such freedoms might be practically achieved, rather than acting as mere frivolous hippy distractions.

If England or Britain represented a kind of psychological prison in the Sixties for artists like Alan Hull and the Animals, then sadly it is even more of one in the twenty-first century – when the old regional and class inequalities are as entrenched as ever, and where there is nothing like the post-war Welfare State to act as a socio-economic counterbalance. Nevertheless, despite – or perhaps because of – the current bleakness of the northern political landscape, acid Northumbria remains a potent dream for those who want to transform the North without having to migrate to new worlds elsewhere. Disparate contemporary pop bands from the Unthanks (from Ryton) to the Orielles (Halifax) offer various colourful versions of northern weird folk and indie psychedelia, while Richard Skelton (Anglezarke) and Richard Dawson (Newcastle) deserve great credit for pushing past parochial stereotypes to come up with genuinely new and bizarre embodiments of the northern terrain. Skelton's glacial ambient drones capture the singular atmosphere of the paleo-industrial West Pennine Moors, while Dawson's solo output – and his work with the band Hen Ogledd ('the Old North') – combines hallucinatory discord with excavations of the medieval history of Northumbria. For Dawson, this psychedelic approach offers a way of transcending portrayals of northern subjects as 'humble worker bees', in the crass, arts-funded version of northern regionalism which goes in for flat caps, exaggerated accents and sentimental reveries of industrial community.

Gateway to Strawberry Fields, Liverpool

Attempting to revise and revoke the limiting clichés of northern identity is in itself, of course, a political gesture. But there have also been attempts to channel acid Northumbria towards more overtly political ends in in recent years. As we saw in the previous chapter, the foundation of the Northern Independence Party (NIP) in 2020 was arguably the most notable development in northern regional politics since the negative result in the North-East England devolution referendum in 2004. In common with previous attempts to create a large-scale pro-North element in Westminster and local government (notably the North-East Party and the Yorkshire Party, both founded in 2014), NIP has very little chance of even moderate electoral success – largely due to Britain's antiquated first-past-the-post system. Nonetheless, it is not implausible that NIP's playful, acid Northumbrian approach might ultimately pave the way for a more substantial political tendency to emerge at some point in the future.

Originally a sort of bedroom joke devised by its Sedgefield-born founder Philip Proudfoot in the 2020 Covid lockdown, NIP has made a virtue of its poor electoral prospects by innovating a sort of high-camp, surrealistic political brand, which is probably best seen as a social media provocation rather than an actual independence campaign. (In this respect, it might be seen as a distant cousin of earlier situationist media experiments like Factory and ZTT's 'Relax' campaign.) Through calls to nationalize the Greggs bakery chain, imagery which juxtaposes pictures of the proverbial northern whippet with the lucid yellow-and-red hues of the ancient Northumbrian flag and Twitter posts which narrate hallucinated encounters with Sean Bean on Ilkley Moor, NIP is in a deep sense the culmination of a long-running, disruptive, psychedelic tradition in modern northern culture. This tendency acknowledges that regional inequality will probably persist for a good while yet. But looking beyond the apparently fixed strictures of the present, it is nonetheless determined to offer provoking glimpses of an alternative northern future in the meantime.

While deep improvements for the North have been rare in recent decades, it remains almost absurdly easy to get a fleeting glimpse of the Northumbrian paradise. At least, that is how it has seemed to me at certain crucial moments in my life.

In May 2013, my partner Louise and I got engaged on Sandham Bay on Lindisfarne, after we got deliberately stranded on this numinous tidal island, a place only someone with no heart could possibly feel to be anything other than sacred. Deciding to get married was itself, of course, a transcendent experience. But it was made even more so by the things we saw and felt in the springtime leading up to our engagement.

After an unusually late winter, the British countryside underwent a sudden, visible revival after the Easter of 2013. In April, a few weeks before we got to Lindisfarne, Louise and I had travelled to Cumbria from our East London flat for another romantic rite – the wedding of the poet Tom Pickard and his partner Gill (I had first got to know Tom a couple of years beforehand, during the course of my PhD on the life and work of his mentor Basil Bunting). From the moment we boarded the northbound train at King's Cross, it was clear that this was going to be a memorable, psychologically transporting trip. After a while, as we passed deeper into the North Country, we could see newborn lambs everywhere, and the returning green of the fields allowed us to slip into a freer mental time signature after a long winter of being surrounded by London's cramped bricks and burrows.

When the train arrived at Haltwhistle, we got into a taxi driven by an ageing farmer, who had only very reluctantly agreed to drag himself away from the unpredictable work schedule of lambing time. But in spite of his grumbles on the phone the week before, the driver–farmer chatted to us fairly warmly as he ferried us to the wedding venue. Mostly, he told us long, rambling stories about the fist-fights and village dances of his youth, in the days when the devastating impact of the closure of the lead mines around Alston had been briefly stalled by the opening of a metal factory in the town. Passing through the barren, depopulated landscape of the modern North Pennines – a place of blanket bog and ruined homesteads, which often recalls the cleared wastes of the Scottish Highlands and the Irish West – it was hard to imagine that even such modest forms of community activity could still exist here in the twenty-first century. Back in 2005, a schoolfriend who had moved to Alston found his way into the national papers after starting a sort of forlorn lonely hearts club campaign – the 'Alston Moor

Re-Generation Society' – which stuck posters up all over the wider North in an attempt to attract young women to this unforgiving backcountry. I don't have access to any statistics, but I'm fairly sure that Stu 'Potsy' Ridley's attempt to plug the gap in social and romantic infrastructure left by the departure of heavy industry from the North Pennines fell some way short of its main objective. In any case, perhaps tellingly, Potsy has since emigrated to New Zealand.

After a meandering journey through the land around Alston, with its circling ghosts of civic absence, Louise and I finally arrived at the wedding venue. Strangely enough, this was the Hartside Café, a popular bikers' haunt in a remote beauty spot high up on the A686 – a dramatic mountain pass which winds snake-like through the heart of the North Pennines, before dropping down suddenly into Cumbria and the edge of the Lake District near Penrith. Tom and Gill had chosen the Hartside as a wedding location because it was Tom's home when they had first met some time earlier, after a courtship enabled by what might be termed the magic of the internet.

A long, convoluted route had brought Tom to this high-up hideout. After his adventures with Allen Ginsberg and Basil Bunting at Morden Tower in Sixties Newcastle, he had continued to develop as a poet in the Seventies while experimenting with other media – notably *Guttersnipe* (a 1971 Geordie *roman-à-clef*), the 1974 BBC TV play *Squire* (soundtracked by and starring his close friend Alan Hull) and a 1976 BBC radio documentary about the Jarrow Crusade. However, through a combination of regional and class prejudice, and his own incurable stubbornness – not to mention the near-impossibility of making a living from poetry away from the twisted crutch of Creative Writing academia – Tom's existence had always been chaotic, cash-strapped and itinerant. After narrowly escaping a long jail sentence for

263

marijuana smuggling in the late Seventies, he spent time living in London and Poland, wrote a documentary history of the closure of the Wearside shipyards (1989's *We Make Ships*) and finally moved back to the North-East permanently in the Nineties. Collaborative work with Paul McCartney on the textual version of his 1997 symphony *Standing Stone* offered the prospect of breakthrough, or at least financial stability through more gigs in the same vein. But that door slammed shut when Tom knocked back McCartney's offer of a charity spin-off commission because it was *pro bono*.

By the start of the millennium, Tom had split up with his third wife and was on the verge of formal bankruptcy. It was at this point, after leaving his former marital home in Alston, that he took out a lease on the tiny attic room in the far-flung Hartside Café. As documented in multiple poems, and at greater length in the 2017 memoir *Fiends Fell*, Tom's time in the Hartside was personally and creatively climactic. On the one hand, this was clearly a breakdown of sorts. At the wedding dinner, the photographer Graham Smith told Louise and I that Tom was so browbeaten and underweight when he arrived at the Hartside, it seemed as though he wouldn't survive for long – especially as he had now sought refuge, at the age of 56, in a dwelling as isolated and exposed to nature as almost anywhere else in England. As Tom wrote in a notebook journal at the time:

My bedroom is an attic, part of the gable end, and has two Velux windows facing east and west on the low slopes of the ceiling. The slate roof concerns me, as houses in this district are traditionally roofed with stone slabs six inches thick … The draughts that burn icily through gaps in the wall and under tiles have blown paint, albeit already flaking, from the walls … It's where two weather systems meet and where, I'm told, winds blow from opposite directions at the same time, thus creating a kind of vortex; which prompted a friend to ask, what's it like living inside a metaphor?

It is tempting to fill in the blanks here and say that the metaphor in question had something to do with the common fate of the northern artist, or at least those who are as hopelessly questing and intractable as Tom. As a poet who had taken to heart his mentor Basil Bunting's Northumbrian-modernist commandment to invent a new form outside the confines of English tradition, and combined it with Bunting's political animus against 'London's England', there is a sense in which Tom had ventured so far beyond the margins of mainstream England by this point that he was in real danger of vanishing altogether. Unlike Andrea Dunbar, Barry MacSweeney and countless other marginalized northern writers, alcohol was not a factor in this case. But the end result – total, exemplary failure – might well have been the same.

The Eden Valley from the Hartside Café, Cumbria

But fortunately, Tom would have another springtime. As described in the 2011 lyric sequence 'Lark and Merlin', he eventually found a way back to life and love – though he would remain a criminally overlooked figure in the staid, businesslike English poetry scene, even after the visionary nature-writing which emerged from his Hartside interlude was published to critical acclaim by the Chicago press Flood. (Notably, much of Tom's popularity, both recently and throughout his career, has been based on his high reputation in the United States – another example of the special relationship between the English North and North America, and further proof that the backwardness-inwardness of England's mainstream literary culture is something of a global anomaly.)

There are deeper morals at work in this narrative, and the first is a bitter one to swallow. Tom's story seems to suggest that we have to somehow look the Medusa in the face, and acknowledge that for most, if not all, northern artists, it will always be painfully difficult to create an authentically new music while somehow flying free of a culture set up to endlessly promote the traditions and rituals of a South-centric establishment (or at least, it will be until a genuine levelling of England's regions occurs). Nonetheless, the example of someone like Tom Pickard shows that it is just about possible to survive as a poet, and a human being, by making a virtue of marginality and the freedom it brings. After his spell in the radical northern wilderness of the North Pennines, Tom's fate seemed to be set. He would probably continue, for the rest of his life, to be overlooked and impoverished, and denied the poisoned chalice of material comfort and creative atrophy which comes with mainstream acceptance – whether through various forms of personal and artistic compromise, or through embrace of those caricatures of northern parochialism which are a passport to prize nominations and professional crossover. On the other hand, he would at least be able to provide glimpses of how artistic and personal release might be achieved without having to relinquish one's homeland and deeper identity, and how the potential for renaissance – or at least a kind of sacred transcendence – is everywhere in the northern soil.

As we gathered together in the strange, elevated space of the Hartside Café in the spring of 2013 for Tom's and Gill's wedding, I realized with passionate intensity how all this might apply to my own life. At the wedding dinner – hearty biker's fare prepared by Tom's former neighbours in the Café kitchen – there was a sort of musical chairs routine, which meant that Louise and I ended up talking to almost all of the 30 or so guests. As time went on, and as the music of the Alston folk band Tarras wound the collective together, it became apparent that this was something like a who's who of the northern counterculture of a certain vintage. As well as the Teesside social-realist Graham Smith (who had documented Middlesbrough's Eighties decline, and told us about Tom's deathly pallor on first arriving at the Hartside), among the guests were Dave 'the Red' Douglass (a Communist union rep and key figure in the 1984–5 Miners' Strike, who had once appeared in the TV series *Living with the Enemy* in harsh dialectic with an Old Etonian Tory peer), Ray Laidlaw (Alan Hull's former Lindisfarne bandmate) and Geoff Wonfor (director of the Beatles' *Anthology* TV series and the seminal Eighties music show *The Tube*, whose late wife, Andrea, had dreamed up the Geordie kids' soap *Byker Grove*). We also spoke to the carpenter Nick Sawyer, who I had first met down in London when Tom gave a reading at the Barbican as part of a 'twenty-first-century happening' featuring Shirley Collins, Alan Moore and Iain Sinclair. It was Nick who had been responsible for bringing his friend Li Yuan-chia to the Deep North back in the late Sixties. As we drank long into the night, Nick told us stories about Delia Derbyshire, when she had lived in Gilsland and been involved with the LYC Museum and Art Gallery, Li's Cumbrian–Taiwanese temple built amid the ruins of Hadrian's Wall.

When the taxi had dropped us off at the Hartside Café several hours earlier, the whole of this weird eyrie at the top of northern England had been shrouded in mountain mist. But at a certain point the clouds cleared to suddenly reveal the whole breadth of the magisterial Eden Valley, a view which Tom describes with lyrical precision in his memoir *Fiends Fell*:

> The ridge forms the watershed and headwaters for three rivers that run into the North Sea some sixty miles away: the Tyne, the Wear and the Tees. On the west side water seeps in springs from the boggy earth covered in sphagnum moss and heather and rushes into tight precipitous cloughs to become tributaries of the River Eden. The escarpment falls steeply into the valley of Eden and across to the mountains of the Lake District and sometimes when the sun is angled appropriately one of the lakes is visible and I can see where Coleridge and Wordsworth walked. Or if I look to the north, across the Solway Firth some fifty miles away, I can see the hills that Burns, Hogg and Walter Scott would have known – and where part of *The Dream of the Rood*, possibly by Cædmon [the first Northumbrian poet], is carved in runes on the eighth-century Ruthwell Cross.

Gazing out at this occluded, other-worldly part of the country – perhaps the North's deepest, most ineffable space – and looking round at the assembled mix of poets, labourers, producers, musicians, radical activists and ordinary citizens gathered at the wedding, none of whom had quite got their due in life, but all of whom seemed creative, solid and soulful, I knew that this was all I ever wanted, and could ever want, from life. As I looked to the future, starting with the ring and the plan to make and gain a promise on Lindisfarne the following month, I knew that I had to somehow get back to the North – and, thankfully, even miraculously, that Louise felt this way too. Outside of the love I felt for her and for my family, I knew that this pride in place and desire to tell the story of my homeland was the most powerful, most unignorable emotion I would ever feel.

This feeling of deep belonging, solidarity and ultimate hopefulness is, in the end, strangely enough, best summarized by the flawed northern dreamer T. Dan Smith. At the height of the optimistic Sixties, Smith recalled flying high over Newcastle Airport for the first time, an experience he later described in the following powerful terms:

> And then, as we brushed the low-lying cumulus, the whole of the North-country offered itself to us. Towns and moors, rivers and forests, coasts and lakes. Counties cut down to size and parochial jealousies ironed out. If ever there was a revelation of togetherness, this was it. We of the North were not just town or country or city dwellers. We were people of a region.

About this much, at least, Smith was right.

Andy Cole (left), like D. H. Lawrence, the son of a Nottinghamshire miner

Let us return, after the end of everything, to the bewildering terrain of recent British politics. In the run-up to the 2017 UK general election, which saw a Jeremy Corbyn-led Labour Party demolish a huge Tory polling lead to produce an unexpected hung parliament, a curious meme started doing the rounds on social media. As is the way with these things, the meme's variations were many, and so difficult to follow and summarize. But all were inspired by the same episode from Nineties football history.

On 29 April 1996, the Newcastle United manager Kevin Keegan gave a post-match interview to Sky Sports presenters Richard Keys and Andy Gray. It has since gone down in football lore, and indeed British culture more generally, as a textbook example of an embattled leader insisting – despite the vast weight of evidence to the contrary – that all is not lost. When Keegan gave the interview, his Newcastle side were trailing Premier League leaders Manchester United by three points, as the last week of the season loomed, despite the fact that they had topped the table for much of the season, and been 12 points ahead of their rivals in mid-January. Faced with the prospect of a tense, ultra-marginal season finale, and responding to claims by the Manchester United manager, Alex Ferguson, that Newcastle's next opponents (Nottingham Forest and Tottenham Hotspur) would go easy on them for certain unknown reasons, Keegan launched into a passionate monologue, insisting that he and his team were still in with a chance:

> I've kept really quiet, but I'll tell you something, he went down in my estimation when he said that. We have not resorted to that, but I'll tell you, you can tell him now if you're watching it, we're still fighting for this title, and he's got to go to [Manchester United's next opponents] Middlesbrough and get something, and ... and ... I'll tell you, honestly, I will love it if we beat them. Love it.

The meme-ification of this outburst in the context of the 2017 general election campaign was predictable. In this later moment, footage and screenshots of Keegan were superimposed with Jeremy Corbyn's face, and polling figures which increasingly pointed to a wafer-thin final result. The Keegan speech came to function in the election campaign as a sort of surreal online rallying cry for young, left-wing Labour supporters. It was one of a series of wry in-jokes in the late spring of 2017, all of which seemed to say: 'Despite what the brainless media establishment thinks and says, *we know* that Corbyn is going to pull off a shock result in this election.'

And in the end, that's exactly what happened.

But let us go back to the starting point of all this – from my point of view at least – to try to work out what it might mean for the fate of the North.

The most utopian civic moment of my life (with the possible exception of the 2017 general election results night) occurred across a five-day period, from 4 to 9 May 1993. On the Tuesday of that week, Newcastle United won promotion to the Premier League, with a 2–0 away victory over Grimsby Town. For me, listening to the match on the radio as a nine-year-old, this was the first time a team I supported had ever won anything (and sadly, this more or less remains the case at the time of writing). For Newcastle manager Kevin Keegan – a quintessential northerner whose life story is a unique mix of the three great northern sub-regions (Yorkshire and the Humber, North-West and North-East) – the victory at Grimsby marked an extraordinary breakthrough. Indeed, in a career full of remarkable achievements, this was in a deep sense a kind of personal apotheosis for Keegan.

He had been born in Doncaster in 1951, the son of a County Durham miner of Irish extraction who relocated to South Yorkshire shortly before his son's birth. No matter where you go in the North, you are always only a short physical and psychological distance away from the legacy of a mining disaster – as Keegan's family backstory underlines. His paternal grandfather, Frank, was on the scene in February 1909, when an explosion at the West Stanley pit in north Durham killed 168 men and boys. In the thick of this unimaginable tragedy, one of the worst in the history of British coalmining, Frank returned to the pit with one of the search parties, shortly after being rescued himself, in a desperate attempt to save some of his fellow labourers. These things do, it is important to emphasize, matter. In the case of Kevin Keegan, it seems fairly clear that the inherited memory of events like the Stanley tragedy – as well as his tough, itinerant family history more generally – was central to the formation of his character. Certainly, these sorts of contexts are meaningful details in a biographical narrative which would see Keegan become an almost literally messianic figure in the history of the late twentieth-century North.

As a player, first at lower-league Scunthorpe United and then, more famously, at Liverpool, Hamburg, Southampton and Newcastle, Keegan was a muscular, ruthless striker, who eventually had a fair claim to the title of most famous football personality of the Seventies. A trademark poodle perm, shrewd understanding of the rapid rise of PR culture and vocal appearances on a series of dire novelty pop songs might have helped Keegan to establish his personal celebrity brand. But the basis of his runaway success on the pitch, which culminated in the England captaincy and two successive Ballons d'Or in 1978 and 1979, was an incredible work rate. Keegan's stoic athleticism was highly unusual for the period. Throughout his career, while many of his contemporaries indulged in hard-drinking, poorly nourished lifestyles, Keegan would spend large portions of his spare time on elaborate fitness and exercise activities – running, weight training and gym sessions – which helped to give him a crucial physical edge over his opponents when it came to match day.

This dedication to finishing first was, I think, something quite different from the duller, more selfish determination to enter heaven which guides the proverbial Protestant work ethic. Instead, when we look at Keegan's biography as a whole, it seems reasonable to suggest that his strict exercise regime and drive to succeed were in some sense fuelled by the peculiar combination of felt historic grievance and desire to lead and inspire an alternative community which arose from his northern, working-class heritage, and which can be seen throughout his public pronouncements and autobiographical writings (perhaps most forcefully and memorably in the 1996 'Love it' tirade). This bittersweet, rabble-rousing instinct, which embodies the philosopher Antonio Gramsci's notion of a 'pessimism of the intellect, optimism of the will', has always been especially strong in Irish immigrant communities in the industrial North. Glancing at other cultural fields, it helps us to make sense of such diverse modern examples as the music of the Smiths and (early) Oasis, the plays and scriptwriting of Shelagh Delaney and Peter Flannery, the Catholic–Marxist literary theory of Terry Eagleton, the entire atmosphere of the city of Liverpool and even, in diluted form, the populist political style of the current Greater Manchester mayor, Andy Burnham.

Keegan's optimism of the will helped to make him a towering hero at Liverpool throughout the 1970s, where he gelled neatly with legendary populist managers Bill Shankly and Bob Paisley (both of whom had also grown up in mining communities, in Ayrshire and County Durham respectively), and with a fanatical Scouse support base drawn from the city's working-class, substantially Irish population. But it was at Newcastle – as a player between 1982 and 1984, and then as manager from 1992 to 1997 – that Keegan finally found his wonderland, to cite the parody Christmas-song-cum-terrace-chant which seemed to echo continuously around Tyneside during his time at the club ('We're walking along, singing a song, walking in a Keegan wonderland'). From the start, Keegan felt himself to be indelibly bound up with the Newcastle supporters, and by extension the wider North-East community. When he scored on his debut against QPR on 28 August 1982, Keegan hurled himself into the crowd at the Gallowgate End, claiming that they had sucked the ball into the net and that he 'just wanted to stay there for ever'. After inspiring a lacklustre side and encouraging certain key younger players to find their feet, Keegan oversaw Newcastle's promotion to the top division, then left St James's Park in a helicopter – seemingly for good – at the end of an emotionally filmic testimonial game in the summer of 1984.

But after this journey out of the wilderness, the club quickly lost its way again. Within five years of Keegan's testimonial, Newcastle had succumbed to boardroom chaos, the financially motivated departure of three incredible local talents (Chris Waddle, Peter Beardsley and Paul Gascoigne) and, crushingly, relegation back into the second tier. The proceeds of Victorian heavy industry were largely funnelled away from the North-East and into the pockets of a wealthy mine-owning class who mostly lived elsewhere. In a similar way, Newcastle's underachieving football club has often been a site of rampant supporter exploitation and corporate asset-stripping by presiding business elites. Over time, this has given rise to a deep mood of fatalism and low self-esteem among its fan base, which has blurred with the region's wider weakness for post-industrial dejection. The late Eighties and early Nineties were one of the gloomiest phases in this sadomasochist cycle. After auctioning off the greatest players of the era, and crashing out of the First Division, by early 1992 Newcastle were mired in the Second Division relegation zone. It was looking highly likely that they would drop down into the third tier for the first time in their history and probably go bankrupt thereafter.

It was at this point that the metaphorical side of the narrative collapsed into full-blown magic realism. In February 1992, Keegan was given the Newcastle manager job, and the Toon Army openly hailed the return of their "messiah." Under Keegan's control, the team avoided relegation and then began a meteoric rise to the top of English football, first winning promotion in 1993, then becoming serious contenders for the Premier League title in successive seasons. They did so while pioneering a brand of idealistic, attacking football, which gave physical expression both to Keegan's inmost character and to the simmering atmosphere of the High Nineties more generally. As the British economy pulled out of recession and into a heady boomtime, and as Newcastle fan Tony Blair posed as PM-in-waiting while Britpop jangled in the background, Keegan's quixotic, high-scoring Newcastle side began to look like a heroic embodiment of the zeitgeist.

But while they were hailed nationally as 'the Entertainers', the 'neutral's favourite' and a symbol of football's new glamorous respectability in an age of all-seater stadiums and corporate investment, there was a more local side to the story. As well as being praised throughout the wider game, Keegan's Newcastle team also enormously boosted the morale of their headquarters in the North-East. The buoyant cultural atmosphere Keegan built-up around his Newcastle team circa 1992–6 transcended the limits of football per se, so that its epicentre in Tyneside began to acquire the look and feel of an ever-expanding carnival.

This was a time of strange occurrences. At some point in the middle years of the decade, a samba band started playing next to Grey's Monument and then outside St James's Park on match days – a sudden, incongruous development at the time, which nonetheless brought out the latent festal spirit lying below the surface of the post-industrial North-East. In a more official context, in July 1993 Kevin Keegan switched on the newly installed lighting system on the Tyne Bridge: a spectral, *Wizard of Oz* conjuring of the North-East's pioneering history of electrification and spectacular engineering feats ('KING KEVIN PUTS A SHINE ON THE TYNE', crowed the local newspaper, quoting boastful claims from local worthies that this would 'epitomise the City' and 'show the country what we have'). Perhaps most famously, in September 1995, an American tourist company placed Newcastle alongside Rio de Janeiro and New Orleans in a list of the world's top ten party destinations. Dovetailing with the examples of cultural regeneration discussed elsewhere in this book, the Keegan phenomenon became a sort of permanent symbol of – and excuse for – celebration on the streets of Tyneside in the mid-Nineties. The internationalism implied by the flamboyant playing of his Newcastle side combined with local pride to create an almost literal Brasilia of the North, about which T. Dan Smith, who died in relative poverty in July 1993, could only have dreamed.

And so, at this cultural zenith for the region, I found myself wandering through the streets around St James's Park with my dad in early May 1993. After the away victory over Grimsby on the Tuesday had secured promotion, Newcastle had to play two final home games close together. On the Thursday night, a clearly slightly hungover team managed to hobble past Oxford United via a 2–1 victory at St James's Park. But despite the so-so football in the game itself, in the surrounding city centre there was an atmosphere of gathering euphoria bordering on delirium, which was verifiably real, for all that my own memory of it is of course partly idealized.

The Keegan Wonderland chant was audible from the moment I opened my passenger door in the Newcastle University car park after the commute from our home in the Tyne Valley, though it now echoed in counterpoint with endless *Campeones* refrains and tributes to our new star striker Andy Cole ('he gets the ball, he scores a goal'). In a poetic socio-historical twist, Cole was the son of a Jamaican immigrant who had worked as a miner in the Gedling colliery in Nottinghamshire (a multicultural 'pit of all nations') while his son was growing up, before retiring shortly prior to its closure in 1991. Though I was scarcely aware of it at the time, some eight years after the collapse of the Miners' Strike, there was a strange, emotional symbolism underlying Cole's elevation to idol status at the centre of the recently ruined Great Northern Coalfield.

Amid this swirling Geordie soundscape, street vendors sold flags and souvenir hats, and black-and-white scarves were everywhere. At the centre of thousands of Umbro replica tops, the distinctive blue-star logo of club sponsor Scottish & Newcastle Breweries supplied a neat visual metaphor for the surrounding mood of overflowing hedonism – not to mention a triumphant *memento vivere* of one of the few Tyneside manufacturing industries to have outlived the socio-economic nightmare of the Eighties. That trauma now seemed to be finally, magically, coming to an end. Something bottled up for a decade or more was bursting out in rainbow colours, and with a tangible sense of civic optimism. While we were walking past a roaring pub on Percy Street, by strange chance my dad bumped into his best friend, Bob Pringle, a Geordie exile back in town for the game. A shipbuilder's son born in 1950, Bob was well placed to look back on the whole panorama of post-war North-East history and say breathlessly, but without hyperbole, that he'd never seen anything like it.

The following week the Newcastle players went on a triumphal open-top bus tour, at the climax of which Keegan addressed thousands of ecstatic locals from the balcony of the iridescent Civic Centre. But for me the really important moment occurred between this postscript and the penultimate match against Oxford, when the season officially ended with a home game against Leicester City at St James's Park on Sunday, 9 May. In rare, dazzling sunshine, a somewhat recovered group of Newcastle players thrashed their opponents 7–1, after a pre-match party headlined by Alan Hull's Lindisfarne, who played their set on the building site of an old, battered terrace now suddenly being extended to the skies. Fully expecting every spring to be like this, or better, I watched through the eyes of a child as an entire city seemed to melt into impossible rapture.

Part of the psychological power – and some might say the lasting harmfulness – of Keegan's Newcastle fable derives from the fact that it was ultimately an unfulfilled dream. This is what historians and political philosophers like to call a *heroic failure*.

To see how emphatically Keegan's dream failed, let us now flash forward to three years after the 1993 promotion week. Despite their manager's now legendary last stand in the Sky News interview, a supine Newcastle team went on to draw their final two games of the 1995–6 season. In the end, they finished a clear four points behind Manchester United – the culmination of a bizarre nervous collapse following their unchecked dominance of the English top flight before March. From this point on, the Keegan project was effectively dead. Though the magic of the 1992–6 interlude would linger on for a while – a poetically just 5–0 thrashing of Manchester United in October 1996, another second-place finish in 1997, a memorable Champions League victory over Barcelona at St James's Park later the same year – Keegan would himself resign within a year of his 'Love it' outburst. Over the next quarter of a century the club he left behind would deteriorate in familiar, dismal ways, to once again become a byword for mismanagement, corruption and serial underachievement.

For Keegan personally, the 1996 collapse seems to have been a blow from which he never recovered. In the words of his striker Les Ferdinand, it was 'almost as though a light had gone out in his head'. He would return to football management, notably by way of an unsuccessful stab at steering the England national team in 1999–2000, as well as a brief, farcical return to Newcastle in 2008 and more mixed spells at Fulham and Manchester City. But this once godlike figure would mostly fade from view in the first decades of the twenty-first century. The civic dimension of his Newcastle campaign would have been impossible to repeat elsewhere – with the obvious exception of Liverpool, who showed no interest in him – and though he tried his hand at television punditry, he never quite projected the mix of conquering-hero smugness and analytical arrogance which allowed lesser figures like Mark Lawrenson and Alan Hansen to enjoy bankable careers in that field. While researching this book, the only recent reference to Keegan I could find on the internet was an announcement that he was due to host the annual Meat Management Meat Industry Awards ceremony at the Hilton Birmingham Metropole on 9 September 2021.

Kevin Keegan in his Liverpool days, late 1970s

For myself, I have never quite been able to get over Keegan's heroic failure in the mid-Nineties. This might sound like a ridiculous thing to admit in a world full of genuine pain and misery, a tiny portion of which I have at times experienced directly. But it is true nonetheless. If Keegan's narrative proves anything, it is that human experience is profoundly shaped by cultural and historical factors, in ways that cannot be fully explained by either the brute economic analyses propounded by academic Marxists or the more cynical rational self-interest theories so beloved of capitalists and liberals. In common with many people from the North-East, I seem to have internalized the fairy tale of Keegan's Newcastle over the years, so that few things I have experienced in the intervening years have come close to emulating this utopic digression of the mid-Nineties. This is the full, real, absurd and tragic implication of what it means to believe in the possibility of a messiah. Holding out for a redeeming populist hero might on the surface seem like a positive form of idealism. But it can also be a psychological disorder – a stupefying mental condition which brings to mind Karl Marx's famous claim that religion is the opium of the people. Cherishing the heroic failure and hoped-for resurrection of a messiah figure is both comforting and absolving. It allows us to assume we have already got the most out of life, while reconciling us to the belief that the status quo cannot be changed except by a form of divine magic. Faced with this combination of nostalgia and learned hopelessness, why bother to improve things, for yourself or for your community, in any practical sense? Far better to wallow in romantic myths about the past and future, to attach yourself to unviable, idealistic causes, to tell tales by the fireside, tumbler in hand, and dream forlornly of the king over the water.

I have written before about how a version of this cultural complex is one of the reasons why English identity – with its nostalgia for vague historical dreams and absurd lack of real constitutional structures in the present – is really a kind of vast melancholic illusion. Northern English identity is a sort of killer variant of this more widespread national disease. There is no doubt, as I have suggested, that northerners feel the messianic impulse especially acutely. Like all attempts to describe a collective unconscious, this is a simplification of sorts. But it is also grounded in historical fact. As we have seen many times already, northern history is defined by a sort of endless back and forth: between surging, energetic bursts forward into a future way in advance of the conservative norms of English culture (most obviously in the case of the Industrial Revolution and its after-effects) and equally drastic recoilings into a radically bleak psychic and actual landscape, which is the inevitable product of enduring marginality from an imperial civilization overwhelmingly centred on London – with one or two short lapses – since the Norman Conquest.

This partly explains why northerners have so often nurtured the messianic impulse. Because of their radical industrial past, and pivotal role in the invention of modernity, northerners have always-already seen the future. But they also learned early on what it feels like to have the future taken away, its profits redistributed among an ancient establishment which continually strives to promote a national identity structured (even today!) around the mythical archetype of the pre-industrial village in the rural South of England. Northerners tend to have felt the dream of an imminent leap forward into a dramatically better life more vividly, keenly and idealistically than their southern English counterparts. They cherish the memory of these moments, by paying tribute to the heroic lore of their football teams, the audaciousness of their civic buildings, the pioneering history of their technological amenities and the passionate collective yearning of their music, from industrial anthems like 'Blaydon Races' and 'On Ilkla Moor Baht 'at', to latter-day folk hymns like 'You'll Never Walk Alone', 'Love Will Tear Us Apart', 'Live Forever' and 'Local Hero'. But there is also an insidious tendency in northern culture to accept the opium rationed out at these rallying points. They speak of times when the ideal seemed within reach, but also of the impossibility of any more material improvements happening in the present.

And so the blend of victimhood and hopeless dreaming is compounded in a seemingly endless and inescapable cycle. In the post-industrial, end-of-history North-East, the only answer to this impasse we could find, rather pathetically, was Kevin Keegan, whose narrative I take to be a kind of fable about the great difficulty – I will not say the impossibility – of real change ever arriving in the North, as in England as a whole. Indeed, in retrospect there is a bitter irony underlying those 2017 memes which brought together Keegan and Jeremy Corbyn to dangle the possibility of an imminent, improbable salvation for their respective teams. In both cases that moment never arrived (despite some heroic short-term victories), and in reality both of these men were doomed messiahs who flourished briefly then failed utterly, and now neither seems likely to come again.

Despite the limits of northern messianism, I still think it is worth believing in, as the title of this book makes plain. This is partly because the alternatives are so much worse. If you don't believe the North will rise again in spite of its immense socio-economic disadvantages and historic low self-esteem, you are thrown back onto a series of equally unappealing plans for its future.

One of these is the common-or-garden conservatism which simply accepts that the North is a marginal backwater of the Anglo-British state, and tries to keep it stranded in this peripheral nowhere-land for ever. According to this view, far more resigned and narcotized than even the most delusional messianic impulse, the North is in essence – like the romantic clichés of Scotland and Wales passed down to us from Victorian leisure culture – a place of sublime mountains, picturesque lakes, welcoming dales and comically boisterous cities: good for stag-dos and a university education, perhaps, but not much else. Certain parts of the North, viewed very narrowly, fit this stereotype better than others – the teashops of Harrogate, the island of collegiate privilege that is the city of Durham, swathes of Cheshire, most of the commercialized Lake District and the posher suburbs of the major conurbations. The North sketched by these coordinates is a mainly rural, mainly rather tame – if often geologically rugged – place. Unlike the high-powered centre of business, finance and technology that is the modern South-East, so the thinking goes, this rustic North should probably see its future in rather modest terms, in a combination of tourism, agriculture, cottage industries, student consumerism and the various forms of hospitality which have rushed into the gap left by the departure of heavy industry (northerners are nothing, after all, if they are not hospitable).

Away from such chocolate-box clichés, which litter the property and travel sections of lifestyle magazines and right-wing newspapers, there are, of course, less mindless ways of responding to the long-term plight of the North, which also stop well short of utopian idealism. One of the most nuanced, most fully developed examples of a self-consciously northern philosophy I know is to be found in Basil Bunting's modernist long poem *Briggflatts*. As well as the broader themes summarized in Chapter 3, there are some valuable – if intellectually layered – lessons to be drawn from Bunting's poem, which I think are well worth examining closely in these concluding pages, as we try finally to chart a way forward for the cause of northern revival.

I know that modernist poetry is an acquired taste, so I will try to summarize the main message of Bunting's *Briggflatts* as succinctly as possible. The majority of this rich, many-sided poem is an abstract retelling of Bunting's own autobiography. However, in its climactic central section this subjective narrative is put on hold. The poem digresses at this point into an adapted episode from the medieval Persian epic *Shahnameh*, part of which tells the story of how Alexander the Great ('Sikander' in the Persian tradition) journeyed to the top of a mountain in the Middle East, to be confronted with the prophecies of the angel Israfel. In Bunting's retelling of this story, the dragons and monsters Alexander meets and kills along the way in *Shahnameh* are transformed into 'turd bakers' (by which Bunting meant members of the London literary and media establishment who had mistreated, rejected or simply ignored northerners like him, such as the hereditary *Times* journalist Hugh Astor). After he has defeated the turd bakers, Alexander is described as a sort of stoical northern fell walker:

> he
> reached to a crack in the rock
> with some scorn, resolute though in doubt,
> traversed limestone to gabbro,

file sharp, skinning his fingers,
and granite numb with ice, in air
too thin to bear up a gnat,
scrutinising holds while day lasted,
groping for holds in the dark
till the morning star reflected
in the glazed crag.

After this dogged ascent, we might expect that Alexander will finally get what he wants at the summit of the mountain. But though he had hoped to hear what is described in the original *Shahnameh* source as 'visions of futurity' telling of his ultimate conquest of the world, the angel Israfel instead warns Alexander of his imminent mortality ('Yet delay! / When will the signal come / to summon man to his clay?'). Magically hurled back to a pastoral landscape which looks a lot like the Northumbrian countryside described elsewhere in the poem, Alexander is recovering in the grass when he hears a quiet voice whispering into his ear. It is the Slowworm, a snake-like creature, and perhaps the most important character in *Briggflatts*. This nimble, unassuming animal, who flourishes while 'lying low', advises Alexander not to overreach himself through overweening idealism and ambition. Instead, he should focus on his immediate surroundings, deriving pleasure from the 'occasional light' he finds in his homeland.

The lesson to be gleaned from all of this, as Bunting commented elsewhere, is that when we human beings accept the loss of our most treasured dreams, we 'may live content in humility'. We might think here of a sort of everyday northern pragmatism, of the kind which has always existed in opposition to the more quixotic tradition embodied in the slogans on display at the Durham Miners' Gala, the quasi-biblical undertaking of the Jarrow Crusade, the hapless idealism of Factory Records and indeed the latter-day hero-worship of Kevin Keegan. For Bunting, a scientifically minded Fabian sceptic, whose politics usually hovered somewhere around the centre-left (with some notable digressions), there was a different, less high-flown way to exist on these islands. In his view (in certain moods at least), the only way to respond to a national culture where politics, journalism, literary publishing, business, finance, education and the arts are all drastically biased in favour of the South-East, is to focus on small, achievable ways of resisting the status quo and its arguably fixed regional inequalities – and not to hope in vain for a great, cleansing reversal of political power.

According to this worldview, which has something to be said for it, England, or Britain, will probably always be economically and socially oriented around the megalopolis that is London (a capital many times bigger and more populous than even the largest northern city). As such, shouldn't we try to find ways within this ancient system of modestly increasing wealth and representation for the North – through investment or regeneration initiatives of the kind which dominated the Thatcher, Major and Blair years perhaps, or else the sorts of mayoral and levelling-up projects favoured by post-2010 Conservative governments? Speaking of something broadly like this practical, one-step-at-a-time attitude in the abstract, Bunting said that people 'resolute to submit' to life as it is may not ever truly flourish or control the world, like the 'turd bakers' of the London establishment. But they might at least be able to achieve a kind of creative productivity, and 'bring something new to birth, be it only a monster'. (We might observe in passing here that Bunting did not live to see the opening of the Gateshead MetroCentre, still less the colossal 'Whey Aye' Ferris wheel due to open on the Newcastle Quayside in 2024.)

But even putting aside the fact that Bunting was a strident Northumbrian separatist with a rather un-pragmatic personal life, who clearly did not always practise what he preached, I do not think that being 'content in humility' is likely to work well for the North, either in practical or in moral terms. As ever, of course, this stance is partly due to personal philosophical bias. As a committed socialist – and indeed a practising Catholic – I do not think that life should be wasted in a condition of mere acceptance of the world as it is. Unless we want to throw in the towel on humanity once and for all, we have to hope and strive for the fact that, on earth, there is always the possibility that life will one day be as it is in heaven (or at least, more realistically, a good bit closer than it is at the moment to a heavenly condition of mutual aid, equality and love). This determination to believe in spite of the empirical reality – we might as well go ahead and call it True Faith, with due respect to the band New Order – is part of what I understand by northern identity. And it is one of the reasons why I think of myself as a northerner above all else.

But this goes way beyond my personal worldview and abstract spiritual truths. Ultimately, I think that even a diehard sceptic has to admit that when it comes to the North of England, some form of prodigal hopefulness – or at least vaulting ambition – is quite simply the only way to go. From an examination of modern northern history, it seems painfully clear that almost all of the more modest, apparently pragmatic, recent solutions to regional inequality in England have been spectacular failures, from the Heseltinite regeneration schemes of the Thatcher years to the Northern Powerhouse delusion of the 2010s (let alone the latest, transparent ruse that is 'levelling up'). Indeed, the cold historical record shows us that the extreme centralization of the islands is only likely to be substantially altered by genuinely revolutionary movements. We might think here of the obvious example of the Industrial Revolution, a radical (and, as it turned out, only temporary) upending of the deeply embedded dynamic of the English system. In turn, of course, the English nation had itself been cemented during another great revolutionary moment: the pre-modern cataclysm of the Norman Conquest, which literally set in stone a centralized power structure which has never really been substantially altered.

Going by such historical precedents, I do not see how, when it comes to the North's place within England, anything other than a great reversal will ever do. Put another way, we might say that the messianic North and the pragmatic North are at this point – as so often throughout history – *exactly the same thing*. Meanwhile, it is gradualist schemes like 'levelling up' that are the real pie-in-the-sky fantasies. This is why, as I have tried to make clear in this book, the only really important question facing us now is: what form should the profound and essential movement towards reform take, and when do we start making it happen?

There is still, even after all, a chance for the deep and dreaming North to find a firmer, fairer reality on the other side of the ideal. If northern culture means anything, and I think it does, it must always imply some kind of belief in the great leap forward, the impossible, gravity-defying feat of technology, the desperate dream of reforming the land and overhauling the ancient map on which the top half of England is consigned to being Britannia Inferior for ever. We might describe this essential facet of northern identity as messianic, or even just hopelessly ambitious. But it is the way we are, and the way life is on these islands. This is the curse and the uncontainable hope at the heart of the northern soul.

ACKNOWLEDGEMENTS

Aside from my family – to whom this book is of course dedicated – I would like to thank several people for their help during its preparation and production.

At Bloomsbury, Robin Baird-Smith was a sympathetic and wise editor; Jamie Birkett was an enthusiastic commissioner and supporter of the project during the difficult days of the 2020–21 lockdown; Sarah Jones and Fahmida Ahmed were always unfailingly helpful and responsive; James Watson designed an incredible Wadsworthian cover; and Rachel Nicholson has been – and continues to be – a superlative publicist. Matthew Taylor's copy-edit was intelligent, sensitive and meticulous.

Mark 'Stan' Stanton is the perfect agent. Without him this book would never have been commissioned.

Marcus Barnett, Harry Stopes, Paddy Lynch, Owen Hatherley and Tom Pickard took the time to read and provide advice on various parts of the manuscript. I am immensely grateful for their help.

Several years ago, in writing the Acknowledgements section for my first book, I tried to list the names of all my friends. I will not try to do that again here, largely for fear of missing anyone out. But I hope you all know who you are, and how grateful I am for your continued faith and love.

NOTES

p. ix   'We are at last experiencing a new empire': Holly Bancroft, 'Revealed: Michael Gove's sexist jibes, racist jokes and homophobic slurs', *Independent*, 13 September 2021; https://www.independent.co.uk/news/uk/politics/michael-gove-sexist-racist-speech-b1918058.html. Accessed 3 June 2022.

p. ix   'Never give in, never give in, never, never, never, never': David Peace, 'My comfort read? Old Labour party manifestos', *The Guardian*, 30 July 2021; https://www.theguardian.com/books/2021/jul/30/david-peace-my-comfort-read-old-labour-party-manifestos. Accessed 3 June 2022.

PROLOGUE: CANARIES IN THE COAL MINE

p. xii   'Different rules are always applied ... pushed around any more': 'Manchester mayor Andy Burnham attacks proposed new Tier 3 restrictions', *The Telegraph*, 15 October 2020; https://www.youtube.com/watch?v=FjCvuZaEQbE. Accessed 3 June 2022.

CHAPTER 1: THE RURAL RETURN

p. 4   'bodies emerged five months later': Basil Bunting, *The Poems of Basil Bunting*, ed. Don Share (London: Faber, 2016), 166.

p. 6   'slow trek to rediscover': quoted in Robert Zaretsky, 'A Man Apart', *Los Angeles Review of Books*, 18 July 2012; https://lareviewofbooks.org/article/a-man-apart/. Accessed 3 June 2022.

p. 7   In recent years, revisionist critics ... 'heroic' account of the Industrial Revolution: Bill Lancaster and Peter Stark, *Releasing the Genie of Coal: The Lower Derwent Valley, the Great Northern Coalfield and the Climate Crisis* (Consett: Land of Oak and Iron Trust, 2021), 43.

p. 14   a chilling 48 per cent in central Newcastle: Jonathan Walker, 'The alarming poverty stats that really should be an issue at the 2019

general election', *The Chronicle*, 20 November 2019; https://
www.chroniclelive.co.uk/news/north-east-news/labour
-conservative-general-election-poverty-17289049. Accessed 3
June 2022.

p. 14   when Britain became a harsher, less equal place: 'How has
inequality changed?', *The Equality Trust*. https://equalitytrust
.org.uk/how-has-inequality-changed. Accessed 3 June 2022.

CHAPTER 2: WALKING ON THE MOON

p. 32   'bourgeois Victorian vistas': Wyndham Lewis, *BLAST 1*
(London: Thames and Hudson, 2008), 18.

p. 32   'wild nature cranks ... wider intricacies than those of Nature':
Lewis, *BLAST 1*, 11–36.

p. 32   'ONCE MORE WEAR THE ERMINE OF THE NORTH':
Lewis, *BLAST 1*, 12.

p. 32   'We assert that the art for these climates ... must be a northern
flower': Lewis, *BLAST 1*, 36.

p. 34   'pyramidal workshop ... discharging itself on the sea': Lewis,
BLAST 1, 23–4.

p. 35   the majority of the ports: Lewis, *BLAST 1*, 23.

p. 36   'For instance, this morning ... nimble pale-blue sunbeams':
Yevgeny Zamyatin, *We*, trans. Natasha Randall (London:
Vintage, 2007), 5–6.

p. 37   'triumphant embodiment ... larger world of planless incoherence':
Aldous Huxley, *Brave New World* (London: Vintage, 1994), xxi.

p. 39   'ragged boys in gangs': Anthony Burgess, *Little Wilson and Big
God* (London: Vintage, 1912), 126.

p. 40   'revelation ... passionate teachers': Kathleen Roberts, 'And the
winner is ... Cleveland College of Art and Design!', 22 February
2018; https://era.org.uk/idea-guide/winner-cleveland-college
-art-design/. Accessed 6 June 2022.

p. 40   'There's a walk from Redcar ... found the beauty in that
darkness': David Bates, 'Ridley Scott's Blade Runner and the
Teesside skyline', *People's Republic of Teesside*, 4 December 2007.
Accessed 6 June 2022.

p. 45   'No poetry before us ... words in freedom': quoted in Martin
Puchner, *Poetry of the Revolution: Marx, Manifestoes, and
the Avant-Garde* (Princeton: Princeton University Press,
2006), 91.

CHAPTER 3: THE FUTURE WE BUILD

p. 51 'The world dominated by its phantasmagorias ... "modernity"':
Walter Benjamin, *The Arcades Project*, trans. Howard Eiland and
Kevin McLaughlin (London: Belknap Press, 1999), 26.

p. 52 'greeted by the most furious ... emissary from another
hemisphere': Alan Sykes, 'Maestro of the all-nude Lysistrata
plans an unforgettable evening at Newcastle's Morden Tower',
The Guardian, 15 November 2011. Accessed 6 June 2022.

p. 53 'celestially decorous ... mechanic illusions of the century': Sykes,
'Maestro of the all-nude Lysistrata'.

p. 55 'sometimes been described as "popular modernism"': Phoebe
Braithwaite, 'Mark Fisher's Popular Modernism', *Tribune*, 18
January 2019; https://tribunemag.co.uk/2019/01/mark-fisher
-kpunk-popular-modernism. Accessed 6 June 2022.

p. 56 'self-described "Anglican-royalist-classicist" phase': T. S. Eliot,
For Lancelot Andrewes: Essays on Style and Order (London: Faber
and Gwyer, 1928), ix.

p. 56 Auden ... rather snootily rebuffed Bunting's attempts: Basil
Bunting, *Letters of Basil Bunting*, ed. Alex Niven (Oxford: Oxford
University Press, 2022), 269.

p. 57 'Southrons' would 'maul the music': Bunting, *The Poems*, 327.

p. 57 reduced reading fees to 'Northumbrian' event organizers:
Richard Burton, *A Strong Song Tows Us: The Life of Basil Bunting*
(Oxford: Infinite Ideas, 2013), 433.

p. 57 advocated devolution of the English regions: Bunting, *Letters*, 239.

p. 57 fond of citing a series of historic northern rebellions: Bunting,
Letters, 302–3.

p. 57 in reality he believed in a form of federalism: Bunting, *Letters*,
239.

p. 58 'cross-discipline and cross-class too ... work for them, and he
did': Alex Niven, 'To reach the moon you need a rocket: an
interview with Tom Pickard', *3:AM Magazine*, 2 November 2012;
http://www.3ammagazine.com/3am/tom-pickard-interview/.
Accessed 6 June 2022.

p. 58 'Gentle generous voices weave ... till bird dawn': Bunting, *Poems*, 43.

p. 59 'sick, self-maimed, self-hating' ... touching acquaintance for
food and tobacco: Bunting, *Poems*, 45.

p. 60 'passion for designing things ran away with him': Bunting,
Letters, 287.

p. 60   'idea was that all the bits and pieces ... arsewipes by the rest':
Bunting, *Letters*, 287.

p. 63   'led Hamilton to encourage his students to derive inspiration':
Michael Bracewell, *Re-Make/Re-Model: The Art School Roots of
Roxy Music* (London: Faber and Faber, 2020), 86–94.

p. 63   Hamilton's famous summary: Bracewell, *Re-Make/Re-Model*,
76.

p. 64   'mechanical conquest of time ... previously denied to him':
Carmen Fernández Aparicio, 'Man, Machine & Motion: Richard
Hamilton', *Museo Nacional Centro de Arte Reina Sofía*, 2014.
Accessed 6 June 2022.

p. 70   'Why do you like water or mountains? ... Athens and Florence
and Rome': T. Dan Smith, *An Autobiography* (Stocksfield: Oriel
Press, 1970), 66.

p. 73   'was told by his legal team ... until they got a conviction': Chris
Foote-Wood, *T. Dan Smith: 'Voice of the North' – Downfall of a
Visionary* (Darlington: Northern Writers, 2011), 256.

CHAPTER 4: ENGLAND'S UNCONSCIOUS

p. 83   'Those limestone moors ... There is my symbol of us all': W. H.
Auden, *Collected Poems* (London: Random House, 1976), 182.

p. 84   'In ROOKHOPE I was first aware ... The reservoir of darkness
stirred': Auden, *Collected Poems*, 182.

p. 84   'the seminal moment of his life as a civilised human being and as
an artist': Auden, *Collected Poems*, lxi.

p. 84   *Urmutterfurcht* ... 'To civilise and create': Auden, *Collected
Poems*, 182.

p. 85   'white water upland empire': Barry MacSweeney, *Pearl*
(Cambridge: Equipage, 1995), 24.

p. 88   Though not directly relevant to our narrative: Max Adams, *The
First Kingdom: Britain in the Age of Arthur* (London: Head of
Zeus, 2021), 95–6; Alistair Moffat, *The Wall: Rome's Last Frontier*
(Edinburgh: Birlinn, 2017), 223.

p. 89   'lightly used': Richard Beeching, *The Reshaping of British
Railways; Part 1, Report* (London: HMSO, 1963), 10.

p. 94   For some early twenty-first-century commentators: Mark Fisher,
'K-Punk, or the Glampunk Art Pop Discontinuum'. *K-Punk*, 11
September 2004; http://k-punk.abstractdynamics.org/archives
/004115.html. Accessed 6 June 2022.

NOTES

p. 96 Though recent critics have tried to shed some light: David Butler, 'Whatever happened to Delia Derbyshire?' *British Art Studies*, 31 May 2019; https://www.britishartstudies.ac.uk/issues/issue -index/issue-12/whatever-happened-delia-derbyshire. Accessed 6 June 2022.

p. 97 her future partner Clive Blackburn would later recall: Butler, 'Whatever happened to Delia Derbyshire?', p. 2.

p. 99 a point ... of everything: Li Yuan-chia, 'Untitled', *Li Yuan-chia Foundation*; http://www.lycfoundation.org/li-yuan-chia/. Accessed 6 June 2022.

CHAPTER 5: COUNTY DURHAM TO ELDORADO

p. 106 'evidence of a collective dream': Benjamin, *The Arcades Project*, 152.

p. 106 'will-power, perseverance ... reality of concrete and glass': 'MetroCentre opening souvenir supplement', *Evening Chronicle* (13 October 1986), 1.

p. 107 'a great deal for the North East ... their shopping revolution': 'MetroCentre opening souvenir supplement', 1.

p. 110 'slave-barracks designed by a team of lunatics': Bunting, *Letters*, 375.

p. 111 In the 1994 article which first popularized the term 'metrosexual': Mark Simpson, 'Here come the mirror men: why the future is metrosexual', *The Independent* (15 November 1994).

p. 111 'more than average interest ... a bit of a mod town really': Taylor Parkes, 'An Unsettling Creation: Bryan Ferry Interviewed by Taylor Parkes'. *The Quietus* (13 November 2014); https:// thequietus.com/articles/16665-bryan-ferry-interview?fb_ comment_id=817070401682803_818145578241952. Accessed 6 June 2022.

p. 112 while it would be perilous indeed ... challenge to undertake: Bracewell, *Re-Make/Re-Model*, 58–9.

p. 113 'cuspate period between the trauma ... salvation and its shadow': Bracewell, *Re-Make/Re-Model*, 59.

p. 115 'sheer coldness and distantiation ... of which he sings': Fisher, 'K-Punk, or the Glampunk Art Pop Discontinuum'.

p. 116 'the deterritority of American-originated consumer culture': Fisher, 'K-Punk, or the Glampunk Art Pop Discontinuum'.

p. 118 'the edge of the edge': Terry Farrell, *Lives in Architecture: Terry Farrell* (London: RIBA Publishing, 2020), 21.

p. 120   I was separated from everything … idolised in America: Farrell,
          Lives in Architecture, 19.

p. 122   the film's narrator, played by Paul Scofield, points out: *London*,
          dir. Patrick Keiller, BFI Production, 1994.

CHAPTER 6: HARD HATS IN THE HEATHER

p. 132   'dreams were all finished … after that, it were gone': Alexandra
          Pollard, 'Andrea Dunbar: The short, troubled life of the prodigal
          Bradford playwright', *The Independent*, 6 June 2019; https://
          www.independent.co.uk/arts-entertainment/theatre-dance/
          features/andrea-dunbar-life-the-arbor-rita-sue-bob-black-teeth
          -brilliant-smile-a8945401.html. Accessed 6 June 2022.

p. 133   According to recent research: 'Adult drinking habits in Great
          Britain: 2005 to 2016', *Office for National Statistics*, 3 May 2017;
          https://www.ons.gov.uk/peoplepopulationandcommunity/
          healthandsocialcare/drugusealcoholandsmoking/bulletins/
          opinionsandlifestylesurveyadultdrinkinghabitsingreatbritain
          /2005to2016. Accessed 6 June 2022.

p. 133   in 2020 there were 20 alcohol-related deaths: 'Alcohol-specific
          deaths in the UK: registered in 2020', *Office for National Statistics*,
          7 December 2021; https://www.ons.gov.uk/peoplepopulation
          andcommunity/healthandsocialcare/causesofdeath/bulletins/
          alcoholrelateddeathsintheunitedkingdom/registeredin2020#:~
          :text=In%202020%2C%20there%20were%208%2C974,time%20
          series%20began%20in%202001. Accessed 6 June 2022.

p. 134   long-term migration patterns have produced a fairly distinct
          genetic mix: Ewen Callaway, 'UK mapped out by genetic
          ancestry', *Nature* (2015). https://doi.org/10.1038/nature.2015
          .17136

p. 135   alarmingly high suicide rates: 'Suicides in England and Wales:
          2020 registrations', *Office for National Statistics*, 7 September 2021;
          https://www.ons.gov.uk/peoplepopulationandcommunity/
          birthsdeathsandmarriages/deaths/bulletins/suicidesintheunited
          kingdom/2020registrations. Accessed 6 June 2022.

p. 135   Blackpool, which has the highest rates of liver cirrhosis in
          England: 'Liver disease profiles: November 2021 update', *Gov.uk*,
          2 November 2021; https://www.gov.uk/government/statistics
          /liver-disease-profiles-november-2021-update/liver-disease
          -profiles-november-2021-update. Accessed 6 June 2022.

p. 135   'the North of England is Stag Do heaven': 'Top 8 Stag Do Destinations in the UK', *Maximise: Stag and Hen by Crazy-Voyages*; https://stag.maximise.co.uk/category/stag-do-destinations-&-ideas/article/top-10-stag-do-destinations-in-the-uk#:~:text=Manchester,off%20for%20your%20stag%20do. Accessed 6 June 2022.

p. 138   'each day [started] with strong tea and rum': John Braine, *Room at the Top* (London: Random House, 2002), 190.

p. 139   'his notion of the artist was formed': Andrew Crozier, 'Barry MacSweeney: Obituary', *The Guardian*, 18 May 2000; https://www.theguardian.com/news/2000/may/18/guardianobituaries. Accessed 6 June 2022.

p. 140   'I had a suspicion … to go to the grave': Robert Fisk, 'Top hack blasts local rags', *The Independent*, 4 August 2001; https://www.independent.co.uk/voices/commentators/fisk/robert-fisk-top-hack-blasts-local-rags-9196235.html. Accessed 6 June 2022.

p. 142   'anti-candidate … trendy hippie of no achievements': quoted in Paul Batchelor, '"I am Pearl": Guise and Excess in the Poetry of Barry MacSweeney', unpublished PhD thesis, 2009; https://theses.ncl.ac.uk/jspui/bitstream/10443/901/1/Batchelor09.pdf, 15.

p. 142   'a sense of exile and a siege-mentality … poetics of opposition': Batchelor, '"I am Pearl"', 16.

p. 144   described by his partner Jackie Litherland as an 'alcoholic's death': Sarah Foster, 'A great love, tainted by the bottle', *The Northern Echo*, 26 September 2006; https://www.thenorthernecho.co.uk/opinion/echowoman/938266.great-love-tainted-bottle/. Accessed 6 June 2022.

p. 145   When I stand on the top road … all my words are homeless: MacSweeney, *Pearl*, 8.

p. 145   'had the most amazing eyes in history … but please don't crush my heart': MacSweeney, *Pearl*, 6–19.

p. 146   at the 'end of the road': MacSweeney, *Pearl*, 14.

p. 146   'I lost my mind in Sarajevo … fiery battleground of the sieged estate': MacSweeney, *Pearl*, 9–24.

p. 146   'They … left harping in the high wind': MacSweeney, *Pearl*, 12.

p. 147   'broken / ovens of manufacture and employment': MacSweeney, *Pearl*, 13.

CHAPTER 7: FLOURISHING

p. 155   overseeing the 'managed decline' of northern cities: Simon Parker,
          'The Leaving of Liverpool: managed decline and the enduring
          legacy of Thatcherism's urban policy', *LSE Politics and Policy*,
          17 January 2019; https://blogs.lse.ac.uk/politicsandpolicy/the
          -leaving-of-liverpool/. Accessed 6 June 2022.

p. 155   Buildings create synergy … This is Dark Ages Manchester: *24
          Hour Party People*, dir. Michael Winterbottom. Film Consortium/
          United Artists, 2002.

p. 158   deliberately intended to be 'a call to insurrection': quoted in
          Simon Spence, *The Stone Roses: War and Peace* (Harmondsworth:
          Penguin, 2014), 16.

p. 164   'Manchester will have you believe … and has been irrelevant for
          too long': 'FUC51: An introduction of sorts', *Fuc 51: Madchester
          Deniers*, 14 January 2010; http://fuc51.blogspot.com/2010/01/
          fuc51-introduction-of-sorts.html. Accessed 6 June 2022.

CHAPTER 8: THE GREAT BETRAYAL

p. 181   This may or may not have been a misquotation: Joe Kennedy,
          Games Without Frontiers (London: Repeater, 2021), 89–90.

p. 181   allegedly also claiming some form of affection: Colin Randall,
          'Tony Blair and Newcastle United: when the truth hurts', *SAFC
          Blog*, 17 April 2010; https://safc.blog/tony-blair-and-newcastle
          -united-when-the-truth-hurts/. Accessed 7 June 2022.

p. 181   'as someone who was brought up in the North-East': Paul
          Joannou, *United – The First 100 Years … and More: Official
          History of Newcastle United F.C. 1882–1995* (Leicester: Polar
          Print Group, 1995), 10.

p. 182   *The Times* reported: Tim Shipman, 'Sedgefield fell, and they
          erupted into song – things can only get better!', *The Times*, 15
          December 2019; https://www.thetimes.co.uk/article/sedgefield
          -fell-and-they-erupted-into-song-things-can-only-get-better
          -9cjfz9hj8. Accessed 7 June 2022.

p. 182   'surreal spectacle … perhaps beyond [Johnson's] imagining': Tim
          Adams, 'In Blair's old seat, the regulars agree: "Corbyn doesn't
          understand us here"', *The Observer*, 15 December 2019; https://
          www.theguardian.com/politics/2019/dec/15/blair-old-seat
          -sedgefield-rejected-corbyn-perceived-unpatriotic. Accessed 7
          June 2022.

p. 183   northern pits had been shutting down at a rapid rate: Huw Beynon and Ray Hudson, *The Shadow of the Mine: Coal and the End of Industrial Britain* (London: Verso, 2021), 49–51.

p. 184   'the house with two chimneys': 'A tale of two constituencies', *The Economist*, 9 December 1999; https://www.economist.com /britain/1999/12/09/a-tale-of-two-constituencies. Accessed 7 June 2022.

p. 185   'man polishing his Ford Sierra ... ordinary suburban estate': Tony Blair, 'Leader's speech, Blackpool 1996', *British Political Speech*; http://www.britishpoliticalspeech.org/speech-archive .htm?speech=202. Accessed 7 June 2022.

p. 186   'nowhere else to go': quoted in Dave Ward, 'Starmer is losing Labour's working-class voters', *The Times*, 6 April 2021; https:// www.thetimes.co.uk/article/starmer-is-losing-labours-working -class-voters-zw3l7prw2. Accessed 7 June 2022.

p. 186   'all middle-class now': quoted in James Bloodworth, 'Does class still count?', *UnHerd*, 29 March 2019; https://unherd.com/2019 /03/does-class-still-count/. Accessed 7 June 2022.

p. 186   Sedgefield was a 'northern working-class' ... them in Benidorm: Tony Blair, *A Journey* (London: Hutchinson, 2010), 135.

p. 188   'identify causes of urban decline ... urban neighbourhoods': *Towards an Urban Renaissance,* final report of the Urban Task Force, chaired by Lord Rogers of Riverside (London: Routledge, 2003), i.

p. 189   'a vision of sustainable regeneration ... environmentally sustainable': Richard Rogers, 'Delivering the Urban Renaissance', *The Observer,* 21 July 2002; https://www.theguardian.com/ society/2002/jul/21/regeneration.comment. Accessed 7 June 2022.

p. 189   'Urban design and planning ... that is our shared space': Rogers, 'Delivering the Urban Renaissance'.

CHAPTER 9: WARK FOREST WITH THE GEORDIE MAFIA

p. 198   'if at any time it appears likely ... form part of a united Ireland': 'The Belfast Agreement', Gov.uk, 10 April 1998; https://www .gov.uk/government/publications/the-belfast-agreement. Accessed 7 June 2022.

p. 199   'the Labour government has said ... to stimulate such demand': John Tomaney, 'End of the Empire State? New Labour and

Devolution in the United Kingdom', *International Journal of Urban and Regional Research*, vol. 24, no. 3, September 2000, 675–88 (at p. 685).

p. 200   Blair thought that devolution in England was 'stupid': Anthony Seldon, *Blair Unbound* (London: Simon and Schuster, 2007), 204.

p. 204   'I've been a member of the Labour Party ... It's time to say No': Johnny McDevitt, 'Dominic Cummings honed strategy in 2004 vote, video reveals', *The Guardian*, 12 November 2019; https://www.theguardian.com/politics/2019/nov/12/dominic-cummings-honed-strategy-2004-vote-north-east. Accessed 7 June 2022.

p. 207   'break [Labour's] links with the unions altogether': quoted in Andrew Roth, 'Stephen Byers', *The Guardian*, 16 March 2001; https://www.theguardian.com/politics/2001/mar/16/byers. Accessed 7 June 2022.

p. 207   a self-described 'cab for hire': Jenny Booth, '"Cab for hire" Stephen Byers to face sleaze watchdog', *The Times*, 22 March 2010; https://www.thetimes.co.uk/article/cab-for-hire-stephen-byers-to-face-sleaze-watchdog-g205fgttpql. Accessed 7 June 2022.

CHAPTER 10: GOING HOME

p. 215   *Canada's a bare land ... for men have made it so*: Bunting, *Poems*, 94.

p. 216   starts laughingly shouting 'I'M HOME! I'M HOME!': *Robin Hood: Prince of Thieves*, dir. Kevin Reynolds. Morgan Creek Productions, 1991.

p. 218   statistically overwhelmingly more likely than their southern counterparts: Gregory Clark and Neil Cummins, 'The Big Sort: Selective Migration and the Decline of Northern England, 1780-2018 (June 2018)', *Centre for Economic Policy Research*, Discussion Paper No. DP13023.

p. 221   The UK is the world's fifth largest economy ... recreation centres have been sold off: Philip Alston, 'Statement on Visit to the United Kingdom'. *United Nations Office of the High Commissioner of Human Rights*, 16 November 2018; https://www.ohchr.org/en/statements/2018/11/statement-visit-united-kingdom-professor-philip-alston-united-nations-special. Accessed 7 June 2022.

p. 222   Cities in the north of England ... South West (excluding London): 'Cities Outlook 2019'. *Centre for Cities*, 28 January 2019; https://

NOTES

www.centreforcities.org/reader/cities-outlook-2019/a-decade
-of-austerity/. Accessed 7 June 2022.

p. 224 an estimated £300 million was slashed from Newcastle City
Council's budget: 'Newcastle City Council budget cuts to reach
£327m by 2020', *BBC News*, 7 March 2019; https://www.bbc.co
.uk/news/uk-england-tyne-47484040. Accessed 7 June 2022.

p. 228 subsequently downgraded to a suggestion: Greg Heffer, 'Boris
Johnson proposes moving parliament to York while Palace of
Westminster repaired', *Sky News*, 16 July 2020; https://news
.sky.com/story/boris-johnson-proposes-moving-parliament
-to-york-while-palace-of-westminster-repaired-12029541.
Accessed 7 June 2022.

p. 229 on average 2.4 times greater in London than in the North: Luke
Raikes, 'Transport Investment in the Northern Powerhouse',
IPPR North, August 2019, p. 3; https://www.ippr.org/files
/2019-08/transport-investment-in-the-northern-powerhouse
-august19.pdf. Accessed 7 June 2022.

p. 229 and a scarcely believable seven times higher: Raikes, 'Transport
Investment in the Northern Powerhouse', 4.

p. 231 a mild and partial leftward shift in parts of the suburban South:
Jon Stone, 'Ed Davey says Lib Dems could win "dozens" of blue
wall seats from Tories after by-election win', *The Independent*, 20
June 2021; https://www.independent.co.uk/news/uk/politics
/ed-davey-boris-johnson-chesham-amersham-b1869299.html.
Accessed 7 June 2022.

p. 231 have in fact been greatly exaggerated: Tim Bale, 'The truth about
the Blue Wall', *UnHerd*, 2 August 2021; https://unherd.com
/2021/08/the-truth-about-the-blue-wall/. Accessed 7 June
2022.

p. 235 The outline of an independent northern English nation:
'Manifesto', Northern Independence Party; https://www
.freethenorth.co.uk/ourfuture. Accessed 7 June 2022.

p. 236 The Northern economy ... security in the North: 'Manifesto',
Northern Independence Party.

p. 238 'real and lasting economic and political devolution': quoted in
David Bol, 'Keir Starmer to warn UK's future at risk without
"real devolution"', *The Herald*, 20 December 2020; https://www
.heraldscotland.com/news/18958316.keir-starmer-warn-uks
-future-risk-without-real-devolution/. Accessed 7 June 2022.

p. 240   'consider how power, wealth and opportunity can be devolved
          to the most local level': Elliot Chappell and Sienna Rodgers,
          'Starmer announces Labour launch of UK-wide constitutional
          commission', *LabourList*, 20 December 2022; https://labourlist
          .org/2020/12/keir-starmer-launches-uk-wide-constitutional
          -commission/. Accessed 7 June 2022.

CHAPTER 11: ACID NORTHUMBRIA

p. 245   'I think we should just restart England ... slam it down around
          Nottingham': James Grieg, 'Sam Fender: is this the heir to
          the throne of British rock?', *Dazed*, 1 April 2022; https://
          www.dazeddigital.com/music/article/55830/1/sam-fender
          -profile-interview-seventeen-going-under-album-review-2022.
          Accessed 7 June 2022.

p. 245   'He saw things through their eyes that other people wouldn't
          see': *Lindisfarne's Geordie Genius: The Alan Hull Story*, dir. Ged
          Clarke. Daisybeck Studios, 2021.

p. 245   according to some accounts: *Lindisfarne's Geordie Genius: The
          Alan Hull Story*.

p. 247   'I looked upon the scene before me ... dropping off of the veil':
          Edgar Allan Poe, *Complete Tales & Poems* (New York: Vintage,
          1975), 231.

p. 248   'I'm worried about the 17- and 16-year-old girls and boys who
          buy it': quoted in John Van der Kiste, *We Can Swing Together:
          The Story of Lindisfarne* (Stroud: Fonthill, 2017), 86.

p. 254   For some they were just another ... my home life, my childhood:
          'Bruce Springsteen – 2012 SXSW Keynote Address', uploaded
          by Pluto Nash, 23 January 2016; https://www.youtube.com/
          watch?v=VW05XedG4zk.

p. 256   Mark Fisher, who coined the term 'acid communism': Mark
          Fisher, *K-Punk: The Collected and Unpublished Writings of Mark
          Fisher (2004–2016)*, ed. Darren Ambrose (London: Repeater,
          2018), 757.

p. 257   '[We'd heard that LSD] alters your life ... never get back home
          again': Mikal Gilmore, 'Beatles' Acid Test: How LSD Opened the
          Door to "Revolver"', *Rolling Stone (Australia)*, 26 August 2016;
          https://au.rollingstone.com/music/music-news/beatles-acid
          -test-how-lsd-opened-the-door-to-revolver-1369/. Accessed 7
          June 2022.

p. 264   'My bedroom is an attic ... what's it like living inside a metaphor?': Tom Pickard, *Fiends Fell* (Chicago: Flood, 2017), 6.

p. 265   Bunting's political animus against 'London's England': Bunting, *Letters*, 319.

p. 268   The ridge forms the watershed ... the eighth-century Ruthwell Cross: Pickard, *Fiends Fell*, 4–5.

p. 269   And then, as we brushed ... We were people of a region: Smith, *An Autobiography*, 78.

EPILOGUE: THE MESSIANIC NORTH

p. 272   'I've kept really quiet ... Love it': '"I will love it!" – Kevin Keegan's infamous rant', uploaded by Sky Sports Retro, 15 April 2020; https://www.youtube.com/watch?v=mk87a7r0V60.

p. 275   'just wanted to stay there forever': 'Newcastle United FC v Queens Park Rangers – Kevin Keegan Debut – 28th August 1982 – St James Park', uploaded by Westend126, 8 March 2018; https://www.youtube.com/watch?v=afzjWSieoLk.

p. 277   'KING KEVIN PUTS A SHINE ON THE TYNE ... show the country what we have': Mike Kelly, 'Power and the Glory', *Evening Chronicle*, 14 July 1993, 1.

p. 280   'almost as though a light had gone out in his head': Graeme Bell, 'Kevin Keegan – I will never ever forget "Black Wednesday"', *The Mag*, June 2021; https://www.themag.co.uk/2020/12/kevin -keegan-i-will-never-ever-forget-black-wednesday-newcastle -united/#disqus_thread. Accessed 7 June 2022.

p. 282   I have written before about how a version: Alex Niven, *New Model Island* (London: Repeater, 2019), 31–40.

p. 285   He reached to a crack in the rock ... in the glazed crag: Bunting, *Poems*, 52–3.

p. 286   'Yet delay! ... to summon man to his clay?': Bunting, *Poems*, 53.

p. 286   'lying low ... occasional light': Bunting, *Poems*, 53.

p. 286   'may live content in humility': Bunting, *Poems*, 348.

p. 287   'resolute to submit ... be it only a monster': Bunting, *Poems*, 345.

IMAGE CREDITS

All photos © the author, except the following which are reproduced by kind permission of the copyright holders. Every effort has been made to contact copyright owners of the photos used in the book.

Page x: Richard Carlile, The Peterloo Massacre (1819) – © Manchester Library

Page 9: Cotton weaving mill, Bolton, Lancashire (1914) – © Adam and Charles Black

Page 26: Newcastle Civic Centre, ref. DT.TUR/4/4356A (1969) – © Tyne and Wear Archives and Museums

Page 33: Newcastle woodcut (1913) – © Edward Wadsworth

Page 40: Redcar Steelworks, Teesside (2009) – © Stuart Kerr – https://www.flickr.com/photos/31838481@N05/3437950597/

Page 43: Cover of Zang Tumb Tumb (1914) by Filippo Tommaso Marinetti (1876-1944), Milan, Italy – © Photo by DeAgostini/Getty Images

Page 48: Newcastle Central Station (1850) – © Newcastle Libraries

Page 63: Victor Pasmore's 'Apollo Pavilion', Peterlee – © Andrew Curtis – https://commons.wikimedia.org/wiki/File:Victor_Pasmore%27s_%27Apollo_Pavilion%27,_Peterlee_-_geograph.org.uk_-_1705684.jpg

Page 70: Dan Smith, Cruddas Park – © Amber Film & Photography Collective

Page 74: Grove Rake Mine (2009) – © Mike Quinn – https://www.geograph.org.uk/photo/1273435

Page 83: The Destruction of Pompeii and Herculaneum by John Martin (1822) – © Tate Britain

Page 93: Delia Derbyshire (1965) – © BBC Photo Archive

Page 100: The MetroCentre, Gateshead (1987) – © ChronicleLive and Reach Plc – https://www.chroniclelive.co.uk/news/history/gallery/day-gatesheads-metrocentre-shopping-centre-13708339

Page 106: Montagu Court, Newcastle – © Waring Netts Architects

304

Page 112: Bryan Ferry (Roxy Music) in AVRO's TopPop (Dutch television show) (1973) – © Beeld En Geluid Wiki – Gallerie: Toppop 1973 – https://commons.wikimedia.org/wiki/File: Bryan_Ferry_(Roxy_Music)_-_TopPop_1973_3.png

Page 119: The SIS Building (or MI6 Building) at Vauxhall Cross, London (2015) – © Laurie Nevay – https://commons.wikimedia.org/wiki/File:SIS_building_(26327425611).jpg

Page 126: Old coal pit, Baildon Moor (2007) – © Humphrey Bolton – https://www.geograph.org.uk/photo/341858

Page 129: Andrea Dunbar – © Bradford Telegraph and Argus – https://www.thetelegraphandargus.co.uk/news/18817850.andrea-dunbar-remembered-30-years-death/

Page 141: 'Basil Bunting in Newcastle in 1970 with, from left, fellow poets Barry MacSweeney, Stuart Montgomery and Tony Harrison' – © ChronicleLive and Reach Plc – https://www.chroniclelive.co.uk/whats-on/arts-culture-news/50th-anniversary-buntings-briggflatts-marked-11412530

Page 148: The Stone Roses Live (July 1989) – © Photo by Joe Dilworth/Avalon/Getty Images

Page 159: MediaCity UK, Salford, Greater Manchester, England (2008) – © Pit-yacker – https://commons.wikimedia.org/wiki/File: MediaCity-UK_%28Feb_2008%29.jpg

Page 169: Frank Sidebottom memorial statue, Timperley, Greater Manchester (2013) – © Duncan Hull – https://commons.wikimedia.org/wiki/File:Frank_Sidebottom_statue_Timperley_Manchester_.jpg

Page 172: Newcastle Quayside – © Ian S – https://commons.wikimedia.org/wiki/File:The_Tyne_Bridge,_Newcastle_(geograph_2895510).jpg

Page 179: Harold Wilson visiting a Retirement Home in Washington, UK ref. 5417/101 – © Tyne and Wear Archives and Museums

Page 191: Tony Blair (2009) – © Andrew Newton – https://commons.wikimedia.org/wiki/File:Tony_Blair_%283182415312%29.jpg

Page 196: Forest Road, Wark Forest, Northumberland (2006) – © Les Hull – https://commons.wikimedia.org/wiki/File:Forest_Road,_Wark_Forest_-_geograph.org.uk_-_301635.jpg

Page 204: Nesno's white elephant in front of the Tees Transporter Bridge – © Young Fabians – https://www.youngfabians.org.uk/north_east_devolution_referendum_2004_the_first_modern_election

Page 214: Sycamore Gap on Hadrian's Wall (2020) – © Clementp.fr – https://commons.wikimedia.org/wiki/File:Sycamore_Gap_Tree_arbre.jpg

BIBLIOGRAPHY

24 Hour Party People, dir. Michael Winterbottom. Film Consortium/ United Artists, 2002.

'A tale of two constituencies', *The Economist*, 9 December 1999; https://www.economist.com/britain/1999/12/09/a-tale-of-two -constituencies. Accessed 7 June 2022.

Adams, Max. *The First Kingdom: Britain in the Age of Arthur*. London: Head of Zeus, 2021.

Adams, Tim. 'In Blair's old seat, the regulars agree: "Corbyn doesn't understand us here"', *The Observer*, 15 December 2019; https://www.theguardian.com/politics/2019/dec/15/blair-old-seat-sedgefield -rejected-corbyn-perceived-unpatriotic. Accessed 7 June 2022.

'Adult drinking habits in Great Britain: 2005 to 2016', *Office for National Statistics*, 3 May 2017; https://www.ons.gov.uk/peoplepopulation andcommunity/healthandsocialcare/drugusealcoholandsmoking/ bulletins/opinionsandlifestylesurveyadultdrinkinghabitsingreatbritain /2005to2016. Accessed 6 June 2022.

'Alcohol-specific deaths in the UK: registered in 2020', *Office for National Statistics*, 7 December 2021; https://www.ons.gov.uk/peoplepopulation andcommunity/healthandsocialcare/causesofdeath/bulletins/alcohol relateddeathsintheunitedkingdom/registeredin2020#:~:text=In%20 2020%2C%20there%20were%208%2C974,time%20series%20began %20in%202001. Accessed 6 June 2022.

Alston, Philip. 'Statement on Visit to the United Kingdom', *United Nations Office of the High Commissioner of Human Rights*, 16 November 2018; https://www.ohchr.org/en/statements/2018/11/statement-visit-united-kingdom -professor-philip-alston-united-nations-special. Accessed 7 June 2022.

Auden, W. H., *Collected Poems* (London: Random House, 1976).

Auden, W. H., *Juvenilia: Poems 1922–28*, ed. Katherine Bucknell (London: Faber and Faber, 1994).

Bale, Tim. 'The truth about the Blue Wall', *UnHerd*, 2 August 2021; https:// unherd.com/2021/08/the-truth-about-the-blue-wall/. Accessed 7 June 2022.

Bancroft, Holly. 'Revealed: Michael Gove's sexist jibes, racist jokes and homophobic slurs', *The Independent*, 13 September 2021; https://www.independent.co.uk/news/uk/politics/michael-gove-sexist-racist-speech-b1918058.html. Accessed 3 June 2022.

Batchelor, Paul. '"I am Pearl": Guise and Excess in the Poetry of Barry MacSweeney', unpublished PhD thesis, 2009; https://theses.ncl.ac.uk/jspui/bitstream/10443/901/1/Batchelor09.pdf.

Bates, David. 'Ridley Scott's *Blade Runner* and the Teesside skyline', *People's Republic of Teesside*, 4 December 2007. Accessed 6 June 2022.

Beeching, Richard. *The Reshaping of British Railways; Part 1, Report* (London: HMSO, 1963).

'The Belfast Agreement', Gov.uk, 10 April 1998; https://www.gov.uk/government/publications/the-belfast-agreement. Accessed 7 June 2022.

Bell, Graeme. 'Kevin Keegan – I will never ever forget "Black Wednesday"', *The Mag*, June 2021; https://www.themag.co.uk/2020/12/kevin-keegan-i-will-never-ever-forget-black-wednesday-newcastle-united/#disqus_thread. Accessed 7 June 2022.

Benjamin, Walter. *The Arcades Project*, trans. Howard Eiland and Kevin McLaughlin (London: Belknap Press, 1999).

Beynon, Huw, and Ray Hudson. *The Shadow of the Mine: Coal and the End of Industrial Britain* (London: Verso, 2021).

Blair, Tony. *A Journey* (London: Hutchinson, 2010).

Blair, Tony. 'Leader's speech, Blackpool 1996'. *British Political Speech*; http://www.britishpoliticalspeech.org/speech-archive.htm?speech=202. Accessed 7 June 2022.

Bloodworth, James, 'Does class still count?', *UnHerd*, 29 March 2019; https://unherd.com/2019/03/does-class-still-count/. Accessed 7 June 2022.

Bol, David. 'Keir Starmer to warn UK's future at risk without "real devolution"', *The Herald*, 20 December 2020; https://www.heraldscotland.com/news/18958316.keir-starmer-warn-uks-future-risk-without-real-devolution/. Accessed 7 June 2022.

Booth, Jenny. '"Cab for hire" Stephen Byers to face sleaze watchdog', *The Times*, 22 March 2010; https://www.thetimes.co.uk/article/cab-for-hire-stephen-byers-to-face-sleaze-watchdog-g205fgttpql. Accessed 7 June 2022.

Bracewell, Michael. *Re-Make/Re-Model: The Art School Roots of Roxy Music* (London: Faber and Faber, 2020).

Braine, John. *Room at the Top* (London: Random House, 2002).

Braithwaite, Phoebe. 'Mark Fisher's Popular Modernism', *Tribune*, 18 January 2019; https://tribunemag.co.uk/2019/01/mark-fisher-kpunk-popular-modernism. Accessed 6 June 2022.

'Bruce Springsteen – 2012 SXSW Keynote Address', uploaded by Pluto Nash, 23 January 2016; https://www.youtube.com/watch?v=VWo5XedG4zk.

Bunting, Basil. *The Poems of Basil Bunting*, ed. Don Share (London: Faber, 2016).

Bunting, Basil. *Letters of Basil Bunting*, ed. Alex Niven (Oxford: Oxford University Press, 2022).

Burgess, Anthony. *Little Wilson and Big God* (London: Vintage, 1912).

Burton, Richard, *A Strong Song Tows Us: The Life of Basil Bunting* (Oxford: Infinite Ideas, 2013).

Butler, David. 'Whatever happened to Delia Derbyshire?' *British Art Studies*, 31 May 2019; https://www.britishartstudies.ac.uk/issues/issue-index/issue-12/whatever-happened-delia-derbyshire. Accessed 6 June 2022.

Callaway, Ewen. 'UK mapped out by genetic ancestry', *Nature* (2015); https://doi.org/10.1038/nature.2015.17136

Chappell, Elliot, and Sienna Rodgers, 'Starmer announces Labour launch of UK-wide constitutional commission', *LabourList*, 20 December 2022; https://labourlist.org/2020/12/keir-starmer-launches-uk-wide-constitutional-commission/. Accessed 7 June 2022.

'Cities Outlook 2019', *Centre for Cities*, 28 January 2019; https://www.centreforcities.org/reader/cities-outlook-2019/a-decade-of-austerity/. Accessed 7 June 2022.

Clark, Gregory, and Neil Cummins, 'The Big Sort: Selective Migration and the Decline of Northern England, 1780–2018 (June 2018)', *Centre for Economic Policy Research*, Discussion Paper No. DP13023.

Crozier, Andrew. 'Barry MacSweeney: Obituary', *The Guardian*, 18 May 2000; https://www.theguardian.com/news/2000/may/18/guardianobituaries. Accessed 6 June 2022.

Eliot, T. S. *For Lancelot Andrewes: Essays on Style and Order* (London: Faber and Gwyer, 1928).

Farrell, Terry. *Lives in Architecture: Terry Farrell* (London: RIBA Publishing, 2020).

Fernández Aparicio, Carmen. 'Man, Machine & Motion: Richard Hamilton', Madrid: *Museo Nacional Centro de Arte Reina Sofía*, 2014. Accessed 6 June 2022.

Fisher, Mark. 'K-Punk, or the Glampunk Art Pop Discontinuum', *K-Punk*, 11 September 2004; http://k-punk.abstractdynamics.org/archives/004115.html. Accessed 6 June 2022.

Fisher, Mark. *K-Punk: The Collected and Unpublished Writings of Mark Fisher (2004–2016)*, ed. Darren Ambrose (London: Repeater, 2018).

Fisher, Mark. 'Requiem for Popular Modernism', *K-Punk*, 7 August 2006; https://k-punk.org/requiem-for-popular-modernism/. Accessed 6 June 2022.

Fisk, Robert. 'Top hack blasts local rags', *The Independent*, 4 August 2001; https://www.independent.co.uk/voices/commentators/fisk/robert-fisk-top-hack-blasts-local-rags-9196235.html. Accessed 6 June 2022.

Foote-Wood, Chris. *T. Dan Smith: 'Voice of the North' – Downfall of a Visionary* (Darlington: Northern Writers, 2011).

Foster, Sarah. 'A great love, tainted by the bottle', *The Northern Echo*, 26 September 2006; https://www.thenorthernecho.co.uk/opinion/echowoman/938266.great-love-tainted-bottle/. Accessed 6 June 2022.

'FUC51: An introduction of sorts', *Fuc 51: Madchester Deniers*, 14 January 2010; http://fuc51.blogspot.com/2010/01/fuc51-introduction-of-sorts.html. Accessed 6 June 2022.

Gilmore, Mikal. 'Beatles' Acid Test: How LSD Opened the Door to "Revolver"', *Rolling Stone (Australia)*, 26 August 2016; https://au.rollingstone.com/music/music-news/beatles-acid-test-how-lsd-opened-the-door-to-revolver-1369/. Accessed 7 June 2022.

Grieg, James. 'Sam Fender: is this the heir to the throne of British rock?', *Dazed*, 1 April 2022; https://www.dazeddigital.com/music/article/55830/1/sam-fender-profile-interview-seventeen-going-under-album-review-2022. Accessed 7 June 2022.

Heffer, Greg. 'Boris Johnson proposes moving parliament to York while Palace of Westminster repaired', *Sky News*, 16 July 2020; https://news.sky.com/story/boris-johnson-proposes-moving-parliament-to-york-while-palace-of-westminster-repaired-12029541. Accessed 7 June 2022.

'How has inequality changed?', *The Equality Trust*; https://equalitytrust.org.uk/how-has-inequality-changed. Accessed 3 June 2022.

Huxley, Aldous. *Brave New World* (London: Vintage, 1994).

'"I will love it!" - Kevin Keegan's infamous rant', uploaded by Sky Sports Retro, 15 April 2020; https://www.youtube.com/watch?v=mk87a7roV60.

Joannou, Paul. *United – The First 100 Years ... and More: Official History of Newcastle United F.C. 1882–1995* (Leicester: Polar Print Group, 1995).

Kelly, Mike. 'Power and the Glory', *Evening Chronicle*, 14 July 1993.

Kennedy, Joe. *Games Without Frontiers* (London: Repeater, 2021).

Lancaster, Bill, and Peter Stark. *Releasing the Genie of Coal: The Lower Derwent Valley, the Great Northern Coalfield and the Climate Crisis* (Consett: Land of Oak and Iron Trust, 2021).

Lewis, Wyndham. *BLAST 1* (London: Thames and Hudson, 2008).

Lindisfarne's Geordie Genius: The Alan Hull Story, dir. Ged Clarke. Daisybeck Studios, 2021.

'Liver disease profiles: November 2021 update', *Gov.uk*, 2 November 2021; https://www.gov.uk/government/statistics/liver-disease-profiles -november-2021-update/liver-disease-profiles-november-2021-update. Accessed 6 June 2022.

London, dir. Patrick Keiller, BFI Production, 1994.

MacSweeney, Barry. *Pearl* (Cambridge: Equipage, 1995).

'Manchester mayor Andy Burnham attacks proposed new Tier 3 restrictions', *The Telegraph*, 15 October 2020; https://www.youtube .com/watch?v=FjCvuZaEQbE. Accessed 3 June 2022.

'Manifesto', *Northern Independence Party*; https://www.freethenorth.co.uk /ourfuture. Accessed 7 June 2022.

McDevitt, Johnny. 'Dominic Cummings honed strategy in 2004 vote, video reveals', *The Guardian*, 12 November 2019; https://www.theguardian .com/politics/2019/nov/12/dominic-cummings-honed-strategy -2004-vote-north-east. Accessed 7 June 2022.

'MetroCentre opening souvenir supplement', *Evening Chronicle*, 13 October 1986.

Moffat, Alistair. *The Wall: Rome's Last Frontier* (Edinburgh: Birlinn, 2017).

'Newcastle City Council budget cuts to reach £327m by 2020', *BBC News*, 7 March 2019; https://www.bbc.co.uk/news/uk-england-tyne -47484040. Accessed 7 June 2022.

'Newcastle United FC v Queens Park Rangers – Kevin Keegan Debut – 28th August 1982 – St James Park', uploaded by Westend126, 8 March 2018; https://www.youtube.com/watch?v=afzjWSieoLk.

Niven, Alex. 'To reach the moon you need a rocket: an interview with Tom Pickard', *3:AM Magazine*, 2 November 2012; http://www.3ammagazine .com/3am/tom-pickard-interview/. Accessed 6 June 2022.

Niven, Alex. *New Model Island* (London: Repeater, 2019).

Parker, Simon. 'The leaving of Liverpool: managed decline and the enduring legacy of Thatcherism's urban policy', *LSE Politics and Policy*, 17 January 2019; https://blogs.lse.ac.uk/politicsandpolicy/the-leaving -of-liverpool/. Accessed 6 June 2022.

Parkes, Taylor. 'An Unsettling Creation: Bryan Ferry Interviewed by Taylor Parkes', *The Quietus*, 13 November 2014; https://thequietus

.com / articles / 16665-bryan-ferry-interview?fb_comment_id
=817070401682803_818145578241952. Accessed 6 June 2022.

Peace, David. 'My comfort read? Old Labour party manifestos', *The Guardian*, 30 July 2021; https://www.theguardian.com/books/2021 /jul/30/david-peace-my-comfort-read-old-labour-party-manifestos. Accessed 3 June 2022.

Pickard, Tom. *Fiends Fell* (Chicago: Flood, 2017).

Poe, Edgar Allan. *Complete Tales & Poems* (New York: Vintage, 1975).

Pollard, Alexandra. 'Andrea Dunbar: The short, troubled life of the prodigal Bradford playwright', *The Independent*, 6 June 2019; https:// www.independent.co.uk/arts-entertainment/theatre-dance/features/ andrea-dunbar-life-the-arbor-rita-sue-bob-black-teeth-brilliant-smile -a8945401.html. Accessed 6 June 2022.

Puchner, Martin. *Poetry of the Revolution: Marx, Manifestoes, and the Avant-Garde* (Princeton: Princeton University Press, 2006).

Raikes, Luke. 'Transport Investment in the Northern Powerhouse', *IPPR North*, August 2019; https://www.ippr.org/files/2019-08/transport -investment-in-the-northern-powerhouse-august19.pdf. Accessed 7 June 2022.

Randall, Colin. 'Tony Blair and Newcastle United: when the truth hurts', *SAFC Blog*, 17 April 2010; https://safc.blog/tony-blair-and-newcastle -united-when-the-truth-hurts/. Accessed 7 June 2022.

Roberts, Kathleen. 'And the winner is … Cleveland College of Art and Design!', 22 February 2018; https://era.org.uk/idea-guide/winner -cleveland-college-art-design/. Accessed 6 June 2022.

Robin Hood: Prince of Thieves, dir. Kevin Reynolds. Morgan Creek Productions, 1991.

Rogers, Richard, 'Delivering the Urban Renaissance', *The Observer*, 21 July 2002; https://www.theguardian.com/society/2002/jul/21/ regeneration.comment. Accessed 7 June 2022.

Roth, Andrew. 'Stephen Byers', *The Guardian*, 16 March 2001; https://www .theguardian.com/politics/2001/mar/16/byers. Accessed 7 June 2022.

Seldon, Anthony. *Blair Unbound* (London: Simon and Schuster, 2007).

Shipman, Tim. 'Sedgefield fell, and they erupted into song – things can only get better!', *The Times*, 15 December 2019; https://www.thetimes .co.uk/article/sedgefield-fell-and-they-erupted-into-song-things-can -only-get-better-9cjfz9hj8. Accessed 7 June 2022.

Simpson, Mark. 'Here come the mirror men: why the future is metrosexual', *The Independent*, 15 November 1994.

Smith, T. Dan. *An Autobiography* (Stocksfield: Oriel Press, 1970).

Spence, Simon. *The Stone Roses: War and Peace* (Harmondsworth: Penguin, 2014).

Stone, Jon. 'Ed Davey says Lib Dems could win "dozens" of blue wall seats from Tories after by-election win', *The Independent*, 20 June 2021; https://www.independent.co.uk/news/uk/politics/ed-davey-boris -johnson-chesham-amersham-b1869299.html. Accessed 7 June 2022.

'Suicides in England and Wales: 2020 registrations', *Office for National Statistics*, 7 September 2021; https://www.ons.gov.uk/peoplepopulation andcommunity/birthsdeathsandmarriages/deaths/bulletins/suicides intheunitedkingdom/2020registrations. Accessed 6 June 2022.

Sykes, Alan. 'Maestro of the all-nude Lysistrata plans an unforgettable evening at Newcastle's Morden Tower', *The Guardian*, 15 November 2011. Accessed 6 June 2022.

Tomaney, John. 'End of the empire state? New Labour and devolution in the United Kingdom', *International Journal of Urban and Regional Research*, vol. 24, no. 3, September 2000, 675–88.

'Top 8 Stag Do Destinations in the UK', *Maximise: Stag and Hen by Crazy-Voyages*; https://stag.maximise.co.uk/category/stag-do-destinations-& -ideas/article/top-10-stag-do-destinations-in-the-uk#:~:text=Manchester ,off%20for%20your%20stag%20do. Accessed 6 June 2022.

Towards an Urban Renaissance, final report of the Urban Task Force, chaired by Lord Rogers of Riverside (London: Routledge, 2003).

Van der Kiste, John. *We Can Swing Together: The Story of Lindisfarne* (Stroud: Fonthill, 2017).

Walker, Jonathan. 'The alarming poverty stats that really should be an issue at the 2019 general election', *The Chronicle*, 20 November 2019; https:// www.chroniclelive.co.uk/news/north-east-news/labour-conservative -general-election-poverty-17289049. Accessed 3 June 2022.

Ward, Dave. 'Starmer is losing Labour's working-class voters', *The Times*, 6 April 2021; https://www.thetimes.co.uk/article/starmer-is-losing -labours-working-class-voters-zw3l7prw2. Accessed 7 June 2022.

Yuan-chia, Li. 'Untitled', *Li Yuan-chia Foundation*; http://www .lycfoundation.org/li-yuan-chia/. Accessed 6 June 2022.

Zamyatin, Yevgeny. *We*, trans. Natasha Randall (London: Vintage, 2007).

Zaretsky, Robert. 'A Man Apart', *Los Angeles Review of Books*, 18 July 2012; https://lareviewofbooks.org/article/a-man-apart/. Accessed 3 June 2022.

INDEX